DYSTOPIA

WHAT IS TO BE DONE?

Garry Potter

NEW REVOLUTION PRESS

Potter, Garry
Dystopia: What is to be done?
ISBN-10: 1453822569
ISBN-13: 978-1453822562

CONTENTS

Dedication

I wish to dedicate this book to a man I have never met. Paul Farmer is a doctor to the very poorest of the world. He is also their best advocate. He is an insightful social analyst and researcher and tireless in his struggle for change. But I hope that the fate of the world does not depend entirely upon men like him because there are far too few of them. No, I think the hope for the world depends upon those who are not so extraordinary but nonetheless bravely strive for a better world. This book is dedicated to them also.

Acknowledgements

I wish especially to thank Georgia Stebbings who listened to me rant for hours as this project grew from a vague notion to a book. She was unfailing in her encouragement and faith in the work, while at the same time providing good analytical commentary. I also wish to thank Julia Welbourne who copyedited the manuscript in its rough draft form and provided very much needed critical insight. Gregory Cameron and Mike Burtt each read large portions of the book and gave helpful suggestions. Finally, I want to thank Judith Brand for her professional copyediting services. The usual disclaimer most certainly applies here: I alone am responsible for whatever flaws or errors are to be found in the book.

Introduction

The Dystopia Thesis

Should we be worried about the next one hundred years?
No, we should be worried about the next five years and
the next thirty years.
　　　Jared Diamond

One generation plants the trees; another gets the shade.
　　　Chinese proverb

If a path to the better there be, it begins with a full look
at the worst.
　　　Thomas Hardy

Introduction: Snapshots

Clock-watching

Klahan wondered again what time it was. He vainly hoped that it was at least mid-morning but knew it probably wasn't. His co-worker Sunan made a small joke about the river of time. Klahan only grunted in response. It was an old joke of Sunan's, and Klahan had long since failed to see any humor in it. The "river" that they both were standing in up to their chests was a thick stream of foul water and waste products in Bangkok's sewage system. Klahan and Sunan were in front of a wire-mesh filter. They were the low-tech solution to clogs and blockages. It was their job to pick out the clumps of solid waste caught by the filter. Klahan had been doing this job for five years. He did not like to talk about it at home, but when he did, he always said the same thing: "You would think that you would get used to the smell . . . but you don't."

Home Is Where the Heart Is

John looked at the mud and broken furniture and rubble where his Biloxi, Mississippi, seafront home had stood. Beside the total destruction of this was the lot where his mother's house had been. Now there was nothing there at all. His mother had died in the hurricane and flood that had destroyed it. John wondered what possibly could cause God to rain down so much suffering on a single family. He had lost his wife and brother as well. He wondered how he was going to support his children. He had had insurance on the house, but the company had told him that in these sorts of mega-disasters they do not pay out.

Playing Dead

Kampanga tried hard to still her breathing. She was playing dead. She was only seven, but she knew that if her pantomime of death was not successful she would soon be killed and in a very terrible way. Her acting was helped by the fact that her hair and clothes were soaked in blood and also that she was partially covered by two mangled dead bodies. The Rwandan church was filled with dead bodies and body parts. The people had mainly been killed by machete blows, but some had simply been beaten to death. Kampanga had seen a great deal of the killing before she had closed her eyes and tried to pull the bodies of her mother and sister over her.

You Have the Right to an Attorney

Lumumba's heart was now racing. He had been sleeping but had awakened when he heard a tiny metallic click. He had gotten up and for some reason pushed gently on his cell door. It gave way beneath the soft pressure and opened slightly. He sat back down on his bed in terror. He wondered if he was mad. He wondered if this was some trick to get him to come outside the cell so that they would have an excuse to beat him again. But they did not need any excuse to beat him.

He started once again the old train of thought. When you have no stimulus except for pain, when you have nothing new to think about; you begin to repeat and repeat the same sequences of thoughts. Lumumba went over in his mind for the zillionth time all the people he had talked to in the last few weeks before he was arrested; he mentally catalogued all the people he had known at university that were even vaguely political; he asked himself again what was it that could have led to this mistake; he questioned again and again what information that he might have that could possibly be of interest to his questioners. He genuinely wanted to help them. But as ever, he could think of nothing.

And then, entirely against his will because he did not want to hope anymore, because it was dangerous and painful to hope, he thought of the lawyer. Two weeks ago, he had had a visit and then last week a second one. The visits were very short, and the man had been cautious concerning anything that could possibly be done for him, including even future visits, in his warning against hope. And now Lumumba's cell door was open!

After a long time repeating the same sequence of thoughts and hopes and fears, he opened the door and began to walk down the hall. The cell next to his was empty. The next one was not. In it a man had hung himself. It was his lawyer.

Microbes, Medicine and Mercy

Bovani held the hand of her unconscious husband. It was only now that he had sunk into a coma that she could touch him. For the previous ten days, his skin had been far too painful to be touched at all. His throat had been swollen, and he needed to be fed intravenously. The doctors could do little for him. They had fed him a morphine drip to try and give him a little respite from the pain and fever that was maddening him. But when the rash had actually begun to peel away all the skin on his body, he had begged Bovani and the doctors to kill him. Now, perhaps mercifully, he was in a coma. The doctors held out little hope that he would get better, indeed that he would ever wake up again. Bovani trusted in the doctors' skills and knowledge, but the doctors did not know what it was that had made her husband so horribly ill. Though there were now some similar cases, many other cases, the doctors still did not even have a name for the disease that was killing her husband.

Dystopia Now

> *The future is here. It's just not widely distributed yet.*
> William Gibson

We live in a harsh world. It is full of mundane suffering. So, so many people have jobs that are simultaneously dangerous and boring, not to mention incredibly badly paid. So many people suffer tragedies that come from nature's powerful destructive forces, where suddenly, out of the blue, their lives are completely ruined. The world contains so many people involved in such desperate struggles for survival. Our world contains genocide and torture. This is not tomorrow; this is now. This is dystopia now, the hell that is life for so many millions and millions of people.

Chapter 2 presents some further snapshots of the harsh realities that are commonplace among the poor of the world. It shows a few pictures of the sudden shocks felt when people used to a more affluent existence are dealt life-changing blows. The situations and problems described are all very different. They are problems to do with the environment. They are the suffering due to simple poverty. Some involve complexities to do with finance and insurance. Yet they have commonalities in their causes. The first premise of the dystopia argument is expanded upon in this chapter: while the dystopia thesis is a dire prediction of our common *future human condition*, for a great many people *that future has already arrived.*

Fifteen million children will die of starvation this year.[1] Eight hundred and fifty million people are living with chronic aching hunger and malnutrition.[2] The World Health Organization

---

[1] http://library.thinkquest.org/C002291/high/present/stats.htm

[2] http://www.bread.org/hungerbasics/international.html

estimates that 54 percent of deaths due to disease have poverty related causes.[3] The dystopia that is the present is much more than pain and disease and suffering. It is also the future that will emerge from our present actions. The causes of this suffering now will also be the causes of a still more terrible future. Social inequality is very definitely one of these causes.

We are running out of fish in the sea. Our forests are shrinking. Clean water is becoming a scarce resource. Global warming is generating more frequent hurricanes, floods and droughts. If oil has ever played any causal role in world conflict, then the coming gap between the supply and demand for oil and natural gas and other sources of energy will be generating much, much more. It is not difficult to see the future. Today's decisions, today's actions and inactions, are creating it.

"Doomology" and the Curse of Cassandra

Knowledge is power.
Francis Bacon

How dreadful knowledge of the truth can be,
when there's no help in truth.
Sophocles

Cassandra could predict future events. Her curse was that she would not be believed. My curse is similar but not the same. This book is a prediction of the immediate future, not in terms of specific events but of general trends, tendencies and the results of such: the global human condition of a few years hence. My curse is not that I will not be believed; my curse is *that I will not be believed by sufficient number so as to make any difference.*

I told my ex-wife I was writing a book about the pain and suffering of the world today. I told her I was predicting the future,

---

[3] *World Health Report 2002*, World Health Organization.

the very near future. I told her I was predicting that the severe problems affecting humanity were going to get worse, very, very much worse. Her reply was as supportive of my endeavors as it usually was, "Yeah, you really need a PhD to figure that one out!" My ex-wife's offhand remark is actually quite indicative of some generalized feelings about the state of the world. Large numbers of people are painfully aware of the enormity of the pain and suffering in the world today. There is a widespread awareness that things look like they may get worse before they get better. Indeed, a definite apocalyptic feeling is quite prevalent. This apocalyptic fascination frequently manifests itself in crackpot Armageddon religious cults or blockbuster Hollywood doomsday films. The dystopia thesis recognizes such things as symptomatic of a generalized cultural malaise and therefore as itself a part of the dystopia phenomenon. But the dystopia thesis of this book is of a wholly different order, though it too belongs to a cultural trend. The dystopia thesis rejects both Hollywood theatricality and mystical pronouncements; it grounds itself in science. But there is today a kind of scientific and social scientific "doomology."

There are many books cataloguing and analyzing our serious environmental problems. There are many careful analytical explorations of the structural forces of the contemporary capitalist political economy and the correspondent misery in the lives of so many billions of people. There is a literature growing in quantity and quality dealing with the problems of the oil economy, with poverty, with the funding of health services, with the negative by-products of development and the negative by-products of under-development. Many of these works, quite unlike the Hollywood films or the assorted apocalyptic religious prophecies, are solidly grounded in empirical evidence; they are cautious in their predictions and careful in their analysis. And so it is with the dystopia thesis. It *does* predict the future, though its predictions are usually merely extensions of existing trends or conditions.

However, the dystopia thesis is distinct from its compatriot volumes in the literature of doomology. Almost all of these works – whether they are concerned with global warming, terrorism or poverty in Africa – can be seen as different in kind from the dystopia thesis. It is not that such books are necessarily narrow in focus, indeed the best of them are not; but it is simply that they are focused upon a *particular* problem, or set of problems or a *particular* region of the world. The dystopia thesis by contrast is truly *global* in its scope and *holistic* in its analysis. Discovering the complex inter-relations between apparently quite disparate problems and their causes is one of a number of ongoing themes in the dystopia argument.

A second crucial difference between the dystopia thesis and other scientific analyses of serious human problems is to do with the degree of pessimism concerning the prospects for the solution to problems or their amelioration. The critical literature of doomology is not by its nature particularly optimistic. It presents evidence of possible catastrophe and gruesome dissections of contemporary evils. Nonetheless, the dystopia thesis is *more pessimistic still*. Usually the analyses of our environmental or socio-political economic problems are couched in a language of possibility concerning what can be done. "If we don't stop doing this . . . or if we don't start doing that . . . then terrible consequences will ensue." This is usually the tone of the conclusions of their not-despairing engagements with even our most intractable and horrific global human problems. They offer us a reasoned hope that we can solve these problems. For example, a recent book by two authors for whom I have considerable respect is titled *Good News for a Change: How Everyday People are Helping the Planet.*[4] Of course, *some* everyday people are helping the planet but many, many more are damaging it. The dystopia thesis is concerned with the causes of the actions of the latter group of people.

But the dystopia thesis does not see the human condition in terms of heroes and villains. The everyday people that are hurting the planet are largely doing so as a result of their structurally constrained choices and actions. The people who are helping the planet are similarly enabled by various social structures. It is not

---

[4] David Suzuki and Holly Dressel (2002), *Good News for a Change: How Everyday People Are Helping the Planet,* Greystone Books: Vancouver.

that human beings do not have any choice or control at all over their lives; it is that some have a very great deal more than others. It is that a great many have so, so very little control at all. It is that the structural forces constraining and often determining choice and action are awesome in scope and terrible in their power. The *only hope* offered by the dystopia thesis is *a despairing hope* that cuts across some of its most salient arguments. The dystopia thesis is not merely a catalogue of our most terrible present and future problems; it is also an *analysis as to why they will not be solved.* The dystopia thesis presents compelling evidence as to why we are not going to stop "this" or start "that" activity that would resolve or even ease any of the serious problems being examined by the other grim analyses of our present and future.

First, while the dystopia thesis *is* a short-term prediction of the immediate future, it is also a compendium and diagnosis of present-day suffering. For billions of people, dystopia is not some future nightmare that may or may not occur; it is an all too present tense of living, suffering reality. Dystopia is nightmare already arrived. Dystopia is nightmare already extremely widespread. Nor did it arrive yesterday. Many people, many politicians, many "experts" intellectually and scientifically engaged with some of these horrendous aspects of the human condition. Many propounded solutions, and some even tried to practically enact them. Yet the problems were not solved! Thus, the dystopia prediction and analysis of the future is grounded in the failures of the present and past.

Time is running out for many things, and the clock is still running without the necessary sense of alarm. Pollution of the earth, the air and water are growing exponentially in some parts of the world, even as these things are being seriously and responsibly engaged with in others. But the effects of the former by far dwarf the latter. Water pollution combines with its depletion even as it is recognized as our most vital resource. Sensible strategies fail to be implemented as precious clean water becomes more and more commoditized. As well as the development of dire emergencies for the future, our water problems translate into the suffering of disease and malnutrition in the present. Agriculture depends upon unpolluted irrigation even as it pollutes it. Chapter 4 clarifies that it is not merely that environmental problems are all inter-related and that a holistic approach is necessary to understand them, the chapter also makes the point that ecology is integrated with economics. The short-term profit-driven rape of the world's rainforests along with a carbon energy wasteful world economic infrastructure literally "fuel" what is perhaps our most serious environmental problem: global warming. The storms and floods that proliferate as a result ensure that suffering from this problem will come (has already come!) to many sooner rather than later.

The dystopia thesis is not that any of these terrible problems are beyond *potential* human solution. There are, of course, possible disasters that could befall us, which even theoretically would be completely beyond our collective capacity to solve. For example, if an asteroid ten kilometers in diameter is now on a collision course with the earth, then very likely the cosmic collision will annihilate the human (and most other) species. The United States has invested a modest amount of money in allowing scientists to track and plot the future courses of all such asteroids as could cause us serious problems in the event of a collision. This project is only about halfway completed, though it should be finished in a few years. However, if we were to learn of a collision trajectory, there would be little we could do about it, notwithstanding Hollywood notions of nukes and heroism. But the dystopia thesis does not concern itself with such unknowns and examples of impotence. It focuses upon humanly created and therefore potentially humanly resolvable problems. The dystopia thesis is perhaps most significantly a prediction and an analysis of why we are not going to resolve that which we could, in theory, resolve. Its only hope is, as previously said, a wholly despairing hope. It is the hope that enough people believe enough of the dystopia thesis to collectively make the decisions and actions that would disprove it. That hope is the motivation for writing this book.

The dystopia thesis depicts present-day horror and a worse future. It argues that our problems will be exacerbated, not resolved. But in theory, in principle, all of these problems *could* be solved. Human beings *could* actually create a thriving global condition for the facilitation of the pursuit of happiness. Human beings *could* become responsible stewards of the global ecosystem. They *could*; but the dystopia thesis argues that they won't. They won't because of key features of our global political-economic system.

Global Political Economy

> *Ruling classes have always sought to instill in their subordinates the capacity to experience exploitation and material deprivation as guilt, while deceiving themselves that their own material interests coincide with those of mankind as a whole.*
>   Christopher Lasch

> *Capitalism is the astounding belief that the most wickedest of men will do the most wickedest of things for the greatest good of everyone.*
>   John Maynard Keynes

Chapter 6 examines three key features of the capitalist political economy most relevant to the dystopia thesis. First, there is that which in the history of sociological thought has been known as the problem of structure and agency. This often very abstract history of arguments focuses upon the degree of influence that social structures have upon our actions. In philosophy this problem has sometimes been labeled the problem of free will versus determinism. The sociological arguments are similar but more grounded in issues concerning social actions and social structures. The extremes of position range from some kind of absolute affirmation of the human mastery of our own thoughts, actions and ultimately fates, on the one hand, and a total determination of all our choices, actions and even thoughts, on the other. Frequently, sociologists have rejected both extremes and tried to theorize some middle ground. It is argued by some that we are not determined by social structures and neither do we "create" them; rather we reproduce existing social relations (social structures) and also transform them through our actions.[5] The dystopia thesis follows in this last vein but also focuses upon *specifically capitalist structural relations*.

In all notions of structural causality, there is an engagement with the issue of unintended consequences and particularly with how a collective sum of individual decisions and actions could result in a collective outcome undesired (and often unpredicted) by any. The dystopia thesis examines the specific logic of the capitalist system whereby *rationally* decided-upon decisions on an individual level convert into incredibly *irrational collective action* with sometimes catastrophic results. For example, it is hard to imagine anybody consciously setting out to ruin ecosystems, yet such is the all-too-frequent result of a collectivity of actions that were each individually chosen. The individuals involved in the collective destruction all had completely different individually desired ends. But the collective result is something quite other. Capitalism as a socio-political economic system promotes just this sort of interchange between individual rationality and *collective insanity*.

Many people are, of course, aware of the preceding argument. They are, to varying degrees, aware of the disjuncture between collective goods and individual desires as a problem. Frequently though, the problem is severely underestimated. This is because of the second key dystopian feature of our world political economic system: the *allowable time frame for planning* in a capitalist economy. Corporate investment is predicated upon the future realization of profit from that investment. This, according to many economists' rationalizations of the capitalist system, is why its ultimate guiding principle – the maximization of profit – will actually result in collective outcomes (for environmental sustainability, for example) that are favorable in the long term. Unfortunately, while this optimistic belief in the market is

---

[5] See, for example, Pierre Bourdieu and Jean-Claude Passeron, *Reproduction: in Education, Society and Culture* [1977] (2000), Sage: London; or Anthony Giddens, *The Constitution of Society: Outline of the Theory of Structuration* (1986), University of California Press.

something of an article of faith for the discipline of economics, there is actually very little evidence to support it and considerable to refute it.

Corporations plan for positions of strategic advantage and financial well-being in the future. These plans always involve *some* consideration of resource reserves and their rate of utilization and replenishment; but there is a time limit to such considerations. Individual investors have concerns and loyalties beyond profit, of course, but collectively capital investment has no such concerns or loyalties. Capital is mobile and follows the opportunity for profit. But this does not mean opportunity for profit 100 years hence . . . or even 50 or 30 years hence. Unfortunately, a great many of humanity's most serious problems have a timeline of causality much longer than that.

Ordinary people, and once again above all economists, would assert, though, that issues concerning long-term collective problems can be dealt with by governments. Indeed, political scientists would assert that governments are there *precisely* to regulate the interchange between private and collective desires, concerns and rights. Governments they would argue, are there, among other reasons, to regulate corporate actions in relation to their long- and short-term consequences. However, the dystopia thesis argues that, in our world capitalist system, the corporate temporal economic logic is "incorporated" within the governmental systems found throughout the world today, whether they be democracies or dictatorships. All too frequently, economists and political scientists wish to compartmentalize politics and economics. The dystopia thesis insists instead that we have a *political* economy (or *economic* politics).

The third crucial aspect to the dystopia thesis about our world political economy is social inequality. The division of wealth and income within all countries is unequal. Some, of course, are much more unequal than others. But *extreme* inequality is the rule, not the exception. This is true for countries both rich and poor. The division of wealth and differences in per capita income between countries is unequal, *extremely* unequal. The dystopia thesis argues about both the cause and consequences of this. With respect to causality, it argues that the extremes of inequality found *are not contingent*. That is, the differences of economic well-being found in the world and the differences of social and political power are not at all accidental. They are the result of *intrinsic features* of the system; indeed, socio-economic political inequality *is* one of the most important intrinsic features of the system.

With respect to the consequences of this inequality, the dystopia thesis argues that it either causes outright, or severely exacerbates, *all of our most serious human problems*. The dystopia thesis analyses the suffering of the poor. It demonstrates how suffering begets suffering. A good deal of this suffering is, of course, to be found in the nations presently referred to as Third World nations. The dystopia thesis locates the greatest amount of human pain in what are sometimes now referred to as the "least developed nations." Indeed, the dystopia thesis's grim prognosis for the future of such countries is perhaps better represented by the phrase "never-to-be-developed nations." However, the dystopia thesis is not exclusively focused upon the poorer nations of the world or even the poorest of the poor. Rather it has a two-fold perspective upon the Third World and poverty.

First, it sees a kind of "Third Worldization" of problems for the First World. Almost all of the wealthy countries of the world, and perhaps the United States most of all, have a large contingent of poor people living within their borders. These people have many of the problems of nutrition, illness and violence of those in much poorer countries. Such problems as these are dealt with at length in chapters 2 and 5 of this book. But disease and violence sometimes escape their poverty-stricken enclosures to impinge upon the health and happiness of the affluent. Not only is the spread of disease and crime facilitated by poverty but so too is terrorism. Perhaps the causal connection between social inequality and terror is so thoroughly intellectually resisted, is because the connection calls so obviously for some form of wealth redistribution as an antidote.

Secondly, the dystopia thesis argues that Third World decisions and actions are significantly determined by structural forces with their power centers in the domains of the wealthy. Governments are corrupted, public health and welfare policies are emasculated, and environmental policies are effectively undermined for corporate benefit. All of these actions will affect not only the future of the poorer nations (those which are affected more immediately) but ultimately the future of us all.

Social inequality is a causal force in terms of exacerbating problems felt by rich and poor alike. The problems usually hit the poor first, but eventually they have a profoundly disturbing affect even upon the rich. Lessons from the past can be suggestive in this regard. Chapter 3 examines a couple of case studies of socio-economic failure . . . complete failure. In each case, social inequality played a contributing role. In the case of the Norse settlements in Greenland, the economic failure actually meant death for everyone. Theirs was a very hierarchical society with large differences between rich and poor. However, the last privilege capable of being bought by those at the top of Norse Greenland society was only the privilege of being the last to die.

The Carbon Bedrock of Society: Oil and Natural Gas

> *Oil is seldom found where it is most needed, and seldom most needed where it is found.*
> > L.E.J. Brouwer, Senior Managing Director,
> > Royal Dutch/Shell Oil Co.

> *If all the cars in the United States were placed end to end, it would probably be Labor Day Weekend.*
> > Doug Larson

Chapter 6 is concerned not only with the structural and dynamic theoretical features of the world political economy but also with what is perhaps its most significant *material reality*: oil. It is not that we are running out of oil; it is that *we are running out of cheap oil!* The development of our world political economy, its industrialization, its globalization, all crucially depended upon cheap plentiful oil. For this entire history, we have treated this resource as though it were infinite. We continue to treat it this way in terms of the facilitating structures of mega-consumption, even as there is a growing realization of a problem in terms of controlling its production.

We will soon pass the world oil production peak. Perhaps we have already. We will not be able to know this until we have experienced several years of production decline. But production decline will take place. It will take place *in spite of* enormous increases in price. At the same time, enormous increases in price will occur because of the decline in production. The enormous increases in price will occur in the context of rising demand at the same time as a decline in availability. And this will change everything. This will change our world!

Once again many economists encourage a kind of blindness to the plethora of new problems and the intensification of old ones that is about to befall us. In the simplistic abstraction of the laws of supply and demand a rise in prices will resolve all the problems of production shortages. Demand may be constrained to some degree by price, but most significantly, supply will be expanded simply because of that demand. The economists are joined in their optimism exactly at this point by the "techno-mystics." a term I give to people who believe in an infinite capacity for technology to solve problems.

This second portion of the equation is most significant for the dystopia thesis because it is mainly false. Of course, a general price rise for a barrel of crude on the world market will make what are at present uneconomic sources of oil production financially feasible. Of course, new technologies will help with this. It will add to world oil production levels. However, this effect will be more than offset by other factors apparently ignored by those who worship the all-powerful god of the market. I am referring here to the laws of physics. There are *physical limits* to oil production potential. Long before the end of the supply of oil in the earth is reached, we will have reached a limit in terms of the energy costs of extraction being translated into economic costs. That is, we will have reached a situation in which the extraction of the remaining oil in the earth is *uneconomic at any price*.

We have already extracted almost all of the easiest oil to get out of the ground. Increasingly, the new oil deposits are found in harsh environments very difficult to access. The amount of energy required to get a barrel of oil out of the ground begins to get close to the amount of energy it can produce. Once it exceeds that quantity, of course, there would be no point at all in trying to extract it. But a very long time before that absolute physical barrier to production is reached, the economic limit would be reached. This is where the physical "energy profit" margins are so small that the economic costs of transporting people and equipment, building the structures and tools and other extraction costs become ridiculously expensive in relation to the *miniscule* money profit it *could* bring. The investment risks (and there are *always* such risks in mega-projects) are simply not worth the potential return.

This process will occur along with growing problems with natural gas production, mainly to do with transport. The rise in natural gas prices compounds the problem of oil because both are used in heating and in electricity generation. Long, long before we run out of either of these commodities, however, we will have reached a situation in which price increases occur that are so huge as to be at present unimaginable. They will necessitate profound economic and social changes everywhere in the world. The question those aware of the coming production shortfalls and price increases are asking is not whether change will be required but rather whether the necessary changes can be managed in a sensible fashion so as to minimize the pain of transition. The dystopia thesis argues that they cannot.

Our current world economy is one in which people and goods are transported everywhere and anywhere at an ever-increasing volume. It is not merely that fresh lobster might be transported thousands of miles inland so as to be a restaurant staple for land-bound gourmets. Rather it is that we ship apples from all over the world to apple-growing regions. It is that we have a North American (and European and Japanese to a lesser extent) transport, distribution and housing infrastructure that is absolutely dependent upon (what from the point of view of any other sort of system would be insane) reliance upon cheap oil.

Cheap goods are produced by cheap labor in China (or other poor countries) for Wal-Mart (or any one of the other big-box superstores commonly found in malls throughout North America). These are sold in workplaces where not only the bargain-hunting, suburban-living shoppers might make easily make a 50-mile return commute, but the minimum-waged employees serving them make a similar commute as well. This system of global shipping, local long-distance driving and suburban living will become increasingly economically unfeasible.

Big changes in the very day-to-day, taken-for-granted ordinariness of the North American lifestyle will be required. The dystopia thesis argues that this adjustment will not be in the form of a smooth transition. It suggests that the transformation will be accompanied by a maximum amount of suffering and social chaos. It suggests that the political efforts leading up to the crisis will not be directed at acquiring an environmentally friendly transition to alternative energies and lifestyles. It suggests increasingly desperate struggles to control remaining supplies for oil. It suggests resource wars and terrorism.

War of the Worlds

> *Where justice is denied, where poverty is enforced,*
> *where ignorance prevails, and where any one class is*
> *made to feel that society is in an organized conspiracy*
> *to rob, oppress, and degrade them, neither persons nor*
> *property will be safe.*
> Frederick Douglass

> *The mother of revolution and crime is poverty.*
> Aristotle

Chapter 2 "The Dystopia of the Present: A Tale of Two Worlds" looks at three examples of serious problems and/or horrific events that occurred in each of the First and Third Worlds respectively. The last of these is the 9/11 attack on the World Trade Center and the Pentagon. This is a bridge to the penultimate chapter of the book, "War of the Worlds."

Is the "war of the worlds" of chapter 8 simply an extension of the suffering tales of the two worlds of chapter 2? Not exactly. Chapter 2 analyses problems found in both First World and Third. The problems examined are diverse – resource depletion, "natural" (in part) catastrophes, exploitation, desperate violence – but have commonalities that cut across the differences between the worlds. The 9/11 case study is the only example of conflict between the worlds. Rather in chapter 2, the main difference between the problems looked at is that the suffering of the Third World cases is both more deeply chronic and severe. So what are the "worlds" that are warring in chapter 8? Is it simply the rich and the poor? Is it Islamic fundamentalism stacked up against Zionism and the Christian fundamentalism of America's Bible belt?

Some would have us believe it is the latter. And there is some truth in this. Certainly it is the subjective truth of some of the participants. But while the war of the worlds is not quite so simple as First World against Third or rich against poor, there is considerable truth in that too. September 11 was by no means the first battle in this war, if we look at things from that perspective. First, there was the entire colonial history of conquest and subjugation of the Western European empires. Then there was the neo-colonial economic domination of the same powers but now joined most importantly by America. School children are taught, and naïve school children grow up and continue to believe into adulthood, that the American military interventions of past and present were and are undertaken to implant democracy and human rights among populations oppressed by wicked dictatorships or insane demagogues. But America's long history of invasions and covert regime changes has been nothing of the sort. They have all been either directly to secure their economic interests or indirectly because of a perceived (whether accurately perceived or not is a different question) geo-political threat to them. With the exception of World War II, America's interventions may have had a rhetoric of democracy or justice attached to them, but they have always been far more self-serving. Interestingly, just about the only people in the world unaware of this fact are the American people themselves. Most ordinary people in the European countries that are America's allies now seem well aware of it. For example, the long history of complete support for America's foreign adventures given by the United Kingdom government (regardless of which party has been in power) has never been matched by UK public opinion. The government (every British government since WWII) always supported America *in spite of public opinion.*

The dystopia thesis recognizes that issues of religion, ethnicity and nationalist identity, ancient grievances and wholly misdirected rage all play a significant role in present conflicts and will continue to do so in future ones. Indeed, all of these issues are liable to be significantly exacerbated. But underlying such issues, feeding them are the injustices that stem from social inequality. Our televised world brings a plethora of images of conspicuous over-consumption to even the most poverty stricken. Those of the affluent societies are envied, admired, aspired to, resented and hated by those who are excluded from the wealth. Political-economic bullying is deeply resented whether the resentment and explanation of the power imbalance is articulated through a mullah or a secular socialist politician. The dystopia thesis argues that as clean water shortages intensify conflict will increase. The dystopia thesis argues that above all there will be intensified struggle for the control of energy resources. The dystopia thesis predicts that because the world's most significant oil repository is in the Middle East, there will be an extreme escalation in the already brutal conflicts occurring in the region.

My ex-wife's sarcastic comment – "that one really would need a PhD to predict that" – would perhaps seem appropriate here. Indeed, the dystopia thesis is certainly not alone in predicting resource conflict. But its understanding of how this conflict will interact with other issues, how it will be stoked by other issues, makes its analysis particularly grim and pessimistic.

The dystopia thesis not only predicts that incidences of terrorism will increase but also that the War on Terror will increasingly erode the civilized veneer of even the most genuinely democratic societies. More rights will be trampled upon, more innocent people will be incarcerated, more people will be tortured, more civilians will be butchered, more refugees will starve.

Cassandra's Curse Revisited

> *This is the bitterest pain among men, to have much knowledge but no power.*
> Herodotus

> *The power of accurate observation is commonly called cynicism by those who have not got it.*
> George Bernard Shaw

As said earlier, while Cassandra's curse was to be able to predict the future yet never be believed, the problem with the dystopia thesis is not that it will not be believed but rather that it will not be believed by *enough* people so as to prevent that which is predicted. There is, however, another dimension to the issue. The dystopia thesis catalogues and analyses serious problems. Chapter 4 does so with respect to the world's most serious environmental problems (carefully integrating the economic dimension to these problems in their analysis). Chapter 5 does so with respect to poverty and disease, paying particular attention to the problems and suffering of children. But the most worrying aspect of the dystopia thesis, though, is that the most significant thing about these problems is not how horrible they are, however horrible that actually is, but rather the argument that the problems are not going to be, indeed cannot be, resolved. The relationship between power and knowledge is a key reason why that is so.

Imagine a near all-powerful totalitarian state that suppresses all dissent. The state must sanction all truths before they can be declared. That is, state power determines what is or is not truth. The distinction between complete fabrications backed up by state power and what actually is the case disappears entirely. The distinction between what is officially said to be true and what actually might be true *ceases to have any meaning*. Truth is wholly determined by power.

But then imagine there is a small group of rebels. There is a small group of seekers after truth. They surreptitiously disobey the powers that be. They circulate their warnings, their subversive knowledges. Their message gets out only to a few. But still, it is heard.

Our contemporary situation is very different from this. Our contemporary situation is in many respects *far worse than this*. It is certainly not the case that all truth, even political truth, is suppressed. *It is that the most important truths can be drowned in a sea of lies, half-truths, irrelevancies and mystifying nonsense.*

Knowledge, real knowledge, can readily be produced. Indeed, the production of knowledge is structurally facilitated in the various societies of the world. It is particularly well facilitated in the affluent societies of the world. Universities, for example, very genuinely are in their very essence institutions designed to facilitate the production of knowledge. Knowledge can also be readily disseminated. The dissemination of knowledge is also structurally facilitated. And again, universities are, in their very essence, institutions that fulfill this role. However, the production of knowledge is also *systematically obfuscated*. Its dissemination is *systematically restricted*. Universities also have this aspect to them; they fulfill these roles too. There is a fundamental contradiction with respect to knowledge production and dissemination in *all* the major institutions concerned with it.

The problem with knowledge with respect to the dystopia thesis is no simple matter of censorship. It is deep and complex. Knowledges, the crucial knowledges relevant to ameliorating present suffering, the key knowledges required to understand the world socio-economic ecology and prevent catastrophic degeneration of the conditions amenable to human and other forms of life, get produced and disseminated. But they are also frequently drowned in an institutionally generated mystifying fog. Structural mystification is the name given to this process. It is fundamental to the production of knowledge in our present world political economic system.

Chapter 7 provides a theoretical understanding of the relationship between power and knowledge through its examination of the education system, the media and the public relations industry. It shows how strong evidentially and analytically supported claims to knowledge are systematically undermined. It demonstrates the effects money and power have upon scientific knowledge. It demonstrates the effects money and power have upon the public's understanding of crucial issues.

The principal contradictions in the institutional production and dissemination of knowledge are general; they are not restricted to issues of particular relevance to the dystopia thesis. But they are most acute there. It is with respect to issues concerning poverty and development, social inequality and the fundamental features of the world's political economy, where one finds structural mystification working most powerfully. The economic logic of the world system conflicts powerfully on just about every level possible with our collective ecological and human needs. Any potential concerning fundamental changes to the structures of inequality is systematically discredited. All coherent holistic explanations of the structural violence so pervasive in the world are countered by individualistic moralizing and causal confusion.

The dystopia thesis contains a prediction concerning its own reception. It will, like many other disturbing prognoses concerning the future, be labeled "alarmist." Bits of it will be believed by a fair number of people who are already "alarmed" about one problem or another that the thesis deals with. A few will believe most of it, and with a supreme degree of "pessimism of the intellect, optimism of the will,"[6] they'll redouble their efforts to change the world and the self-destructive course humanity is on. The dystopia thesis will be the world view of a tiny minority for many years. However, within no more than two decades at the most, what is now an "alarmist" and controversial thesis will have become the commonplace understanding of the world by everyone (sure "don't need a PhD" for that) who is educated at all. This is because the problems will have become so acute. This is because the extremities of action and reaction will have made some things that are perhaps obscure now, very, very

---

[6] The Italian Marxist Antonio Gramsci coined the phrase initially but it has since passed into common usage.

obvious. In two decades, no more than three at the most, almost everyone will certainly be aware of dystopia. But it will not have a correlate thesis that anyone would be interested in articulating. By then people will be too busy living and dying its painful distressing reality.

What Is to Be Done?

> *What is to be done?*
> *V.I. Lenin*

There is a paradox with respect to dystopia; or rather there is a paradox with respect to the *articulation* of dystopia. The dystopia thesis articulates the conditions of its own reception; it asserts that it will not be believed by sufficient numbers of people for the collective political will to be brought into existence to save us. We are doomed! Why bother to write about it?

The answer is contradictory. Our inevitable doom will be clearly proved by this book. We are on a destiny track to horror. Tracking back from it, we can say that if we had done this then we would have survived; had we done this and that and that, then not only would we have survived but something like a utopian future, or at least a better world than this would have been made. So if we can see it; if we can see the nodal points of the inevitability of horror, let's change them. Chapter 9 engages with this. It considers the flaws in the "logic of historical inevitability." It ponders the possibilities of avoiding barbarism and species extinction. It considers this on a philosophical level; but it also elucidates the urgent practicalities and politics and strategies for action. It asks and answers the always-all-important question: *what is to be done?*

Chapter 1

Dystopia of the Present: A Tale of Two Worlds

*It was the best of times, it was the worst of times,
it was the age of wisdom, it was the age of
foolishness, it was the epoch of belief, it was the
epoch of incredulity, it was the season of Light,
it was the season of Darkness, it was the spring
of hope, it was the winter of despair.*
    Charles Dickens

*If rich people could hire other people to die for
them, the poor could make a wonderful living.*
    Yiddish proverb

Introduction

The fearful, painful moments before death came suddenly and unexpectedly for Carol. She had no idea what had happened to rock her workday world. She had been alone in the reception area. Now it was unrecognizable. Things had collapsed. Things were in flames, and she was bleeding from the glass fragments that had blown in from the window that was no longer there. The man had asked her if she was okay. She didn't know his name, but she knew he worked on her floor. She had answered yes, but that was before they had properly assessed their situation. She asked him a question: "Do you believe in God?" "No" he replied, "do you?" She was going to answer yes, but then the thought was driven from her mind and instead she said: "It hurts; it hurts!" The heat from the flames was beginning to peel their skin. They knew there would be no rescue. The man took her by the hand and led her to the window. She looked at him. She crossed herself. They jumped. They died on September 11, 2001.

The dystopia thesis presents certain challenges to our understanding. Ironically, the greatest difficulty in fully comprehending it is not principally one of analytical reasoning.

True, the present human condition is complex and human problems are multiple with complicated inter-linkages of cause and effect. Nonetheless, the detailed analytical arguments that shall be presented in later chapters are not difficult to follow, however unpleasant some of the conclusions may be. No, probably the greatest challenge the dystopia thesis presents is one of individual imagination. The difficulties are two-fold. The first is simply one of scale. It is impossible to fully grasp the immensity of the problem. I mean here not merely the full panoply of human problems present and future that form the dystopia argument. Rather, I mean *any one* of the many problems that compose it. Though the problems "go all the way down," so to speak, and manifest themselves through the pain of *individual* suffering, so many, many people are affected that our imaginations are simply not capable of grasping such an immensity of pain.

The second difficulty is one of perspective. It is not only that none of us can see all of reality all at once, but also that any part of reality we do perceive has its perception profoundly affected by where we are socio-economically, culturally, politically and geographically situated while perceiving it. In this regard, the most likely reader of this work is in some respects the most poorly placed to understand the dystopia of the present, and I am among the worst placed to write it. That is, our comfort and relative affluence present significant barriers to our potential understanding.

I am Canadian, and the vast majority of readers of this work will also live in North America or Western Europe, Japan, Australia or New Zealand. If you don't live in one of these countries, then it is likely you belong to one of the proportionately small middle classes of the world's poorer countries. The flip side to this fact is that this is exactly the population least likely to be experiencing very much of the dystopia of the present.

I have problems, just as I am sure you have problems. We all have (to varying degrees) problems of romantic relationships, families and friendships. Most of us worry about money. Our jobs and careers are variously stimulating, frustrating, fascinating or boring – a source of satisfaction or unhappiness. Some of us have serious health problems; some of us have minor chronic pain. All of us will someday die; and all of us have seen, are seeing, or will see someday, some loved ones die too. Such is the human condition. Some number and degree of problems are inevitable. But none of this is part of the dystopia of the present. *Our* world is still a world of affluence, technological wonder and pleasure. Inequality is a major cause of dystopia; and as such it ensures that it is to be the poor who will not only bear the brunt of the suffering in the future but shall also be the first to experience it. Dystopia has already begun. It is not only humanity's future but its present.

It is the fact that few of us have even come close to experiencing the dystopia of the present that makes our imaginative grasp of it so difficult. The philosopher Jean Paul Sartre argued that we should all attempt to see the world through the eyes of the most oppressed. But this is very difficult. It is hard to see the problems of dystopia when your present problems are nothing like them. It also makes it more difficult to imagine the future where they will be.

Nonetheless, the cataloguing of present-day dystopia begins in the First World, with Newfoundland and New Orleans. Dystopia is not a single problem with a single cause. On the face of it, one would be inclined to say that the problems associated with the decline of the Newfoundland fisheries and those of Hurricane Katrina have nothing in common. And on some level, this is quite true. The Newfoundland problem is a simple one of resource depletion. New Orleans' problem can also be expressed simply: a severe weather event. But the dystopia thesis argues that there is a cause-and-effect inter-linkage of *all human problems.* Newfoundland and New Orleans have commonalities of cause and effect. The chapter begins with them before considering three Third World case studies: Nigerian gangs, Mexican women workers in the Maquiladoras and the Rwandan genocide. The chapter finishes with a return to September 11.

Newfoundland: In Cod We Trust[ed]

Get the facts, or the facts will get you. And when
you get them, get them right, or they will get you
wrong.
                    Thomas Fuller

The Canadian province of Newfoundland has one of the coldest inhospitable climates on earth. Newfoundland consists of a huge island off Canada's Eastern coast and a large chunk of equally cold and inhospitable mainland (Labrador) cutting into the province of Quebec. The island, approximately the size of England, has relatively few inhabitants – a little over a half a million people. Though comparatively speaking this is a very small population, one might well wonder why anyone lives there at all. It is not only that the weather is severe. Human beings thrive and survive in many places on the earth with climates hostile to human well-being. No, the island portion of Newfoundland is known affectionately to the locals as "the Rock" for very good reasons. It is more or less exactly what Newfoundland is . . . a cold windswept enormous rock thousands of miles from anywhere. There is nearly no agriculture to speak of. Compared to the rest of Canada, also frequently a very cold place, Newfoundland has very little of what the country has a lot of – mining and logging. In human terms, it really is close to being simply a barren rock. Before its European colonisation, the small population of aboriginal inhabitants followed the caribou and supported themselves by hunting and fishing. But though a half a million is a very small population for all that cold windswept space, given the climate and scarcity of resources, the number seems large rather than small. One wonders why anyone would choose to live there at all!

If one was to visit St. John's, the capital, however, one would see a quaint and picturesque, but nonetheless very much First World, town. Leaving the old-world-flavoured town center and the beautiful harbour (perhaps with an iceberg floating serenely within it), one would find a modern sprawling suburb. One could blink one's eyes and readily believe it was Toronto or Vancouver or any other North American haven of middle-class life. One would find a large modern university with 10,000 students or more. The denizens of the sprawling middle-class suburb work as university professors or social workers or insurance claims brokers or government officials; in short, they live their lives very much as millions of other middle-class Canadians and Americans do. The climate is harsh, but it is dealt with competently and efficiently, so as to produce the First World middle-class lifestyle. The streets are snow ploughed, and not only the homes but the shopping malls are climate controlled. There are fruits from all over the earth to be found in the many supermarkets. The economic structure is as complex and diverse as that of any First World nation – Newfoundland is a *Canadian* province after all, and though the poorest of Canada's provinces, its inhabitants work and live like Canadians.

But though the busy complexity of this economic superstructure gives thousands of reasons to individuals for living there, one can still ask why anyone lives there at all. St. John's is a Canadian city, but it is a long way from anywhere else in Canada. It is a similar distance from there to London as from there to Toronto. The First World kitchen pantry of the consumer choice lifestyle has to be *imported from a great distance.* Why is this happening? Why are all these people there? There is a very simple answer: fish. Fishing, for the entire history of Newfoundland, has been the economic *infrastructure*, the raison d'être of the Rock. The Grand Banks of Newfoundland's east coast was one of, if not *the*, richest fishing spots on earth.

Just as it is an oversimplification to say that Newfoundland's entire economy was based upon fishing (there is *some* mining, logging, manufacturing, agriculture, tourism etc.), it is also an oversimplification to say that the fisheries were dominated by a single kind of fish. However, it is no exaggeration to say that cod was king. King Cod was the heart and soul of Newfoundland's culture and economy. But on July 2, 1992, John Crosbie, Canada's then Federal Minister of Fisheries and Oceans, declared a *moratorium upon cod fishing!* This initially a two-year moratorium, was the belated governmental response to an unprecedented ecological and economic disaster: the economic mainstay of hundreds of years, the cod, were gone!

There was, of course, an orgy of retrospective blame and anger. The question of what was the cause for this dilemma was intertwined with a much more bitter question: *who* was to blame? Politicians and the government were, of course, rather obvious targets. There was enormous anger but relatively little bloodshed. There was a tiny mini-riot of fisticuffs and curses at one public meeting with governmental spokespersons. But angry response was muffled not only by police and the notions of public order held by a loyal citizenry but also by the answer to a pressing immediate question: what was the government going to do about the situation? The answer given was one that was possible for a wealthy First World country such as Canada to give. It was an answer, however unsatisfactory to many of Newfoundland's fishers, that would not have been possible on the same scale (if possible at all!) in many other countries. If such a disaster struck a Third World nation, there would be *no compensation package*. There was, of course, public quarrelling over both the organisation of the distribution of this financial relief and the amount. But Canada is a wealthy democratic nation, and the Newfoundland fishers were not simply going to be left to drown. "Drowning" and death is exactly what one could expect would (and does, and will) happen to Third World communities when faced with this sort of ecological-economic tragedy.

The population of Newfoundland can approximately be divided in half – half that live in St. John's and another half that live in very small town/villages whose entire reason for existing was fishing. "Baymen" (the term applies to women as well), these people call themselves. Were these Baymen to be found in a Third World country whose fishing economy and lifestyle was suddenly stopped, then they would *have to move*. Their communities, their way of life, would die; and were they unable to find a new means of supporting themselves, they and their children would die too. The world capitalist core of the economy has a brutal indifference to the fate of its peripheral workforce once it has exploited the last drops of its resources. Canada, though a First World capitalist-core country, retains some of the peripheral status features of its early history. This is nowhere more evident than in Newfoundland. That is, it has an enormous dependence upon a single primary resource industry. If the fish are gone, then one might well expect the people to disappear soon after. But, still Canada is a First World country, and the Baymen aren't leaving. They can't. They have put a lifetime of saving into the purchase of their middle-class homes. Who will buy them now? They cannot afford to leave and chase work elsewhere. This is the human cost of ecological-economic disaster in the First World: the people will not physically starve, but debt, bankruptcy and a lost future still crush them.

There were culprits to point blaming fingers at that gave the local disaster an international dimension. Cod is not the only fish in the sea, and fishing takes place in all the oceans of the world. The Grand Banks fishing area was not only a local problem but also, in some sense, international. There was a "fish war" with Spain. This was not, of course, an all-out shooting war. These were two First World countries within the same NATO military alliance. Canada arrested a Spanish fishing trawler, and there was a diplomatic incident. Eventually an international agreement was reached. As this little drama unfolded, other international fishing disputes were connected in the minds of fishers if not governments. British fishing vessels flew the Canadian flag as a symbol of Spanish blame for over-fishing and the destruction of *their* fishing industry in quite a different set of contested areas and international quota agreements and regulations. There are global problems that are not global in one sense but yet are in another. That is, fishing and over-fishing is a *global ecological and economic problem* that *manifests itself locally*. Certain regions face dramatic ecological changes with tremendous negative economic impact, while other regions continue to flourish. Each situation has its own unique particularities. There are plenty of fish in the sea. The problem of one region is not that of another . . . except that the same problem will likely recur. Regional disaster should be regarded as a *warning signal* to another. There is some limited consciousness of this, but the warnings by and large go unheeded.

Yet another group received blame for the over-fishing of the

Newfoundland cod: the scientists. Local governments and international agreements set the limits as to what can be harvested from the sea. It is a complex set of political economic interactions within and between governments that determines the regulation of fishing. It is a complex political economic and sometimes even military process that determines how and to what degree such regulation is enforced. It is but one factor among many, but government policy is influenced and/or justified by the "expert advice" they receive. This advice is provided by the scientific community. From the perspective of most Newfoundland fishers, the advice with respect to fishing quotas given by the "experts" was not only woefully inadequate but flat out wrong! They *knew* they were over-fishing!

But if they knew this, and were not simply claiming knowledge after the disastrous fact, one could well ask: why didn't they stop? There is a simple answer. They each had very good financial reasons. They needed money to pay the orthodontist to work on one of their children's teeth, or to pay off credit card accumulated debt from last year or simply to make the mortgage payments on their home and boat. But while the answer is simple on one level, it is quite complicated on another. There is the complexity of the relationship between an individual action and that of a collectivity. There is a complicated relation between individual decision and powerful structural forces. There is the peculiarly dialectical formula, whereby a collection of individually taken rational decisions translates into a collective phenomenon of extraordinary irrationality. It may be crazy to knowingly over-fish when you know the stock is reaching depletion. But individually one decides to fish up to quota even if one believes the quota set is too high.

Capitalism on one level is exceedingly rational. There is the easy-to-comprehend logic of supply and demand: fewer fish, higher prices; more fish, lower prices. The price of fish, of course, is determined by both a local market and an international one. However, even at the local Newfoundland market level, the economic forces are far too powerful to be dealt with individually. If the supply of fish is to be controlled, for whatever reason, the mechanisms for doing so must be set at a collective level of decision making. Individual fishers might have made altruistic decisions, at considerable financial cost to themselves, in the name of a saner ecological management of the cod stock. But this restraint could not have saved the cod. There is a logic to the relation of the individual decision to the collective outcome such that what sounds on one level like a moral cop-out is in fact perfectly true: "If I don't do it, somebody else will; it won't change the final outcome . . . so I may as well do it." Individual fishermen simply could not financially afford to fish below the quota set by governmental regulation. What they could and did do was to urge the government to set lower quotas. They could shout their warnings of a budding ecological disaster. But they were shouting into the wind.

Why did the scientists, whose advice the government took far more seriously than that of local fishermen, get it so badly wrong? Or did they really get it wrong at all? Of course, on one level, they apparently did. There were far fewer fish than they had estimated. Nonetheless, they went against even the advice of their own Department of Fisheries scientists (DFO) concerning quota reductions.[1] On another level, however, the issue is far more complicated. It is the reason for opening this chapter with this description of the socio-economic ecological problem of the Newfoundland cod industry. It is because this problem, one of many, many similar problems besetting humanity, is very significantly, amongst all its other aspects, a problem of knowledge. Karl Marx famously wrote that humanity only sets itself such problems as it can solve. A major part of the pessimistic thesis of this book is that this proposition is mistaken! It is not that the problems are in theory irresolvable. They could be satisfactorily resolved if the right decisions were made and the correct courses of action taken. But reliable knowledge is required for this to be done. And the production of knowledge is interwoven into the fabric of the political economy in such a

---

[1] Fred Mason, "The Newfoundland Cod Stock Collapse: A Review and Analysis of Social Factors," *Electronic Green Journal*, Issue 17, December 2002.

fashion as to ensure such knowledge will be obscured.

It is not, as some have concluded, our culture's over-reliance upon scientific expertise. It is a false opposition to set up local "common sense" experiential knowledges against those of the scientific community. Ideally these knowledges could and should reinforce and enhance one another. In fact, this is precisely what happened with respect to local and scientific knowledge concerning cod stocks. In 1987, the Newfoundland Inshore Fisheries Association commissioned an independent analysis of the cod stocks, and of the DFO science.[2] The calculations concluded that estimations of the number of fish were wildly over-optimistic, by as much as 100 percent.[3] The Newfoundland inshore fishery thus knew that cod stocks were much lower than the figures that the Canadian Department of Fisheries were using to determine cod quotas. They knew it on two levels. The independent scientific study essentially confirmed the local knowledges. However, both sorts of knowledge are situated within the powerful forces of the political economy. The report was ignored.

So, too were other scientific voices. Perhaps even more disturbing is the fact that not only were dissident scientific voices not listened to, but that they were actively suppressed! Ransom Myers, now the Killam Chair of Ocean Studies at Dalhousie University, worked for many years at the DFO. He asserted that he and other scientists warned that fishing must be curtailed. Myers stated:

> I did work for them that showed the cod stocks were not increasing at the time   the DFO was claiming. It was dictated, or it was attempted to enforce, bureaucratically enforce a scientific position that is that the cod stocks were increasing

---

[2] Harris, Michael, (1998), *Lament for an Ocean: The Collapse of the Atlantic Cod Fishery, a True Crime Story*. McLelland & Stewart: Toronto.

[3] http://www/tv.cbc.ca/national/pgminfo/fish/index.html

by great leaps and bounds that the mortality due to fishing was low, and it simply was not so.[4]

New Orleans and Katrina: The Perfect Storm (Prediction)

Considering the dire circumstances that we have in New Orleans, virtually a city that has been destroyed, things are going relatively well.
        Michael Brown, FEMA Director

Most Canadian readers would have been familiar with the problems of the Grand Banks and the cod fishing moratorium. But the *whole world* saw the dramatic images of storm and flood that was Hurricane Katrina. This is perhaps the first difference between the two dystopian situations. One was presented to the world with far greater emotional force and visual drama. We all saw the New Orleans images of flame and looting and heard innumerable hours of commentary concerning the failures of the relief effort.

This is another difference between the New Orleans and Newfoundland situations: the "relief effort." Though undoubtedly there were many disgruntled and angry fishers who saw the Canadian government's efforts as far less than laudable, such things are to some extent a matter of degree. Essentially, the fishers were looked after; those other workers dependent upon the fishery industry were looked after; Newfoundland was looked after. As I said, such an assertion is one of degree, and I am sure there are many today who would find shameful the overall handling of the problem from beginning to end. However, let us imagine what could have been. Newfoundland, other than St. John's and a handful of lesser towns, consists of a string of little villages scattered around the coast – little *fishing* villages. Like most Canadians,, their home is the greatest financial asset these village residents have. Without government support and aid (either direct or indirect), fishing village life would become

---

[4] Ibid.

wholly uneconomic and the villager left with the "between a rock and hard place" choice to stay and starve or to leave the house that they had thus far worked their whole life to buy. In any event, their chief financial asset would have been wiped out. The house values would go down to nothing because no one would want to buy them. Thus, though for very different reasons, the Newfoundlander would have experienced something quite similar to many New Orleans residents: they would have lost their entire life savings and been forced from their home. But, as I said, this is in fact one of the chief differences. Newfoundland was looked after.

The dystopian thesis asserts inequality as one of the chief problems of humanity, either causing directly or exacerbating the worst effects of every problem. To some extent, this translates practically into a First World/Third World difference. The Third World is usually the first to suffer the direst consequences of every problem. In the case of Newfoundland, we see this First World/Third World difference. Over-fishing is occurring worldwide, and Newfoundland is not the only region to experience a catastrophic resource depletion. But the painful effects were ameliorated by the fact that Canada is a wealthy country and Newfoundland is a part of Canada. New Orleans demonstrates for us that the First World is not immune to dystopia; while New Orleans demonstrates the conceptual weaknesses of a simple First World/Third World categorization. The Third World is present in the First.

Leaving aside the human tragedies of loss and death for the moment, we can assert an economic disaster for New Orleans (and other parts of Louisiana and Mississippi) of colossal proportions. As of this time of writing, approximately half of New Orleans' population has yet to return. Not all of these people are suffering greatly, of course. Some are among the most well off and are simply cutting their minimal losses and moving on with their lives. But most are truly suffering. In New Orleans, it was the poor who suffered the most. It was the poor who could not afford the transport necessary for early evacuation. It was their neighbourhoods that were among the most vulnerable to flooding. Thus, an extremely disproportionate number of them were among the seriously injured and dead. It was mostly them who were directly robbed and personally terrorized.

But again, as I said at the beginning of this chapter, I have begun with Newfoundland and New Orleans because of a question of perspective and imagination. The average Canadian and American perhaps might find it hard to imagine lacking the bus or train fare to get out of town to avoid a hurricane. The average Canadian and American owns and drives a car. However, the dystopia thesis is that not only do the world's problems belong to the third world, the dystopia thesis is that there is a time lag with respect to most problems. At present, most aspects of dystopia are confined to the poorer countries of the world, but as time passes that will become less and less true. The middle classes will increasingly be infected by dystopian nightmare. There will be many effects that even the very rich will not be able to escape. Newfoundland and New Orleans, with their very different types of problem, are among the first instances of dystopian manifestations in the First World.

The difference is that, in many respects, Newfoundlanders were protected by Canadian wealth and the country's social democratic ideals and policies. The poor and middle classes of New Orleans have instead been left to the individual vicissitudes of luck, charity, neo-liberal indifference and a hapless bureaucracy. As stated earlier, the poor of New Orleans were most affected by Katrina, and that is true in many respects but not all. As an economic disaster, it is the middle-class homeowner or small-business operator who has been most affected. The poor will move from one slum to another, one rented accommodation to another, one unskilled occupation to another; whether one is unemployed in New Orleans or Atlanta makes little difference. Your home was destroyed by a hurricane, or you were evicted for failure to keep up with the rent; the small business you worked for was flooded, or you simply got fired; one cause is far more dramatic than the other, but if you are poor in America, the result is all too familiar. As the saying goes, "If you ain't got nuthin', you ain't got nuthin' to lose." For the middle classes though, it was very different. They had *equity* in their homes.

The thousands of people who lost their homes in New Orleans

had a wide variety of circumstances affecting them. Some had very little or no equity at all. Their situation in this regard sometimes turned out very similarly to that of the poor described above. It depended upon the detail of their mortgage arrangements and insurance policy. This is more generally true of those who lost their homes and much of their possessions. An awful lot depended upon their insurance policy. Some were mostly all right. Most were not. Percentage reimbursements, acts of God clauses, specific circumstances disallowed and many other of the technical details of home insurance "ensured" that it was the homeowner that lost out rather than the insurance company.

The consumer protection group Americans for Insurance Reform produced a comprehensive report detailing the industry's shameful response to the Katrina tragedy. that highlighted the most common problems:

- Companies attempting to avoid any liability under homeowners' policies declaring all damage to be flood related, which insurers said was not covered, even though this position was not supported factually or legally. As one hotline caller who was told this said, "I'm basically going to be hung out to dry by my insurance company."
- Incredibly slow response to policyholders, with two callers typifying the problem: "Our money is running out, and our insurance companies can't tell us when or if any help is on the way," and, "I haven't paid premiums to two companies all these years to be starving, struggling and homeless."
- Insurance carriers unreachable or simply refusing to respond at all. "I'm a 70-year-old woman, I need to pay rent at the place I'm living, and I just don't have any money," said one caller who could not get any response from her carrier.
- Homes further damaged by Hurricane Rita when companies failed to send adjusters after Katrina, which would have allowed people to make repairs. "There wouldn't be half as much water damage if they had been

able to get an adjuster out here in a reasonable amount of time," said one hotline caller.[5]

Thus, it was the case that thousands who were middle-class ceased to be so. All they had of value in the world was wiped out in an instant, including sometimes their job and career. Starting all over again was an option, indeed for many the only option, but though individual situations were quite diverse, it is safe to say that a very great many faced extreme hardship.

This kind of individualized collective hardship is not such to be very much affected by donations of canned goods or emergency temporary housing. America's self-congratulatory media portrayal of the various celebrity charity efforts is a case in point. Such are a part of dystopia, not steps toward overcoming it. Most Americans cannot even begin to understand that *charity is barbarism*. If, as a reader of this book, you are among that number, you need seriously think about this. Charity applies band-aids to serious wounds. It does little to solve or even very seriously ameliorate the suffering it addresses. Its principal function is to allow those unaffected by the problem to sleep well at night while maintaining the conditions that led to the problem in the first place.

The reader unhappy by the explicit and implicit criticism of the preceding paragraph might at this point object "but the problem in this case was caused by a hurricane." A hurricane, if one is religiously inclined, certainly qualifies as an act of God, if anything does. True, there was real suffering; true we could have done more for the victims; true the government's response was wholly inadequate; but it was a *hurricane!* The hurricane was the ultimate cause of the death and destruction and the later individual financial disasters. Well, yes and no. The hurricane was, of course, the immediately proximate cause. But what caused the hurricane? Why did the levees fail? Why was the

---

[5] *The Insurance Industry's Troubling Response To Hurricane Katrina,* Americans for Insurance Reform, report was released to the media January 11, 2006.

public evacuation such a dismal failure? Why have the victims of the disaster seen so little of the billions in aid that were promised? Why when all house mortgages have compulsory insurance coverage as part of the contract is payment to the Katrina victims such a legally contentious issue in so many cases?[6] Why does so much of New Orleans today *look exactly like it did three days after the hurricane?* These questions have answers.

The Independent Levee Investigation Team's report[7] concluded that there were three main reasons for the flood damage, of which the hurricane is given only as the proximate cause:

(1) a major natural disaster (the Hurricane itself);

(2) the poor performance of the flood protection system, due to localized engineering failures, questionable judgments, errors, etc. involved in the detailed design, construction, operation and maintenance of the system, and;

(3) more global "organizational" and institutional problems associated with the governmental and local organizations responsible for the design, construction, operation, maintenance and funding of the overall flood protection system.

The answers demonstrate the complex inter-linkage of structural causes and effects that is the dystopian thesis.

There were several predictions that were made with respect to this disaster that powerfully illustrate this thesis and bode very ill

---

[6] Ibid.

[7] *Investigation of the Performance of the New Orleans Flood Protection Systems in Hurricane Katrina on August 29, 2005,* Independent Levee Investigation Team commissioned by The University of California, Berkeley and the National Science Foundation published July 31, 2006.

for the future. First, and perhaps most importantly, is global warming. It is *still* a debated concept. We shall engage with this debate and the socio-economic causes for its perpetuation later. But let us simply say here, that just as the depletion of Grand Banks fish stock was predicted, so too are increases in average hurricane intensity levels. The so difficult (but possible) to measure, incremental warming of the planet produces effects considerably easier to measure: the frequency and force of storms. Average hurricane intensity has increased by fifty percent since the seventies.[8] All such extreme weather events – storms, floods, droughts etc. – are predicted to greatly increase in intensity and frequency with global warming. The scientific community widely believe that this is already underway. Thus, while we cannot know for sure that global warming played any causal role in the formation and intensity of Hurricane Katrina, we can reasonably assume that it is likely.

No matter about global warming increasing their frequency and intensity, hurricanes have always formed in warm Caribbean waters, and every year some will hit the American coast with varying degrees of force. Everyone has known for years that eventually, simply by the law of averages, a hurricane would hit New Orleans and that powerful flood surges very likely would go with it. Flood protection is why New Orleans' levees were built in the first place. However, we now know a great many things about this "risk amelioration" effort. First of all, that is exactly what it was designed to do – *ameliorate* risk *not eliminate it*. Thus, a probabilistic calculation was involved in the levee design in the first place. They were designed to completely protect the city in the teeth of some levels of hurricane intensity and expected flood surge but not others more powerful.

Secondly, shoddy workmanship was involved in the levee construction; there was under-funding and disorganization at the different levels of government agencies, as well as incompetence

---

[8] National Science Foundation, *Hurricanes Growing More Fierce Over Past 30 Years,* Press Release 05-128 July 31, 2005. http://www.nsf.gov/news/news_summ.jsp?cntn_id=104325

and corruption connected with their maintenance.[9] Thus, the levees proved wholly incapable of doing even the job they were intended to do. All of this received considerable media attention in the immediate aftermath of the storm. There was an orgy of finger pointing and buck passing that they facilitated. But one might be tempted to engage in some issuance of blame to the media themselves. Why, when all the preceding issues were well-known long before the hurricane did the media not engage in some investigative journalism and critical analysis, and do some finger pointing *before* the hurricane, when it might have done some good.

The critical accusations directed at the media of the preceding paragraph apply to the emergency evacuation "plan" as well. It was well-known to people within a number of different government agencies that many thousands of people would lack the means to get out of New Orleans. The "plan" was for them to go to the Superdome. The inadequacy of this arrangement was apparent to a great many experts long before the hurricane actually hit. It was pre-decided that a total evacuation would be beyond the available resources, an interesting conclusion to be made in one of the richest countries of the world when we have poor Cuba to consider in comparison. Faced with their own probable hurricane disaster, Cuba managed to evacuate to safety one million and a half people (a much greater number than the New Orleans situation) apparently without serious difficulty or any loss of life.[10]

The year following Hurricane Katrina's preparedness mirrors that prior to the disaster to an amazing degree. Hurricane season

---

[9] *Investigation of the Performance of the New Orleans Flood Protection Systems in Hurricane Katrina on August 29, 2005,* Independent Levee Investigation Team commissioned by the University of California, Berkeley and the National Science Foundation, July 31, 2006.

[10] CNN Student Reports: *Hurricane Rita, Lessons from Cuba* September 20, 2005.
http://www.cnn.com/2005/EDUCATION/09/20/transcript.wed/

"officially" begins in June, and one might think that all emergency preparedness would have been completed by then. But no, the pumping system was still in a dire state of damage and disrepair; many emergency communication centers are in trailers (just about the worst place for them in the event of a storm emergency situation) with the 911emergency lines still dependent upon highly vulnerable land lines. Only one hospital emergency room is now open in New Orleans. It has only a 17-bed capacity.[11] In addition to other deficiencies in the hospital and health care system as a whole, people already cannot get proper *emergency* treatment. But what if there were to be a multi-car crash with multiple victims and injuries? This is the Third World reality brought home to the United States.

Repair of the levees was completed in 2006, but though they were known before Katrina[12] to be inadequate in design, this has not been rectified. In theory, they should be fully able to handle tropical storms and hurricanes below a category three. *Probably* the system would be adequate for a fast-moving category three, but if a hurricane of that strength was actually slow moving, Katrina's devastation or worse would likely be the result. The "bet" is that such like or worse weather events won't happen for quite some time.

The damage and suffering of New Orleans gives us our "First World" dystopian vision of the future and its lessons for how it will affect ordinary middle-class people. There will be physical suffering and injury for large numbers of poor people as a result of disasters even if they are predicted long in advance. The necessary safety measures simply will not be invested in. There will be property damage sufficient to financially ruin the middle-class people it by such extreme weather events because of a

---

[11] As of September 2006.

[12] *Investigation of the Performance of the New Orleans Flood Protection Systems in Hurricane Katrina on August 29, 2005,*
Independent Levee Investigation Team commissioned by The University of California, Berkeley and the National Science Foundation published July 31, 2006.

number conjoined factors. First, there will be an economic infrastructure collapse owing not only to the engineering difficulties of repair and rebuilding but because of the under-financing of this effort; thus jobs will vanish. Secondly, there are two virtual certainties with respect to property damage and insurance: 1) that lawyers will do very well in the lawsuits that will go on for years; and 2) that huge numbers of people will find themselves waiting forever for their claims to be settled or they will be inadequately reimbursed. This last may well be such a financial blow for many middle-class homeowners that they will move from "middle class" to "working class"; that is, the losses will be a disaster from which they will never recover but instead will find their world permanently altered in very unpleasant ways. This is part of the general dystopian thesis to do with rich and poor, middle class and working class, First World and Third – there will be large-scale, downward social mobility.

Safety precautions in the face of known risks, the welfare state "safety net" and other costly expenditures for government, ultimately depend upon some level of taxation of capital and the affluent. This has been eroded by neo-liberal capitalist reform. It is a part of the dystopia thesis that neo-liberal policies, unfettered by government regulation or taxation, is the natural way to maintain free enterprise political systems most in accord with the underlying dynamic of a world capitalist system. Social democratic "liberalism" or "socialism lite" once served a purpose in deflecting demands for more fundamental revisions of the system. But this seems now to be fading everywhere in the First World. The British Labour Party's embrace of neo-liberalism and the "American Way," for example, is merely symbolic of a much wider world trend. Thus, though the depletion of the Grand Banks fish stock is a small aspect of the dystopia of the present, the various Canadian and Newfoundland government responses to it are not so much so. With respect to political responses to economic and environmental disaster, New Orleans, not Newfoundland, is the future in the present.

Much of the First World middle classes are at risk to be affected by the events and issues that we shall discuss in later chapters. If we look at New Orleans as any kind of model for the future, we can conclude that neither government nor big business will be much help to ordinary people. All that will be left in a world full of much greater levels of suffering will be charity. And even in this, Hurricane Katrina and New Orleans demonstrate an old Third World pattern of response to disasters. Extravagant promises are made by First World governments. Yet most often, for most wealthy counties, and almost always in the case of the United States, such promises are not kept. For example, "Nearly 96,000 people in Louisiana have applied for the Road Home federal grants of up to $150,000, but the money has only reached about 100 applicants so far."[13] The billion and half dollars promised by the Bush administration to revamp and improve the southern levee defences was rescinded before the next year's hurricane season. The justification for this reneging on the promises made during the media frenzy of disaster coverage: the area was declared to be simply not viable. . . an apt description for the dystopian realities already found in much of the third world.

The Other World (1): Children, Crime and Gangs in Nigeria and Brazil

> *He sees it in the juvenile street gangs, who live in*
> *fear of death and who propagate fear by inflicting*
> *death to banish fear.*
>   Ed McBain

> *What we were after now was the old surprise visit.*
> *That was a real kick, good for laughs and lashings*
> *of the old ultraviolence .*
>   Alex, in the film *A Clockwork Orange*

The poor of the world experience ills of dystopia first and

---

[13] New America Media,(*Katrina Relief Funds: What Happened to the Money?* January 28, 2007.
http://news.ncmonline.com/news/view_article.html?article_id=990d632
2afec4e8a001f82f2a81fb200

most intensely; in fact, the suffering exists on a whole different level than that of the First World cases we have thus far discussed. Still, the little disaster on Christmas day 2006 in Nigeria[14] was not an event of anything like the scale of destruction wrought by hurricane Katrina. No, it was simply a little explosion and a fire that incinerated perhaps 200 people. The explosion and fire came from an oil pipeline not too far from Lagos, Nigeria's poverty-stricken, violent capital. It was not exactly an accident, and the victims were not exactly innocent. They had punctured the pipeline to steal oil.

Such explosions are relatively rare but not exactly unusual either. A much larger pipeline explosion outside Lagos in 1998 killed 1,000 people. Attacks on the pipeline, and theft of oil, though, is very common in Nigeria. Local people in the oil-producing areas complain that they see little benefit from the country's massive oil production. They respond politically and criminally in a contextual scale of poverty and desperation that is hard for us even to imagine.

Personal safety, the perception as well as the reality of some level of security, are freedoms most of the first world takes for granted. The perceptions and the realities of risk are not identical but are nonetheless related. True, repeated studies of perceptions of risk show rural and suburban middle-class elderly women to have the greatest fears of violent attack. This perception is out of sync with actual probabilities of robbery or attacks. It is actually urban young men that suffer the greatest risk of attack. Some social scientists find this disjuncture perplexing; they can deduce why the elderly women may be quite afraid – the constant exposure to media reports of crime fuel their fears – but they cannot understand why the young men are not more afraid. It doesn't occur to most social scientists that actually the young men *are* afraid, in fact, are very afraid. That they don't freely admit this fear to social science researchers, that they seldom if ever

---

[14] CNN, *Pipeline Explosion Kills at least 200*, December 26, 2006. http://www.cnn.com/2006/WORLD/africa/12/26/nigeria.blast/index.html

admit it to anyone is an easily understandable coping mechanism for living in a very violent, very insecure world. If one is constantly living with dangers, then there is, of course, a manner in which one becomes to some degree inured to them. The fear and the awareness of risk are consciously and unconsciously repressed; but though they are buried, they are not eliminated. Those that live in very violent worlds are suffering a constant fear. Being violent oneself does not alleviate that fear, though it may be a response to it. The frequent observation of brutality does inure one to it; but this familiarity does *not* eliminate the manner in which life in a brutal frightening world is *suffered*.

There is, of course, organized and articulate political struggle in Nigeria with respect to the unjust manner in which the oil wealth is distributed. But on a much broader and deeper level, one of the major proactive responses is simply organized criminal violence. The "area boys" gangs of Lagos are famous for their violence. An American blogger writing about them once asserted they "make the Crips look kind of wimpy!"[15] Part of the dystopia thesis is that the existence of suchlike gangs is an entirely understandable and predictable response to the extremes of inequality and social exclusion produced by world capitalism. The economic realities of life for a substantial proportion of the Nigerian population are not only harsh but increasingly desperate. Those close to the bottom struggle to ensure that they do not actually reach the very bottom, because the very bottom is death! The "legitimate" social structure of society, the agencies of law enforcement and the military, exist only to protect the interests of capital (e.g., the oil installations and the pipelines) and the security and safety of the rich and small middle class. The rest of society is on its own, locked in a vicious struggle for survival. Of course, gangs would emerge, big and small mafias develop and fight and steal and bully and generally terrorize. They are about two things principally: self defence and making money.

---

[15] The Crips are the larger of the two principal black criminal gangs that originated in Los Angeles but are now spread throughout the US and have thousands of members. The Bloods are the other one.

Let us turn to Brazil to make the former connection clear. The number of homeless Brazilian street children is enormous and incalculable. Children as young as five or six are on their own . . . or would be, if it were not for the way in which they link up and look after one another. They beg. They steal. To a store owner who has the misfortune of having some of them hanging about in his neighbourhood, they are not some sad tragedy or even a nuisance. No, they are far more than that last designation. They are perhaps what is actually ruining his business. The presence of these street children embarrasses his customers; they are frightened and irritated by them, and sometimes robbed and assaulted by them. They look to shop elsewhere.

Such problems occur in the First World as well. The same motivations for gang formation exist in the US. The aforementioned Crips (of LA origin) are guesstimated to number in the hundreds of thousands now. The same motivations for gang membership would have been present in New Orleans too – that is, self defence, a sense of belonging and cultural identity, as well as simply employment in organized criminal capitalism. One of the serious aftershocks of Hurricane Katrina is the significant rise in Houston's violent crime rate. The New Orleans gangs were "evacuated" to Houston. They are now fighting for crime control and territory with the local Houston gangs.

But there are differences between the First World and the Third. American six-year-olds are sometimes dealt with badly by an underfunded child welfare system. But they are never simply left to look after themselves on the street. Older street kids who become annoyances to merchants are moved on by the authorities; they are harassed and often treated callously. But they are never literally hunted down and killed! But that's happened in Brazil. "Citizens groups," vigilante organizations were formed. They formed death squads. And the prey of these hunters was young children!

Vast numbers of Brazilian children are street children. Estimates vary from two hundred thousand to eight million. Death by violence is normal; most of these children do not expect to reach their eighteenth birthday. They are executed by the police as well as by the vigilante death squads. But mostly they are the victims of the normal violence that is simply part of the violent criminal world that is life in the favelas (slum neighbourhoods). Estimates vary from a high of eight to the conservative figure of two child deaths by violence a day!

When children cannot be looked after by deceased, absent, ill, seriously impoverished or abusive parents, and the underfunded and generally inadequate state welfare agencies cannot provide safe havens for them, then such children live in the street. Criminal gangs become their fathers and mothers. They do not receive a formal education, but they learn. And if they survive, the lessons in brutality they have been taught make them a force to be reckoned with, making it increasingly impossible for anyone to feel any sense of safety and security.

The gangs of delinquents evolved over the years to become serious criminal organizations. Because the Brazilian police force is underfunded, because it is corrupt, because it only protects those with money and does nothing for the millions of poor, this situation left a vacuum in social organization in which the power of the criminal gangs grew beyond their criminal activities to be the enforcement agencies with the poorer districts. The gangs, of course, have many members in prison . . . which means, on some levels, they run the prisons, and many incarcerated leaders continue to run their extensive criminal activities outside the prison from within. Conditions within the prisons are appalling, and thus there is extreme dissatisfaction there. Dissatisfaction within the overcrowded prisons is mirrored in the impoverished and overcrowded favelas. Thus, we find a situation in Brazil where it appears at times that the Mafiosa-style violent struggles for power evolve into something more political, though devoid of any plan or ideology. For a few days in the middle of May 2006 in Sao Paulo, Brazil's largest city, a virtual state of war existed. The PCC, Sao Paulo's most powerful gang, openly challenged the power of the state. They attacked the police in their patrol cars, precinct headquarters and homes. They seized large numbers of buses and burnt them. Essentially, they brought the daily functioning of the economy to a standstill. The government was ultimately forced to negotiate with the imprisoned gang leaders.

Exactly the same sort of events occurs in Nigeria. There is a fusion between the day-to-day desperate struggles for survival and an inchoate political challenge to the established order. In Brazil, the economic heart of poverty and crime contains all the usual things of society's vices: robbery, extortion, prostitution and drugs. This last most extensively links up with the world criminal economy (though other activities such as prostitution do as well, of course). In Nigeria, though, we have the same situation as Brazil, where the sheer violent force of the criminal gangs drawn from the nation's impoverished youth dares to challenge even the country's armed forces. But in Nigeria, the interweaving of poverty, disenfranchised youth and organized criminality connects up with the fundamental working of the world economy in an even more obvious way: oil! It is estimated that criminal gangs siphon off from Nigeria's oil export pipeline more than 200,000 barrels a day.[16] Thus is the wealth of between five and ten percent of the output of the world's seventh-largest oil producer being redistributed to a desperate local population . . . but not according to any principals of rational justice; no, the redistribution occurs in the context of lost children on the one hand and organized brutality on the other.

But let us return to Brazil to put the relations between homeless children, crime and world capitalism into its proper context. There is a perfectly logical vicious circle of children, crime and capital. The high Brazilian levels of poverty have two sources. Brazil's internal socio-economic structure is very, very unequally balanced – just one percent of the population owns approximately fifty percent of the wealth[17]. But notwithstanding

---

[16] Karl Maier, "Shell 'Feeds' Nigeria Conflict, May End Onshore Work (Update6)", June 10, 2004.
http://www.bloomberg.com/apps/news?pid=newsarchive&sid=aC3m6A
FYzJjM&refer=europe

[17] "Street Children in Brazil". *http://www.answers.com/topic/street-children.*

that inequality, overall it is very much poorer than a First World country. Thus, in part, Brazilian poverty derives from its relatively poor status among the world nations. The inequality of the former is very much related to the inequality of the latter. The wealthy elite is able to retain its relative privilege, in part, by selling out its country in cooperation with the wealthy corporations, governments and inter-government institutions (e.g., the IMF and World Bank) of the West.

> From 2003 to 2005, the federal government exclusively applied to the interest of the debt (without considering the values paid for paid-off bonds) R$230 billion, which is equivalent to 2.4 times the expenditure on healthcare in land reform over three years. is equivalent to 2.4 times the years[18].

This sort of prioritization is, of course, part of the neo-liberal ideology imposed upon Third World countries. As creditors, they not only demand repayment of loans made in good faith but they interfere in governmental decision making by making loans conditional upon less social spending.

This imbalance between debt repayment and social spending thus goes quite some way to explain two things: 1) the general impoverishment that leaves children uncared for with nowhere to turn except to criminality; and 2) the underfunding of police that leaves them, on the one hand, underpaid, undertrained, undermanned and frequently outgunned by the criminal gangs they must contend with, and on the other hand, open to corruption to the point of being interwoven with the very criminal organizations they are supposed to protect the public from. The fear, the bloodshed, the pain and suffering are tragic; their proportions are monstrous and truly dystopian. But the causes are clearly and easily understandable. The dystopia of the present Third World possesses a very definite logic.

---

[18] Maria Lucia Fattorelli Carneiro (2006), "Foreign Debt and Human Rights Violations in Brazil," *Rede Social de Justica e Direitos Humanos.*

The Other World (2): Dystopian Development and the Development of Dystopia, the Case of the Maquiladoras

This shirt sells for $14.99, and the women who made this shirt got paid $0.03. Liz Claiborne jackets, made in El Salvador. The jackets cost $178, and the workers were paid $0.74 for every jacket they made. Alpine car stereos, $0.31 an hour. It's not just sneakers. It's not just apparel. It's everything.
Charles Kernaghan

A plethora of terms refer to the poorer countries of the world – the "Third World," the "underdeveloped world," the "periphery," the "undeveloped world." Each term captures grains of truth depending upon which aspects of which countries one wishes to look at. Perhaps the most optimistic term used is "developing world." It implies not only progress but a specific progression. Wrapped around the term is a whole theory of development. It implies the theory of *stages* of development.

The end stage is the "developed world" of the knowledge and service economy that is in the process of exporting not only its pollution but its older industrial activities to the less-developed nations. The industrial past of these "developed nations" is the present of many of the "developing" ones. Through the lens of this optimistic theory, we can clearly see the futures of the "tiger economies" (once upon a time, so-called anyway) of Southeast Asia. We can see many of the citizens of these countries possessing some of the luxury goods they manufacture and export; we can see some of them achieving the lifestyles of the richest citizens of the West that at present they merely facilitate. Well, this scenario is actually highly unlikely according to the dystopia thesis of development that will be explained in chapter 6.

In this section, though, through our examination of the Mexican Maquiladoras, we will see that, though the adjective "developing" is very apt to apply to these areas, the aforementioned set of theoretical propositions concerning development are not. The Maquiladoras show us that dystopia cannot be simply equated with a lack of development but how it can embody suffering all the more terrible for the hopes of the poor upon which it feeds.

The Maquiladoras are the Mexican example of a global phenomenon. The phenomenon is the formation of "special economic zones," whereby their host country voluntarily relinquishes a number of the political rights and privileges of sovereignty. This is not the usual way this is explained. Rather it is usually simply explained as the formation of special import and export areas. However, this more neutral description hides some of the ways whereby local and democratic constraints upon foreign capital are forfeited. In zones such as the Maquiladoras, tools, machinery and raw materials of one sort or another are imported duty free. A special workforce is locally recruited (only relatively locally, as people may travel long distances within their own country to work there). This workforce then manufactures goods for export. In Mexico's case, this includes textiles, electrical goods, toys, automobile assembly, furniture assembly and sporting goods. Foreign companies situated in the Maquiladoras include such American household names as General Electric, Chrysler, Ford and Mattel; Japanese ones like Honda, Toshiba and Mitsubishi, as well as the German Mercedes and other international giants.

It is with reference to cars that we can most clearly show that the conventional "evolutionary stages of development theory" can be seen to clearly be wrong. The theory would liken the development of auto assembly in the Maquiladoras to the Fordian revolution of Detroit auto manufacture in the early part of the 20th century. Later the "developing" Maquiladoras would become a fully "developed" economic zone, with its accompanying higher standards of living for the workers. There are reasons why this is very unlikely to happen.

The Ford revolution in early Detroit was threefold. First, there was assembly-line production to make automobile manufacture a mass production. Secondly, though Ford's vicious attacks, worker intimidation and strong opposition to union formation would seem to belie it, Ford's mass manufacture was based upon good wages for the workers. The attraction of these wages caused one of the largest mass migrations of the 20th century: from the economically declining and impoverished rural South to the northern city boom in manufacture. The "good wages" paid these newly arrived urban assembly-line workers was not done out of some spirit of generosity or altruism on the part of Henry Ford. Rather the mass production of cars was set to coincide with the mass purchase of the same. This is the third portion of the tri-partite Fordian revolution: mass consumption.

But the Maquiladoras Ford and other auto-assembly plants have a very different connection to mass consumption. In early Detroit's history, it was the workers themselves who later became (along with others) consumers of the products they produced. There was then a reciprocal logic between mass production and mass consumption that does not exist in the contemporary Mexican case. The mass consumption is occurring elsewhere; the consumers of this Mexican product are not Mexican (or Philippino or other Third World workers of the "special" economic development zones). These workers will *never* be buying the products they make. The average Maquiladoras wage (for manufacturing workers) is one dollar an hour.[19]

Not only will executives of the foreign companies of the Maquiladoras, or the hack politicians of both the US and Mexican governments, publicly praise the operation of these zones and justify them in terms of making life better for the workers but one will often find workers themselves joining in with the right-wing free-enterprise cheerleaders in asserting that life has been made better for them. They often assert that they are grateful for the opportunity. Chapter 7 explains the working of this ideological yet material phenomenon. But here one could simply ask: how can I be claiming the Maquiladoras as part of the dystopia of the present? That $1.00 an hour manufacturing wage looks pretty good in comparison with Mexico's $3.40 a day minimum wage.

---

[19] Wear, Avery (2002) "Class & Poverty in the Maquila Zone," *International Socialist Review*, May-June.

Many of the Maquiladoras workers maintain a good deal of hope and optimism. Yet from the dystopian perspective, both hope and optimism can be painful. Both hope and optimism are dystopian realities when the grounds for them are not reality based and the unpleasant sides to the hopeful situation lie concealed. For the majority of the female Maquiladoras workers, the hope and optimism break upon the unpleasant reality of aging.

I am not talking about old age in this context. The unpleasant realities connected with age in the Maquiladoras hit while the workers are still very, very young. The Maquiladoras workforce is both age and gender specific. It is temporary. Or rather, while the Maquiladoras are not temporary but permanently inserted into the Mexican economy, the individual workers have a limited employment span that stops a long, long way short of a "job for life." Rather it is a job for a few years. The young women who make up this workforce not only have the optimism and hopefulness of youth but are sometimes escaping the sexist limitations of an oppressive family regime and rural living. They now have their own money (though, of course, most are sending money home). They have money to spend on themselves, upon little luxuries. However much they take real pleasure in this, however hopeful they arrive, it does not take long for them to realize just how expendable they are. They wear out their bodies, they inhale poisonous chemicals, they destroy their eyesight or they simply get injured. Amongst other restrictions the international corporations escape from by investing in such economic zones, are the safety regulations that would govern them at home. It does not take long for the young women workers to realize that their future with these companies will not last too long – because there are *no older workers*. People have dreams, people have little luxuries. But no one has a new car!

The economic structural realities of the age dynamic of the Maquiladoras go something like this. If you agree to live apart from your family packed into a dormitory with a bunch of other women, and work 12 tedious, repetitive hours a day (and don't get injured or try to join a trade union or in any other way complain), then at the end of six years or so, you can take away the toaster and portable radio you saved so long for and start your new life . . . as a peasant again, or a whore or a beggar or a toilet cleaner.

Human beings can cheerfully submit to a good deal of misery. They can perform an awful lot of drudgery. But they need not only hope for some reward at the end of it but some realistic basis for that hope. It is not that they will not keep trudging on without these things; it is simply that doing so involves a psychological suffering beyond the experience of virtually all North Americans and Western Europeans . . . no matter how bad their jobs are. Not all of the suffering of dystopia is violent; not all of the suffering of the dystopia of the present is dramatic. Rather a good deal of it is simply mind-numbing, body-breaking, soul-destroying drudgery.

Interwoven with this drudgery, of course, is also a fair measure of violence. We have the ruthless use of police and hired thugs to destroy the self-organization attempts of the workers. This too is reminiscent of the early Detroit days and the formation of auto-worker unions. We also have a phenomenon that occurred later in the US inner cities – an emasculation of men accompanied by a hyper machismo and criminality. Sociologists used to write books about the marginalization of men in Black American families. The women not only maintained the homes but also had the jobs. Men came and went . . . to other women or to prison or the gang. And with this structurally created male unemployment came the personal tragedies of domestic violence. So it is now in the Maquiladoras.

The Other World (3): Rwanda: The Horror, the Horror

The people whose children had to walk barefoot to school killed the people who could buy shoes for theirs.
A Tutsi teacher

I think if people see this footage, they'll say oh, my God, that's horrible. And then they'll go on eating their dinners.
From the film *Hotel Rwanda*

While human misery is for the most part mundane, dramatically extreme violence is also very much a part of dystopian horror. The Maquiladoras have both crime and political struggle. There is both company- and state-sponsored repression. Violence continues to attend the struggle for unionization and worker's rights. Violence is also very much a part of the everyday life of even First World cities, and we have seen how extreme it can get in parts of Nigeria and Brazil. But there are nightmare extremes that go way beyond even this. Part of the dystopia of the present is genocide!

Events have occurred in history that are so monstrous that they boggle the human imagination. Questions are asked and asked again for a long time after. There are, for example, whole departments of Holocaust Studies in many universities. And rightly so. Along with the horrific dreadful simplicity of such occurrences, there is considerable complexity. However, that complexity of fact, and the matching complexity of explanation, should not be allowed to obscure some of the important simplicity of causation. The Rwandan case we shall discuss has its complexities too. But we should not forget that some of the *simple* reasons for its occurrence also form part of the horror of dystopia.

When the Europeans conquered and colonized the world, they often employed the rather simple but nonetheless effective strategy of divide and conquer. Generally, they built upon existing differences, alliances, inequalities and grievances to control a divided subject population. They would favor one group at the expense of another; if there were any pre-existing status and wealth hierarchies, they would utilize them and exaggerate them in their administration of the colonial society. Over time, the very identities of the colonized thus came to reflect not merely pre-colonial differences and loyalties but a much stronger, virulent sense of ethnic difference.

Such was the case for Rwanda. The Hutus came first and the Tutsis later as conquerors . . . or so one story tells it. There is no substantial proof of this; it may simply be the case that the two groups divided and evolved locally in relation to power, wealth and inequality at different points in their history. By the time the Belgian conquerors came, the differences between the two groups were relatively minimal. They shared a common language, culture, economy and way of life. They intermarried to quite a considerable degree and sometimes even changed their ethnic grouping self-identification. The Belgians thus had considerable work to do to exaggerate an initially minimal social division.

Tutsis *on average* (only on average!) are taller with narrower, more-European facial features. The Hutus are smaller with broader faces. Again, this is only on average. In practice, neither the Belgians nor the Tutsis and Hutus themselves could consistently tell the two groups apart. Thus, an order for ethnic identity cards was given by the colonizers. What was once somewhat vague and of minor interest, came to assume more and more importance. The Belgians made the Tutsis their colonial administrative assistants. That is, they gave them economic privilege and higher social status in exchange for facilitating their rule.

The preceding is merely a variation on a theme in the very old story of colonization. The post-colonial story for Rwanda is the same. The Europeans negotiated their respective departures with the other colonial powers, and the boundaries of the "countries" they left behind in no way resemble either pre-colonial boundaries, "natural" economic or environmental divisions, or the ethnic demography of the post-colonial areas. In short, in virtually every case, they left behind a mess – a seething caldron of colonial-sponsored envy, hatred, distrust and ethnic division. Almost always, there would be vulnerable minorities living in one country side by side with another country in which they would often be the persecuting majority. Such was the case for Rwanda. The distribution of Hutus and Tutsis extends to Zaire, and crucially to Burundi. In Burundi, the population distribution of Rwanda reverses itself.

Thus, we have the complicated inter-country and inter-ethnic history of persecution and reprisal. We have an economic dynamic of class division ideologically understood in terms of ethnic identity in response to the history of relative privilege, oppression and also reprisals across the border, where the power dynamic was tilted in the opposite direction. We see dictators maintaining their rule through the shifting of blame for corruption, chaos and a seemingly permanent economic crisis onto racial scapegoats.

Rwanda's history[20] and present are complicated, and the detail is, of course, important. Understanding the manner in which Hutu mythology was exploited to whip up hatred, as well as understanding the post-colonial politics of Belgium, France and the United Nations, is crucial to a full understanding of the tragedy of the Rwanda genocide . . . even to understanding the ideological political struggles involved in the debate as to whether to call it a genocide or not. However, all of this detail, as important as it is, should not be allowed to obscure the understanding of the simple and single powerful causal force that produced the horror. That is, all the ideological and political complexity of the Rwandan past and present took place in the context of inequality and extreme poverty.

Farms in Rwanda can frequently be as small as half an acre. Perhaps a way of dramatizing the fact of this poverty is to make the observation that in this world of incredible high-tech weaponry, that in this world where M16s and even rocket launchers seem to be easily within the budgets of the poorest peasantry in the world, in Rwanda it was machetes and axes that were mass purchased to produce the killings that the country's murderers could not afford to do with guns. So, 800,000 people were killed with axes, machetes or simply beaten to death.

---

[20] A number of excellent books have been written that detail the genocide and the history leading up to it. See, for example: Dallaire, Romeo (2003), *Shake Hands with the Devil: The Failure of Humanity in Rwanda,* Avalon: New York; Mamdani, Mahmood (2002), *When Victims Become Killers: Colonialism, Nativism, and the Genocide in Rwanda,* Princeton University Press; Gourevitch, Philip (1998), *We Wish to Inform You That Tomorrow We Will Be Killed With Our Families: Stories from Rwanda,* Picador: New York; Prunier, Gerard (1995) *The Rwanda Crisis,* Columbia University Press.

War of the Worlds

The great nations have always acted like
gangsters, and the small nations like prostitutes.
Stanley Kubrick

Every gun that is made, every warship
launched, every rocket fired signifies, in the
final sense, a theft from those who hunger and
are not fed, those who are cold and not clothed.
This world in arms is not spending money
alone. It is spending the sweat of its laborers,
the genius of its scientists, the hopes of its
children.
Dwight D. Eisenhower

We all know that Osama bin Laden is a fanatical Muslim extremist. We also all know that he and many others of his kind were not born poor; we know that many of his kind are actually quite rich. We thus know that the September 11 attack upon America and the myriad other suicide assaults were motivated not out of a sense of the injustices that derive from inequality and poverty. We know that, instead, there is an insult (real or perceived) to Islam that they feel must be avenged. And, of course, we have heard of the many virgins waiting in paradise for the martyrs to jihad. We know that the forces of hate ranged up against America and the free world are a monstrous form of insanity and thus are *fundamentally inexplicable.*

The dystopia thesis is not simply that very bad things have happened to people, are happening to them now and that more is on its way in the future. It is also a thesis about causality. It is also a thesis about knowledge and understanding in relation to that causality. It is a thesis that important knowledges are obscured by mystifying nonsense. The mystification can obscure even what is screaming-in-your-ear obvious. So, a little laugh at the forty-seven or seventy-three or however many virgins the Muslim martyrs of holy war allegedly believe they have waiting for them after their violent deaths, seemingly can blot out any possible connection of terrorism to the very real suffering of an unjust world. Our knowledge of Osama bin Laden's birth into wealth and privilege is allowed to discredit any speculation concerning the consciously chosen and extremely obvious symbolic aspects of the September 11 targets.

The World Trade Center and the Pentagon are the symbols, first, of all global capitalism and all of its attendant injustices and, secondly, of the military might that ultimately guarantees the privileges of one world on the back of the suffering of another. So, just as the Rwanda genocide was the result of irrational ethnic hatred and nothing to do with poverty and social divisions, 9/11 was merely a religious matter. The thesis that there are explicable reasons and material causes for the terrible things human beings do to one another is discredited on the basis of being "too simplistic." It is apparently not possible to understand material motivation as being inextricably intertwined with various forms of ideology and complex senses of group and self, and a host of other non-economic grievances. This is in itself an extraordinarily simplistic thesis. It is the proposition that we must read everything from the surface of events and take every stated motivation in the most literal manner possible. But could there not be a linkage between the Muslim objections to American military forces based in Saudi Arabia, the general Arab world opposition to the Israeli oppression of the Palestinians and something akin to the understanding of the global capitalism manifest in the worldwide "anti-globalization" movement? This label for these protestors is also an example of the mystification process at work, as they are not exactly against globalization, just its accompanying poverty, injustice and environmental harm.

True, the motivation of a suicide bomber may have crucially important religious underpinnings. True, the Palestinian suicide bomber may well be focused upon issues to do with land, or revenge or any number of things that are connected to the conflict but apparently quite removed from any context of economic inequality. But we can ask if it seems likely that the ideological fuel for the Middle East fire that comes from the Israeli/Palestinian conflict would be so potent and flammable if there were not the most basic and primitive effects of inequality being daily felt by the people in the region.

One perhaps feels thirst more strongly in a desert. But there are swimming pools even in there. Israeli kibbutzers use ten times the water of an average Palestinian[21]. In some cases, a single kibbutz[22] could supply forty average-sized Palestinian villages that currently have no running water.

How could the suffering associated with this inequality not be a causal factor in the conflict? How could the fact that the millions of Palestinians were driven from their land not be of the essence of the conflict? I don't mean by this latter question simply the historically disputed title to the land. That is another one of the things "we all know." We know the roots of the Jewish claim to their "promised land." We know the Palestinian claim that they were there for all the thousands of years in between that time and the time they were expelled from the land their great-great-grandfathers had known as their own. No, the question I was asking to do with land was that of a more fundamental inequality. Why are the people driven from their land still landless? Why was all the money spent upon guns and bombs instead of an attempt to mitigate the suffering that derives from simple economic disparities? But we know the answer to this question too. The guns and bombs are connected to oil . . . another thesis discredited as "too simplistic." This thesis we shall explore in depth in later chapters because humanity's dystopian future is very much bound up with oil and war.

---

[21] "The Politics of Water" Mideast Water Series: *Living on Earth*, Public Radio, Program first aired March 13, 1998.

[22] Ibid.

Chapter 2

Lessons from the Past

If history repeats itself, and the unexpected always happens, how incapable must Man be of learning from experience.
George Bernard Shaw

Human history becomes more and more a race between education and catastrophe.
H.G. Wells

Introduction

The present global human situation is absolutely unprecedented. Novelty is generally the case for any given moment in history: history does *not* repeat itself. What we do have available to learn about the future from the past, however, are instructive similarities. Yet we must be cautious in our search for such. This chapter will focus principally upon the causes for the collapse of two past societies and the question of just how instructive the analogies between their grim fates might be concerning our own future. The argument will be made that similar causal factors to those that produced their societal collapses are at work in our own. The chapter will also examine a much more recent historical phenomenon: a failed experiment in biodiversity and sustainability that sheds light upon a different aspect of our present predicament. It will conclude with a new perspective upon an infamous incident of brutality in the recent past – the My Lai massacre – that demonstrates dystopian lessons about the clouds that surround all silver linings.

Different sorts of comparative analysis are used by the social sciences with different degrees of success in producing authoritative understandings of problems. The historical comparisons that will be used here have too great a difference in circumstances belying them to give them any direct predictive power. Both the early societies being examined – that of Easter Island and Norse Greenland – are pre-capitalist and pre-industrial. Both are very small in terms of numbers and in socio-economic cultural terms are incredibly simple in relation to the enormous complexity of today's global political economy. However, though the confidence of a scientific pronouncement upon the relevance of the implicit comparisons being made cannot be claimed, the analysis possesses a different sort of power: *metaphorical power.*

Many of the analogies are very clear and present us with inescapable conclusions simply on the level of common sense. Among them is a single one very much part of the dystopia thesis that will elsewhere in the book be argued for on quite different grounds. The single most powerful conclusion is this: a socio-economic, cultural, political system with major structurally ingrained inequality between its members will causally contribute to, and later fail to adapt to, an environmental crisis that will ultimately undermine the viability of the whole society.

Of the two examples that we will focus upon, the Greenland Norse is more extreme. Societal collapse is a matter of degree, and theirs is the most extreme. They all died. However, we will begin with the Easter Islanders whose descendants still populate the island to this day. That small number is in part due to the later contact with the outside world. They contracted diseases for which they possessed no immunity and died in great numbers. Some of them were captured and taken as slaves to South America. But this later cruel fate is not what shall concern us here. The collapse of their civilization occurred *before outside contact.* Their descent into warfare, starvation and cannibalism was entirely brought about by themselves. In both cases, environmental factors ruined their economies but also in both cases social inequality played a crucial role. We shall begin with Easter Island.

The Mystery of Easter Island

> *The greatest mystery is not that we have been*
> *flung at random between the profusion of*
> *matter and of the stars, but that within this*
> *prison we can draw from ourselves images*
> *powerful enough to deny our nothingness.*
> Andre Malraux

The title of this section has a certain irony. The term "mystery" has been applied so often for so long to Easter Island that its accuracy possesses all the certainty of a cliché. And indeed there is a mystery. But it is not the one that most people would associate with Easter Island. That mystery is that of the massive stone statues found on the island. Why were they constructed? How were a people of only stone-tools technology able to build, transport and erect these huge statues? Well, we shall come to the real mystery of Easter Island somewhat later. The perceived mystery, though, is in fact not very mysterious at all. Though we cannot know many things about this pre-literate oral culture of the past with a great deal of certainty, modern archaeological technique of some deduction can tell us quite a lot about the statues and the role they played in Easter Island society.

There has been considerable past debate and many bizarre theories concerning Easter Island. Thor Heyderdahl argued that the Islanders were descendants of the Incas or some other South American tribe and famously sailed his Kon-Tiki raft from that continent to the island to prove the migration possible.[1] Modern genetics powerfully suggests that this is not very likely at all. The Easer Islanders were part of the same wave that discovered and settled the rest of Polynesia. Evidence for this rests upon not only genetic similarities but linguistic and cultural. Erik von Daniken's quack theory that the famous statues were constructed by aliens has only the difficulty of constructing a more plausible

---

[1] Heyerdahl, Thor (1950), *The Kon-Tiki Expedition* and (1958) *Aku-Aku: The Secret of Easter Island*, Allen & Unwin: London.

alternative, to support it.[2] However, more reasonable people have indeed been able to do so.

The Easter Islanders did not possess iron tools, cranes, modern engineering knowledge or even draft animals. The statues were dragged miles and erected by human muscle power alone. These statues (called *moai*) were big: 32 feet the tallest (75 tons) and 87 tons the heaviest, but on average "only" about 13 feet tall and 10 tons. However, the size of these is dwarfed by that of the platforms (*ahus*) that they were erected upon. These ranged from 300 to 9,000 tons! On top of many of the statues was an additional feature: a red scoria cylinder (called a *pukao*) weighing up to 12 tons. There were not just a few of them either; rather there were 887 of them (only a little over half transported out of the quarry) and about 300 ahus. How *did* they manage it?

The more massive ahus were not solid stone but rather rectangular structures with quite large facing stones (about ten tons the largest) and simply filled with stone rubble. Their massive weight is of interest to us, not so much as an engineering challenge successfully managed by the Islanders, but simply in terms of the massive expenditure of energy required by the population to carry and lift so much rock. It is the transport of the statues that provides the challenge to understanding how they managed it – that and the erection of the larger and taller moai and the placement upon them of the heavy *pukao* headdresses.

We actually do not know for sure exactly how the Easter Islanders transported and erected these heavy statues. But both reasonable speculation and modern experiment show the feat to quite possible within the technological limitations of these early artists and engineers. The principal quarry, Rano Raraku, contains statues of every production stage, from the wholly complete and ready for transport, to mere crude outlines roughly hewn from the

---

[2] Daniken asserts that the stone the statues are carved with is not to be found on Easter Island and is as hard as steel. This might make the aliens theory more attractive if either alleged fact were true. They are not. See von Daniken, Eric (1972), *The Gold of the Gods,* Putnam and Bantam Books.

rock but still attached to the ground. Beside the statues, the craftsmen's tools were found littered about. The transport roads are still plainly visible on the island, following the contours of the land to minimize the difficulties of steep inclines. Jo Anne Van Tilburg proposed the quite reasonable hypothesis[3] that the Easter Islanders used a variation on the outrigger canoe ladders used elsewhere in the Pacific for transporting heavy logs. These are parallel tracks held fast by unmovable wooden cross pieces that the logs or in the Easter Island case statues would be dragged over. The application of some kind of lubricant would of course make the task easier and some kind of system of movable rollers much easier still. Tilburg actually experimented with the transportation of an average sized moia. She found that it took a week for fifty to seventy people to drag such a prone statue the nine miles, which was the maximum transport distance from quarry to destination on the island.

Erection of the statues was, of course, quite tricky. A modern archaeologist failed to do so successfully even with the use of modern machinery. Other moderns broke them in transport, and there is evidence that accidents occasionally occurred to the ancients as well. However, there is no question that the job can be done. Modern-day Easter Islanders, perhaps somewhat irritated that no one had deigned to ask them how the job was done, erected one themselves. The task involves some clever calculation and ramp construction but was entirely within the means of these stone people, given their evident intelligence and determination.[4]

That the carving, transport and erection of these amazing statues was entirely within the very human powers of the Easter Island people should not diminish them as a source of marvel. First, of course, is the artistry, its skill and spiritual inspiration. This, one could say, is the qualitative dimension of the Easter

---

[3] Van Tilburg, Jo Anne (1995), *Easter Island, Archaeology, Ecology and Culture*, Smithsonian Institution Press: Washington DC.

[4] Jared Diamond (2005), *Collapse: How Societies Chose to Fail or Succeed*, Viking Penguin: New York.

Island accomplishment. The second more-quantitative aspect is no less impressively marvelous and more relevant to the dystopian theme of this book. The sheer effort on an individual and most importantly collective scale is horrifying. The reader might find "horrifying" a rather peculiar choice of words to connect with one of the most beautiful and wondrous collections of artifacts of a complex vanished civilization in the world. And indeed it is. The explanation of my use of it is to be found within the next section's reflections upon the "real mystery" of Easter Island.

The Real Mystery of Easter Island

Madness is something rare in individuals – but in groups, parties, peoples, ages, it is the rule.
Frederick Nietzsche

The size of the expenditure of resources that Easter Island society devoted to the construction and transport of *moia* and *ahu* was truly enormous. It was not only material resources such as food, stone, rope and wood but also human resources. This last was mainly an astonishing amount of physical labor. But the creativity and "social energy" was also impressive.

This energy expenditure is a source of wonder in itself. Bear in mind that unlike our present-day society where perhaps only two percent of the population is engaged in agricultural activities, *all* pre-industrial societies need to have a much, much greater proportion of the time and energies of their populations directly engaged with food production. Some societies, of course, had need of greater energy outputs to this end than others. Some were blessed with richer natural resources and climates and/or better techniques of farming, animal husbandry, hunting and fishing. Easter Island was, we know, relatively wealthy in this way. We know this because of deductive reasoning. If they were not, they would not have been able to produce such a collection of massive statues and platforms. They simply would not have had the time and energy to spare from the more mundane activities of survival. But this is something else we know: though they did not all die out, nonetheless, there was a dramatic population reduction and starvation on an extensive scale. We need think about this expenditure of energy upon statue building in relation to this eventual fate of the society.[5]

A calculation has been made, again speculative, but nonetheless speculation based upon reasonable premises, that during the 300 years of peak *moai* production, the Easter Islanders expended physical energy equivalent to *one quarter of their entire food consumption*.[6] This is a truly astonishing proportion of collective energy to be devoted to such a task. It is particularly so when we consider the social relationships underpinning such an effort, the relations between the functioning of religious symbolism, social hierarchy and the division of labor.

Many of the *moai* have been re-erected in modern times as it was perhaps recognized that standing statues were much better tourist attractions than prone and broken ones. This modern effort was required because *all* the statues were toppled. The toppling of the statues is entwined with the *real* mystery of Easter Island. The social rage that brought these statues down is easy enough to understand; no, the real mystery of Easter Island is *why they waited until it was too late* to attempt social change.

---

[5] Jared Diamond's excellent book *Collapse* devotes a chapter to the failure of Easter Island society to socially and economically sustain itself. Another chapter is devoted to the Greenland Norse settlements. The respective sections dealing with these topics in *Dystopia* are significantly indebted to Diamond's work. However, there are a number of other interesting and informative books devoted to Easter Island and its famous statues. See, for example, J. Flenley and P. Bahn (2003), *The Enigma of Easter Island*, Oxford University Press: New York; and Jo Anne Van Tilburg (1995), *Easter Island, Archaeology, Ecology and Culture*, Smithsonian Institution Press: Washington DC.

[6] Diamond (2005), *Collapse*, p. 179.

Easter Island was first discovered and settled around 900 AD.[7] The society flourished, and the population steadily expanded until approximately 1500,[8] when the production of *moai* also reached its peak. One could thus also assert that this is when their civilization reached its peak. Shortly after this, their complex social hierarchy and culture broke down, their economy collapsed, and their quality of life totally degenerated to the point of mass starvation and constant internecine warfare.

Easter Island society was actually twelve or thirteen separate "nation states" (though not exactly the modern equivalent of such). These states socially and economically interacted with one another in a kind of competitive cooperation. They traded with one another, they intermarried, but they also competed. The island's economy was interdependent. Each part of the island, each state, possessed things the others needed but were unable to obtain elsewhere. For example, the largest quarry where virtually all the *moai* were carved was in a single territory, but transport of them to some states required passage through several others. Sometimes there was conflict and violence, but most often the competition for prestige took the form of *moai* building, while peaceful trade was the norm.

This all seems very admirable until one examines the social order a little more closely. A hierarchy of inequality was structurally inscribed in it. It ranged from slaves to chiefs – an elite of military, political and religious leaders. The importance of

---

[7] There is scientific controversy surrounding the dating of the first habitation of the island, and there are much earlier estimates. But that it was settled by *at least* this date is not debated.

[8] Jared Diamond's estimate is between 1400 and 1600. Making such estimates is a complex and difficult process involving reasonable deduction, speculation and the empirical labors of such things as bone counting in middens. In *Collapse* he describes the archaeological process in detail and at a level accessible to the average layperson.

the *moai* to Easter Island culture shows how religion was integral to political leadership. It also suggests how crucial was the status competition between the members of the elite to the organization of the economy. It is the key to our practical and moral lesson to be derived from Easter Island: *the interests of religious political elites can run directly counter to the interests of society at large.* Their dominance can prevent sensible actions being taken to protect the economy . . . and the environment.

Easter Island before its human discovery was nearly entirely forest covered. But after arriving upon the island, the people must have begun cutting down the forest. Trees were valuable for many things crucial to Easter Island society. They provided lumber for housing and other domestic structures. They provided wood for boat construction. They provided the means for statue transport (thick ropes as well as the transport tracks). They provided some wild fruits. They provided firewood for cooking and warmth. Some of the forest needed to be cleared for agriculture. By the 17th century, though, the island was *entirely deforested*! This is the key factor in their economic collapse.

With the tall trees good for canoe building gone, the Islanders were unable to build the sort of ocean-going craft that they had arrived in. As a result, dolphin and tuna and other offshore fish that had previously formed a substantial portion of the Easter Islander diet disappeared as a food source. With total deforestation came the total extinction of all land bird species and the vanishing of a great many visiting sea birds who used to come there to breed. Wild fruit also disappeared from their diet. Inland fishing deteriorated through what became a necessary (for simple survival) overfishing. The kinds and numbers of shellfish shrank in size and quantity. Deforestation led to significant soil erosion and thus to a major decline in crop yields. In essence, the Easter Islanders quite literally destroyed the material base for their economy and survival! This is the real mystery of Easter Island. They must have watched themselves doing it and kept going anyway! Why?

Jared Diamond explores this mystery by speculating about what the Easter Islander who chopped down the last big tree must have been thinking. I think this is not difficult to imagine. By that time, all the serious problems caused by deforestation would have been all too readily apparent. He would also have known that it was too late to reverse the damage done. Not only that, but the problems would have been so severe that all time for philosophical or sociological reflection would also have been long past; he would have been far too immersed simply in the struggle for survival to have thought much about it. It is very doubtful if he would've even had time for any nostalgia for "the good old days" when trees were plentiful. No, what captures my imagination is the imprecise time span between a dawning but remote worrying conjecture and the later terrible certainty that all the trees would soon be gone. How did they socially process this gradual realization?

Essentially, the real mystery of Easter Island is how it is possible that an obviously creative and intelligent people, with such a highly evolved and complex culture, could have been so incredibly stupid? How could they destroy such a valuable resource, when its necessity for so many crucially important aspects of their life was so obvious? Diamond's phrasing of the question in terms of the last tree being cut down and the thoughts of a hypothetical individual, while certainly possessing dramatic force, nonetheless obscures some key elements of the situation. It actually obscures the most significant parallel between the Easter Islanders' world and our own. That is, it obscures the fact that the Easter Island deforestation was a product of *structural* rather than *individual* causality. Individual decisions were made, individual actions were taken, but both decisions and actions were made within a social context, within a social *system* of economy and culture.

The Solution to the Mystery

> *The important thing in science is not so much to obtain new facts as to discover new ways of thinking about them.*
> Sir William Bragg

First of all, the awareness of the deforestation problem was inextricably interwoven with a lot of religious nonsense. Secondly, the problem would've been connected with another one that is ongoing and persists to this day: the relation of structure to agency and the division of labor in relation to knowledge. Let us look at these in turn.

We do not know much detail of the Easter Island religion. However, we can easily deduce some broad generalities. The Easter Island cosmology would have related each individual's identity and place in the social hierarchy to a larger system, in which the place of human beings in the natural order of things would also have had an explanation. The boundary between the entirely abstract and "spiritual" and the material basis for daily life in most religions is usually not quite so absolute as one might at first be inclined to think. Religious rituals, rites and symbols are usually connected both to the natural order and to a system of morality. The latter usually contains an explicit (or at the very least implicit) justification and legitimation of the social hierarchy.

We know that Easter Island society was stratified, and we know that they put enormous energy into the production of religious icons. We know that the building of the *ahu* and *moai* served to sublimate the social tensions between the different tribal groupings ("states") and preserve the peace. This peace allowed a more complex economy because of the division of labor that accompanied the trading between the different groups. We can deduce a competition between the chieftains and the different social elites of each of them. And we can readily imagine some kind of religious cosmology that placed each individual in their place. But as religious cosmologies usually involve the natural world as well, we can readily imagine a symbolic quid pro quo between the different strata of the social order. That is, if the statues were the symbols of gods, then the religious and political elite were implicitly responsible for a great deal of the profane prosperity of everyday life, i.e., the economic well-being of the populace. On some level or another, with some symbolic expression or another, the gods and the political elite were responsible for health, good harvests, successful fishing and the like.

How do such conjectures connect with the problem of deforestation? Well, first some observations can be made before directly answering that question. We can observe that with respect to either farming or fishing there is always an element of luck involved. Obviously, both involve considerable skill, but that only affects success probabilities over what is usually a relatively lengthy time. The time periods involved with respect to "luck" may not be sufficient to wholly obscure individual skill variation, but all fishing and farming peoples know that both harvest and catch are variable due to factors beyond their control – the weather for example. Yet, on the other hand, individual variability of success obscures some of what otherwise might be a collective awareness of the collective variance of success or failure.

The success of farming is greatly dependent upon good soil, and this is where deforestation powerfully affected it: erosion. But while one might think that, given the small size of Easter Island, the connection between cutting down the forest and soil erosion would have been readily easy to spot, this is not entirely true. The daily activities of a great many people would have given them little occasion to notice the gradual deforestation of the island. Human beings tend to live with an unreflective acceptance of the present without considering even the quite recent past in relation to the future. Related to this is the division of labor with respect to knowledge. It would not have been most people's job to worry about either deforestation or a *new* explanation for a poor harvest.

I say "new" explanation here, because there would always have been a ready-made one within their cosmology. In some manner or another, the gods and their human representatives are responsible. Today's fashionable cultural relativism and epistemological tolerance for religious dogma fails to take into account some of the harm such belief systems can do. Today's tolerance and respect for any and all religious beliefs only stops short when confronted with religious-inspired intolerance, hatred and violence. But religious belief systems can do much more harm than that. Their false causal explanations can greatly impede arriving at the truth. Thus, what might seem fairly clear to us retrospectively, as to the causal connection between deforestation and soil erosion, would have been concealed within a mystifying cosmological fog involving gods, chiefs, rituals and statues.

The problems of firewood shortages, the connection between trees and comfort and warmth, would have come very late on. It would not have manifested itself until the society was economically collapsing because brush and smaller trees could satisfy that need. But the disappearance of the larger trees would have been evident much sooner because of their utility for statue transport on the one hand and boat building on the other. This is a problem that quite a number of people would clearly have seen before it reached a crisis. It is also a relatively complex issue to analytically reconstruct. It involves time and generational relations. It involves the structural disconnect between individual interests and collective ones in social systems of hierarchy. And again, of course, awareness of everything in relation to these issues would have been obscured by the cosmological fog of their religion.

Carvers carved, fishers fished, and farmers farmed. The political religious elite depended upon the labor of these people as well as those who actually dragged the statues to their places. We might recall here our speculative figure of twenty-five percent of the entire physical energy of the society being expended in this effort. But this twenty-five percent of calorie expenditure would not have been divided at all evenly. For some, virtually the entirety of their life's energy would have been devoted to it; while it was left to others to ponder the meaning of it all. While in reality the physical well-being of the elite and the construction of their symbols were entirely dependent upon the material activity of those lower in the hierarchy, the general understanding would have been just the opposite. Everyone's health, success and general well-being was directly dependent upon the power of the gods . . . mediated, of course, through the political religious elite. Many people would have noticed the forests diminishing, but they would have reflected upon it from their situation in a natural and social hierarchy as explained by their cosmology. Some may have been well aware of the effect of their own activities upon the forest. But again this awareness would have been contextualized within a system that told them it was not really their place to worry about such things.

The elites upon the island, however, would surely have noticed the accelerated diminishment of the large trees so necessary to deep-sea boat building, as well as the transport tracks for the *moai* they were so obsessed with creating. Reality must have intruded upon their religious cosmology to some degree. One can speculatively ask of the Easter Islander elite the same sort of questions often asked today's politicians: do they really believe the bullshit they spew, or is it cynically uttered to pacify an ignorant multitude? I expect the truth of the situation was much the same as now – some are true believers, and some are cynics; some wholly believe, some wholly disbelieve, and some maintain considerable contradictions of belief and understanding.

But two further matters must be considered to properly imagine how the elites would have cognitively processed the deforestation problem. First, there is the issue of temporality. When we later analyze contemporary capitalism, we shall see that temporality is a key aspect of its dysfunctionality. Until Easter Island society neared the end, that is, neared collapse, the problems accompanying deforestation would have possessed a certain remoteness and thus an accompanying air of unreality – particularly in relation to much more immediate concerns. The tracks would be made, the boats would continue to be built until there was no more lumber to do so. Now while this later eventuality might well have been quite clear to the last generation of boat builders, still in a sense, it was not their problem – it was their children's problem. They might have worried about it in an abstract kind of fashion, but such concerns would quite likely be overtaken by the problems of everyday life, their lifelong rivalry with Chief X perhaps. It was imperative that the latest *moia* be completed soon. *This* was a matter of honor and honor was all important. Easter Island society's socio-cultural peak and its collapse followed directly on from one another.

The starvation, warfare and societal breakdown came very quickly after the peak period of statue building. One can see statues at every stage of completion in Rano Raraku quarry. It was as though they kept living with the old system's plans for the future until it was absolutely clear to all that they were not viable. Then all of a sudden everything changed. Their societal collapse took the form of a kind of anarchic revolutionary catastrophe. When one looks at the statues in the quarry that had just been started, one can clearly imagine then the planning that was going on right up until the end . . . a planning for a future that was never to be. It is the dystopia thesis that such is precisely what is being done by most of humanity today.

The second crucial thing that must be understood about the self-inflicted ecological disaster of Easter Island and the role of the elite is the disjuncture of interests between the collective whole and particular groups. The interests of Easter Island society as a whole are obvious with respect to the environment. Deforestation was disastrous, and one is thus tempted to say that deforestation was certainly in no one's interest. But while that is true on one level, it is not so on another. The status competition among the elites was very important to *them*. Their individual and small-group interest was not identical to that of society as a whole. Yet they possessed the power to assert their interest against that of other social groups. Their short-term interests (the status competition) could be, and likely was, weighed against the future of society as a whole. Quite likely other social groups with less at stake in the social honor contest would have more significantly weighted the welfare of future generations. But they were not asked.

Perhaps the major point of the Easter Island lesson for us today is that, when faced with similar problems (oil depletion, global warming and the like) concerning our children's futures, we are not being asked what to do about it either. Some of us, both in a wider metaphorical sense and actually concerning trees, can see our forest disappearing at an alarming rate.

One of the theses of this book is that of structural mystification, the processes whereby the production of knowledge and its distribution are systematically obfuscated owing to the power relations of capitalist society. It is not some simple conspiracy but rather a complex dialectic contained within the various social institutions concerned with the production and reproduction of beliefs. Much more shall be said about this later, but we can observe, even at this early point in our argument, that forces are at work to systematically discredit it.

The writing of this section was very much indebted to the thinking and research of people such as Clive Ponting,[9] Jared Diamond (particularly the latter) and others concerned with environmental issues. Such thinkers and researchers see the history of Easter Island deforestation and socio-economic collapse as instructive with respect to our present environmental and social problems. But many of the relevant "facts" are subject to debate for a large variety of reasons to do with both science and politics. Thus, those like Diamond, who would use the Easter Island case as a warning, have been subject to considerable critique of both a frivolous and serious nature.

I have tried to ward off such criticisms in advance by propounding the relevance of the previously sketched Easter Island scenario as of *metaphorical relevance only*. However, even with respect to metaphor, the relative truth of factual propositions counts considerably. Cannibalism is a particularly controversial and emotionally loaded alleged fact. It is that very emotiveness that gives it its dramatic metaphorical potency as well. I am convinced by the evidence available that such did, in fact, take place. But it is controversial and there is counter-evidence as well.

More important than the cannibalism issue, though, is the anthropological and archaeological controversy concerning the essence of our Easter Island "story." That is, there is doubt that the mass starvation, serious depopulation, severe suffering and general socio-economic collapse ever took place.[10] There is no dispute over the proposition that *eventually* most of the

---

[9] Ponting, Clive (1991), *A Green History of the World: The Environment and the Collapse of Great Civilizations*, Penguin: New York.

[10] Readers may wish to look at some of the evidentiary and scientific grounds for critiquing the Easter Island "ecocide thesis." See, for example, Peiser, Benny (2005), *"From Genocide to Ecocide: The Rape of Rapa Nui,"* Energy & Environment, 16:3.

population was wiped out and that their rich culture disappeared. There is also no dispute that European contact was devastating for the Easter Islanders. At one point, virtually half the population was captured, taken into slavery and transported to South America. Nearly the whole population eventually died of Western-transmitted disease. No, the dispute concerns the *pre-contact* social collapse and de-population. I find the evidence for this convincing, as I believe most who seriously look into it will; but it *is* in dispute.

Some of the descendants of the Islanders themselves, other aboriginal peoples who have been the victims of colonialism and near genocide at Western hands, and anthropologists of a certain romantic political persuasion, all strongly desire to disbelieve the notion of self-inflicted harm by a pre-industrial people and culture. And there is some evidence for this "story."

There are variable limits to the relative certainty with which we can sensibly believe different accounts concerning the past. Though the Easter Islanders eventually invented a system of writing (rongo-rongo), there are no written accounts by them of the period we are concerned with. The oral testimonies that Diamond utilized in part as evidence for such things as cannibalism are part of what is questioned by the "ecocide skeptics." Thus, there can always be debate.

The very existence of scientific debate can always be used to cast doubt upon the arguments of "environmental alarmists." The potency of the Easter Island story, even just as instructive metaphor is weakened. But, as was just said, the relative certainty with which our credibility may pertain to an account of the past is variable dependent upon the quantity and quality of the evidence. Thus, we now turn to a case to which a *stronger degree of certainty* adheres. There is no controversy concerning this group of people's eventual fate. Theirs was the ultimate example of socio-economic collapse: *they all died!*

Lessons from the Greenland Vikings

*Every civilization that has ever existed has
ultimately collapsed.*
    Henry Kissinger

For 450 years, there were Norse settlers living in Greenland. They lived in two separate settlements, confusingly named the Eastern and Western settlements when actually they were both on the West coast and the "Western" settlement lay approximately 300 miles to the North of the "Eastern" settlement. In the mid-14th century, the remaining residents of the Western settlement met their final fate, and by the early 15th century the Eastern settlement was no more. Perhaps some had managed to return to Norway or to another of the Norse settlements such as Iceland. But there is no question concerning the fate of most of them: they died!

Why did they all die? Why did their society collapse? There is a simple and obvious answer that contains a good deal of partial truth. It got too cold, and they died. During the 450 years of their residency in Greenland, a profound climate change occurred. When they first settled there in 987 AD, it was during one of the warmer periods of northern climate fluctuation. They died out during what has been called the "Little Ice Age." The generally colder weather, longer winters and shorter growing seasons caused considerable difficulty for the survival of them and their animals. The shorter and cooler the growing season, the poorer the hay harvest, which the animals depended on during the longer winters when they were confined to the barns. The colder weather also iced up the navigational waterways and made the connection to the outside world much more tenuous. And the Norse were actually quite dependent upon their trading relations with other Viking colonies and Norway. No question about it, climate change was certainly a factor in the perishing of the Norse settlers.

But not all of their destruction can be attributed to the harsh climatic conditions that they faced. The Norse shared Greenland with another people whose society flourished. Greenland's cold barren ecosystem made survival difficult for the Inuit as well. But they adapted and survived and live there to this day.

This fact illustrates another of the differences between my perspective and Jared Diamond's. He is as ever the optimist when he writes: "The tragedy of the Greenland Norse (Greenland Scandinavians) thus carries a hopeful message: even in difficult environments, collapses of human societies are not inevitable; it depends on how people respond."[11] Well, yes, that is true. But, more pertinent to our present predicament, there is another implication to be aware of as well. Just because it is *humanly possible* to adapt to difficult conditions, and even flourish, does not mean that we will! The title of this section is not hopeful "Lessons from the Inuit." No, the lessons from the Greenland Vikings are (or should be!) frightening in their metaphorical parallels with our own probable future. They failed to learn! They failed to make necessary changes! And they failed to make peace with their enemy!

There is considerable speculation as to the degree that hostilities with the Inuit played in the demise of the Norse. Trade with them was minimal, and off-and-on warfare was chronic. But there is no doubt that the Norse failed to learn some of the most important survival lessons from the better-adapted Inuit. They never learned to make the fleet and maneuverable kayaks that served the Inuit so well in fishing and hunting seal, walrus and whales. All of which could have made a valuable protein contribution to the Viking diet.

There are other factors that contributed to the Greenland Norse collapse that one could argue were not their really their fault. As with Easter Island, soil erosion was an important factor in reduced agricultural yields. However, unlike the gradual deforestation on Easter Island, the damage in Greenland was done relatively quickly, before the Viking farmers could quite figure out what was happening. In this, they cannot really be blamed. At the time of their arrival, Greenland must have looked very like their Scandinavian homeland. There was rich soil underneath the treed and grassy valleys. It probably looked at first sight as being ideal

---

[11] Diamond (2005), *Collapse,* p. 179.

for cattle grazing. But while the Greenland ecosystem might have resembled Scandinavia, in reality it was much more fragile. Trees, shrubs, sedges, grasses and other plant life play a key role in keeping the loose topsoil from simply blowing away. In Norway, the Greenland Viking home of origin, the soil is heavier; many more generations of organic decomposition have contributed to its buildup. Plant life that is lost to animal grazing has a much longer growing season. It can easily be replenished. In Greenland, plant life does not recover so easily, partly due to the colder climate and partly because of a vicious positive feedback loop. The soil with less plant life to hold it in place is washed or simply blown away. The soil that remains does not support so easily the sometimes very fragile hold that the plant life had, and less regeneration occurs, leading to further soil erosion, and so on and so on, toward an ever-worsening condition.

Many types of agriculture simply became impossible and were abandoned. Increasingly, the Greenland Norse farms were devoted to hay production to support their domestic animals. The Norse kept all the usual European animals: horses, pigs, chickens, goats, sheep and cattle. The latter proved to be the most difficult to maintain and the most damaging to the fragile ecosystem; therefore, it was drastically cut back upon. Sheep and goats, most particularly the former, became the domestic animal mainstays of the economy. Though they cut back upon cattle rearing, they did not abandon it entirely, for reasons that will be discussed below. They ought to have. In fact, the sheep, though more economically viable, were still inflicting environmental damage. They ought really to have fundamentally changed their culture and lifestyle to something much more like the Inuit.

We have not yet got to the main lesson for us from the fate of the Greenland Vikings. But there are a few minor lessons we can reflect upon already. First, the fact that we cannot really blame the Vikings for a good deal of the environmental damage they quickly inflicted upon their fragile environment is, perhaps, a lesson itself. Humanity should tread very cautiously in its engagement with the natural world. There are perhaps *hidden dangers* involved with a great many activities. The risks that immediately come to mind here are to do with the likely future attempts to harness the potential energy of methane hydrate and with the dangerous kinds of biological experimentation being conducted. But these issues will be discussed much later. We can simply observe now that human practices can have a profound effect upon the environment in ways that are ultimately extremely detrimental, before we have any knowledge or awareness of the problems we are creating. We might also observe that cultural conservatism can be a very bad thing. Clinging to old habits of lifestyle, taste and economy can exacerbate problems and prevent their happy resolution.

However, though the collapse of Greenland Norse society has a great many interacting causes, there is one principal cause to direct our attention to. With respect to it, the fate of the Greenland Norse presents us with our most dramatic and relevant metaphorical lessons relating to our own future.

Inequality in Greenland Norse Society

> *Once the game is over, the king and the pawn go*
> *back in the same box.*
>   Italian Proverb

In the previous section on Easter Island, we considered the issue of socio-economic inequality in terms of exacerbating their problems and, in conjunction with religion, contributing to a sufficient understanding of them so as to allow their solution. The same factors are at play in the Greenland situation, though they are manifest somewhat differently and perhaps even more dramatically.

Greenland Norse society also had a religious-political hierarchy, but one that we are much more familiar with. They were not Christian when the land was first settled but became so in the 11th century, along with the rest of Scandinavia. This meant Roman Catholic. Their civilization did not last long enough to embrace the potential freedoms of the Reformation, which well might have benefited them. They were tithed by the Roman church. Thus, along with other inequalities, there was a straightforward transfer of wealth from the marginally surviving

Greenland settlements to the wealthier European homelands. This net transfer of wealth to the European center was something that the often-struggling Greenland farmers could ill afford; but, of course, this was not the only manifestation of a socio-religious element in the distribution of wealth.

Greenland has its own bishopric, but it was frequently an absentee one; the Greenland bishops quite understandably preferring the comforts of the relative Norwegian affluence. Regardless of the absence of God and the Pope's official representatives, tithes were duly collected for the Church by the lesser mortals of the religious hierarchy. These people were the real permanent elite of Greenland society. They were the large landowners.

Greenland was only semi-feudal in social structure. There were freemen and slaves, serfs and "nobility." Principally though, there were simply very poor small farmers and relatively wealthy ones, with different statuses and privileges corresponding to the relative wealth. Cattle, which we described earlier as being profoundly unsuited to the Greenland ecosystem, nonetheless played a very important role in the Norse socio-economic status hierarchy. It formed less and less a portion of their diet as time went on and became one of the prime signifiers of wealth – a status consumer item, as it were. It provides a handy reference point to imaginatively grasp the quantitative division of wealth in Greenland. Evidence suggests that the richest farm had something of the order of 160 cows, while many of the poorest were lucky to even have one.[12]

To understand the full significance of inequality as a causal force for the catastrophe in Greenland society, another aspect of their economy must be considered: trade. Unlike Easter Island, which was virtually entirely isolated for the whole of its history until the disasters of Western contact, Greenland maintained an infrequent but nonetheless fairly regular contact with their fellow Norse back in Norway and in their other settlements (e.g., Iceland). Trade was very important to the Greenland economy

---

[12] Ibid., p. 232.

and *could have been* the crucial factor in maintaining their survival. But it wasn't.

Iron was a particularly important commodity. The Greenland Norse were an Iron Age people with tools and weapons more sophisticated than those of their Inuit neighbors. Such might have given them an edge in times of conflict. But gradually the Greenland Vikings were forced to return to stone and bone because they could no longer afford the imports and the trading ships stopped coming. It is true that climate change also played a big part in this; as they entered the Little Ice Age, the passage to Greenland always dangerous became more so, the deep fjords of the Greenland coastline became increasingly filled with ice. But as always, even in relatively "simple" societies such as the Norse in Greenland, there exists a complex interaction of mutual causality. Frequently these turn into disastrous positive feedback loops. The weather-caused greater infrequency of visits by trading ships contributed to the impoverishment of the Greenland Norse society as a whole. As the overall economic level declined, there was a greater concentration of productive activity devoted simply to survival, and less time and energy was expended in accumulating the necessary goods for export . . . necessary, that is, if the ships carrying the much-needed imports were to hazard the journey. Thus, just as the Europe-Greenland trip grew more dangerous, just when the Greenlanders needed the imports the most, they actually had far less to trade, and the incentive to make the excursion at all declined to the vanishing point. So iron and other *crucial* import items became scarce to non-existent.

Actually, most of the Greenland imports were not at all crucial to their economy. Here is where inequality truly manifests itself as a factor pushing a marginal society over the brink. The bulk of their imports were "luxury items," status markers for the relatively affluent. The church is involved here again, too. They imported such things as ceremonial vestments made of jewels and rich cloth and stained glass windows for the churches. While undoubtedly more-utilitarian commodities were imported (e.g., the aforementioned iron tools), a disproportionate share of their imports was not of any practical use at all. And this is a society, remember, that tipped over the edge into eventual starvation and death.

There are elements involved in our present human condition and present activities that, when analytically measured against some of the dire probabilities of our collective future, can only be seen as quite literally insane. Such is also the case for the Greenland Norse. If their selection of imports can be seen as unwise in the context of the struggle to survive, their activities and energy related to *exports* can only be seen as completely mad!

As with any agricultural society, not only is it the total expenditure of effort on different activities that success and failure depend upon, but decisions concerning timing are crucial. In farming societies generally, but in ones of such bitter extremes of weather as Greenland, it is even more the case. The organization of activities is highly seasonal. Two activities fundamental to their very survival coincided. There was, of course, the hay harvest that their animals depended on to stand any chance to make it through the winter. And increasingly the annual caribou hunt became more important to the protein intake of the Norse diet. With two such critically important activities taking place at roughly the same time of year, one would think they would have had little time for anything else. But they made the time; they made the time for polar bear hunting!

Remember, they are hunting these animals not with guns but with Iron Age, and later sometimes even Stone Age, implements and weaponry. As difficult and dangerous one might imagine such a hunt to be, we still have not got to the heart of the Norse madness. They captured *live* polar bears! Live polar bears were one of their important exports, though they had no tranquilizer darts to keep the bears sedated for the long, rough and very dangerous sea journey home to Norway.

The mind truly boggles attempting to imagine the execution of this exercise. The skill and daring involved is truly impressive. But so is the very madness of the effort. The Greenland Norse population was small, perhaps 5,000 at its peak, and they needed all able-bodied people to contribute to the harvest and the caribou hunt. Yet they not only sacrificed labor hours to this pursuit, they also undoubtedly lost many lives. People risked their lives for what back home in Norway was a fashionable novelty for a time. This did little for their survival needs but partially paid for the stained glass windows in Greenland churches. We can see here a parallel madness to the Easter Island statue building; perhaps we can see it as even more so, as we attempt to construct a mental picture of a rope-tied struggling polar bear in a small boat in the middle of an Arctic storm. Could there be a parallel between such activity and the many thousands of dollars that rich people pay to risk their lives (and the lives of others who are not rich of course) climbing Mount Everest; or the millions of dollars now beginning to be spent upon "space tourism," just as our society is perhaps reaching its peak and beginning its collapse?

The Greenland Norse societal collapse can be summarized easily in terms of its causal factors and its lessons for us. Climate change played a role in their demise and may also in our fate. Though, as we shall see in the next chapter, human causation is very much a factor in global warming, there are other possible "natural" contributing factors. That the climate changes were not caused by the Norse is not really the point; the lesson derives from their incapability to properly adapt to their environment. The Norse failed to learn the survival strategies that could have saved them. The dystopia thesis argues that we seem to be similarly failing. The Norse failed to achieve peace with the Inuit. Conflict rather than cooperation played a role in their final fate and shall almost surely do so in ours. Finally, social inequality played its part in their economic failure. The interests of the elite are seldom the interests of the rest of society. Extravagance is a relative concept. Norse society was simple; our world is complex. But the effects can and may be the same: the rich of our world may well end up exactly as did the Norse; their wealth only buying for them the privilege of being the last to die.

The Heroes of the My Lai Massacre

> *No good deed goes unpunished.*
> Clare Booth Luce

The previous sections dealt with the fate of societies from quite a long time ago. This section concerns far more recent history – the late sixties – and does not deal with whole societies or their fates. It focuses upon a single historical incident, a shameful episode of brutality amid a larger context of brutality: the Vietnam War. Though the event is indeed shameful and brutal, that is not the reason why it is reconsidered here. That humans are capable of disgustingly cruel and violent behavior is not the lesson from the past that we need to engage with. No, there actually were heroes involved with the My Lai massacre. It is their fate that is instructive concerning our present and future.

On March 16, 1968, after an aerial bombardment and shelling of the village and its surroundings, American forces entered My Lai without receiving any enemy fire. Events then took place that later became known to the world as the "My Lai massacre." In the context of adrenalin, fear and confusion that accompanies any potentially dangerous situation, soldiers first killed sixty or seventy civilians. Most of these killings, though casting some aspersions upon the effectiveness of the American command and control over the operation, could still be considered "accidental."

A woman carrying a baby with older child in hand suddenly bursts out of the bushes; a pumped-up, scared American soldier shoots her, before really knowing who or what he was firing at. There were a great many such incidents at My Lai. An old man, severely wounded from the strafing and shelling that had occurred earlier, was shot in the head at point-blank range. The American soldier who did it later claimed he did so as an act of mercy. One can question such acts on many levels. But the events that later followed possessed *no such ambiguity*. They were *mass executions* of innocent civilians: old men, women and children.

The first of these executions took place on a trail leading out of the village. Approximately sixty villagers were being held captive under watch by American soldiers. Lieutenant Calley, the commander of these soldiers, had ordered them to "look after" these villagers. His orders had been misunderstood. He had meant: kill them all! He made this clear upon his return when he and another soldier then did so.

The second major incident involved the herding of villagers into an irrigation ditch and then firing upon them en mass. Some children managed to crawl out. They were chased down and fired on. Some children managed to survive the first few rounds of firing as their mothers threw their bodies on top of them in a futile effort to protect them from the fusillade of death. But the Americans were thorough. They went after the wounded. Sometimes it took three additional bullets to finish them off. The events took place over four hours, and to this day, it is not known exactly how many were killed. Estimates range from 400 to 500. But there is no doubt about some things. A great many children were murdered in execution fashion. Soldiers received direct orders to engage in these killings. Others gave those orders.

It was a particularly shameful episode in a shameful history of, first, colonial oppression and, then, neo-colonial oppression. The Vietnamese had been fighting for their liberation for a long, long time before the Americans became involved in the violent attempt to prolong their subjugation. The 30 years of wars fought by the Vietnamese against the French, the Japanese and finally against the Americans contain many, many stories of atrocity, even perhaps some that the Vietnamese freedom fighters conducted against their foreign occupiers. However, this in itself is not the reason for bringing up the events of My Lai in the context of dystopia. One might think that moral reflections upon war crimes, in and of themselves, would be prime lessons to learn about future dystopian scenarios. One might even go so far as to suggest that a species capable of engaging in such barbarity perhaps actually deserves to perish. But that is *not* the dystopian perspective that is about to be presented here.

Explanations for dreadful moral iniquity that begin on the level of humanity, that begin with phrases such as "man is destroying himself," do little to enlighten. Most often it would be an improvement upon such explanations to substitute the generic use of "man" as representing humanity, and gender the term so as to mean only men. Though women have collaborated with men in a great many evil and harmful things, and in a minority of cases have played the leading direct causal roles, the recognition that, when it comes to human responsibility for events, it is seldom the case that all are equally responsible is an important step toward better understanding. Humanity has a collective history of performing barbaric acts of horrendous cruelty. But that does not mean that *we* are all capable of engaging in such. The pathetic excuse often given by the perpetrators that "if you were in my position, you too would have done the same" at best stretches only to a maybe. The dystopia thesis of this book recognizes that both heroes and villains exist, and such despairing hope as it possesses rests quite strongly with the former. But the dystopia thesis is not a *moral* thesis, it is a *causal* thesis, and as such, its major focus is upon structures rather than individuals. Here the My Lai massacre provides its more subtle lessons.

As the events of the My Lai massacre became known to the American public, they provided a focal point for debates among a public already divided upon the war in general. For many who supported the war, the My Lai war crimes needed somehow to be justified. Chapter 6 presents the aspect of the dystopia thesis called "structural mystification," the process by which the production of knowledge is frustrated and the dissemination of knowledge is restricted. Half truths, partial truths, absences of truth along with disinformation and honest mistakes and calculated lies create mystification. The debate concerning the conduct of some of the American military at My Lai is an excellent example of structural mystification. In this case, it is the "absence of known" information from the public discourse that is most interesting.

Captain Medina, the overall commanding officer of the three platoons of American forces at My Lai, tended to vanish from the story, and is far less well-known than Lieutenant Calley. Calley became the focus of the debate and even had a pop song about him widely played on American commercial radio stations.[13] It seems very possible that Medina gave orders for the atrocities and even participated in some illegal killing. It is also quite possible that he had received orders for the mass executions from higher-ups in the chain of command. But all of this remains indefinite.

---

[13] *Battle Hymn of Lt. Calley* C Company featuring Terry Nelson.

What is known for sure is that Captain Medina was cleared of all charges and that none were filed upon any higher officer. Lieutenant Calley was not the only one who had charges filed against him, but he became the clear focal point for the moral justification of "just following orders", as well as pro-war emotive patriotism. Lieutenant Calley was made into a hero, and though convicted of war crimes, he was given a presidential pardon that commuted his sentence to only house arrest for three years.

If there was real justification for his "only following orders" rationalization, those who had given these orders were never brought to justice. And he, of course, provided an undisputed case for the only following orders defenses of all other participants in the massacre. That is, he had *given them the orders*. Altogether, we can conclude that, for the participants in the massacre at whatever level within the hierarchy of command and responsibility, the personal consequences were very minor. If punished at all, they were not punished severely. If we consider the scale of the atrocity and the fact that so much of it was visited upon children, then the conclusion is inescapable: they got away with murder! They got away with mass murder!

Others were not so lucky. I am referring here to *those who refused orders*! Military law is clear about the refusal of orders:

> . . . all orders which do not involve explicit violation of the Law of Land Warfare are presumed to be lawful and must be obeyed. The dictates of a person's conscience, religion or personal philosophy (let alone fear or misgivings) cannot legally justify or excuse the disobedience of a lawful order.[14]

In theory, the punishment for the refusal of orders could actually be summary execution. This was not the fate of those who refused Calley's orders. Their fate was not dramatic; they were simply given dishonorable discharges. Such a discharge most frequently carries later consequences in civilian life, such as

---

[14] http://www.globalsecurity.org/military/ops/battle.htm

problems in securing employment, and in the main, these men did not fare too well in their post-military careers. But their lives and fates were played out outside the media spotlight upon the perpetrators of the massacre. Such people, their moral courage, their actions and the consequences for them form the absence that functioned in the structural mystification of the debate over My Lai. It is peculiar that, during the debate concerning the moral responsibilities of following orders or not, the actions and fates of those who did not, *were not even discussed*! Indeed, it was not for twenty years that any knowledge that there even were such refusals truly entered the domain of public awareness.

In addition to the stands taken by these people, there was an even bigger absence. That is, not only did some soldiers refuse the orders to murder but some Americans even actively intervened to protect the villagers. Captain Hugh Thompson Jr. put down his helicopter gunship between the unarmed Vietnamese and the Americans who would've executed them. He ordered his crew to turn their guns against their countrymen and warned they would shoot if the killing did not stop. Thompson then called in support from other US helicopters, and together they airlifted nine Vietnamese civilians to safety.

Thirty years later, in 1998, Thompson was officially recognized as a hero for this, and with his two crew members, was awarded the Soldier's Medal for bravery.[15] However, this was certainly not how he was seen at the time. He was shunned by his fellow soldiers. He received death threats and was told by a congressman that he was the only American who should be punished over My Lai. Indeed, Thompson seriously feared court-martial. It is worth noting here that the chief investigator for the massacre was none other than Colin Powell. Powell reported relations between US soldiers and Vietnamese civilians as "excellent." Powell's whitewash became the foundation of his meteoric rise through the ranks.[16]

---

[15] "Heroes and Massacres," *Storm Warning*, Issue 36: Summer 1998.

[16] Sigal, Clancy (2006) "Hugh Thompson and My Lai," *CounterPunch*, January 12.

There is a pattern here that is not accidental in its linkage with the present. Structures are in place that facilitate butchery and murder, even as they exert power against making moral stands against barbarity. It is not that people do not have choices or that they are not morally responsible for their actions. But which choices they make are conditioned by a great many situational factors. For example, there is the structural force of military law and the conditioning to obey orders without question. There were the political forces at the time that wished to exonerate the military of any systematic wrong doing.

Colin Powell made cognitive, intellectual and moral choices in his investigation of the My Lai incident. We may hold him morally culpable for the way he handled things back then, just as we may hold him morally culpable for his part in the Bush administration's misleading of the American people concerning the alleged weapons of mass destruction possessed by Iraq. But the way in which structural forces work in such cases is that we can be sure that, had Powell behaved differently with respect to the investigation of My Lai, it would have been someone else who presented the case for invading Iraq to the United Nations; Powell would not have reached the higher echelons of power.

There were also other discursive structures in place, including but not be limited to the institutions of the media and their relations to the political economy. There is also the manner in which logically unbound together positions nonetheless cohere. In the case of the My Lai massacre and Lieutenant Calley's responsibility, the American public by and large split down the middle with respect to it just as they did concerning the war in general. That is, the vast majority of people who were against the war considered him a grotesque child murderer and war criminal, while those who supported the war saw him as a hero. Now, one would think it quite possible, to be against the war and yet accept Calley's "only following orders" defense. One would think it even more likely that the majority of people who supported the war could still find shameful acts of barbarism unacceptable. Yet such was not the case. The entire set of debates concerning anything to do with Vietnam was quite definitely structured. While it was possible to think outside the parameters set by that discursive structure, it was very difficult, and not too many people managed it. Lack of crucial information, of course, was part of the discursive structure. Thus, the American people morally pondered Calley's case in a complete lack of any knowledge of the behavior of Thompson to compare it with. The structural mystification aspect of the dystopia thesis asserts that such absences of information are certainly not accidental nor any matter of simple ignorance. The dystopia thesis asserts that the My Lai incident and the way it was dealt with and discussed is a guide to the present, to the torture chambers of Abu Ghraib and Guantanamo Bay.

A Decade in the History of Uruguay

> *The healthy man does not torture others; generally*
> *it is the tortured who turn into torturers.*
> Carl Jung

> *People were in prison so that prices could be*
> *free.*
> Eduardo Galeano

> *Words divide us, actions unite us.*
> Slogan of the Tupamaros

History suggests that the capacity of human beings to torture other human beings is not a subject to be understood through a reflection upon the mysterious workings of evil in the human heart. It can easily be grasped through a cataloguing of quite mundane factors. We can see commonalities between the American atrocities in My Lai and Abu Ghraib. One such commonality is *difference*. While back home in America the civil rights struggle was achieving immense success, the newly achieved understandings of the dynamics of racism was not something that was transported across the Pacific and applied to the Vietnamese people and their culture. The Americans conducted that war in a state of great ignorance with respect to their "enemy," just as they are doing today in Iraq and Afghanistan. The cultural differences when combined with sufficient misunderstanding and ignorance provide an initial starting point for a dehumanization process. And dehumanization, history tells us, is a crucial ingredient in the psychological dynamic that allows cruel atrocities to be committed. The complex dynamic of American racism as it was and is played out with respect to dehumanization is, of course, a structural force and a very complicated one in its workings. I do not wish to oversimplify it. Thus, a simpler example can be helpful in clarifying how the systematic process of producing torture and torturers works. Uruguay provides the perfect example.

Uruguayan history also demonstrates the possibility of extremely rapid negative change from democracy to a hell on earth. In 1962 Uruguay was known as the Switzerland of South America. This was because of its prosperous economy and democratic institutions. Uruguay had a civilized history to be proud of. It was very progressive. Women achieved suffrage and began to vote in Uruguay many years before most European countries. Its prosperous economy and well-educated urban populace gave it a slightly misleading First World veneer. Uruguay is in fact an object lesson in the dependencies and economic vulnerability in its relation to the global political economy (see Chapter 5). Its economy was small and not sufficiently diverse to fare well when there was a fall in both price and demand for its meat product exports. Extreme political change quickly followed economic downturn. Within a decade, Uruguay's nickname changed from the Switzerland of South America to the Torture Chamber of South America.

How could such a nasty change occur? It was a very simple process actually, quite easy to understand with clear lessons for the First World affluent concerning the fragility of their political freedoms. Uruguay's economic fall was largely a result of market-driven global forces outside of its control. It did not, of course, respond well to these forces and instead helped the economic decline along through bad policy decisions undertaken by a series of corrupt governments. It is an old story in the Third World; some people in power get rich selling their country down the drain. This is not impossible but still rather more difficult to do in a polity with democratically accountable institutions. Therein lies the initial lesson for the First World. How did these institutions come to be eroded?

Uruguay's democracy possessed interesting similarities with that of the United States; not so much with the state's specific form, as in the party political culture and tradition. People in Uruguay (most of them, most of the time) voted for one of two political parties: the Colorados and the Blancos. These color designations held no extra meaning. The Colorados were certainly not "Red" in the sense of association with socialism or even social democracy. Rather they were the party of the city's commercial elite, the big bourgeois and the proxy representatives of international capital. The Blancos' power was land based; they were the old aristocracy. Of course, most of the people who voted for either one were neither bourgeois nor aristocrats, though voting habits tended to be inherited from one generation to the next. People traditionally voted Blanco or Colorado in more or less the same way as people vote Republican or Democrat in the US. That is, they made their ballot choices on the basis of tradition and a manipulated, politically apathetic ignorance.

The people voted but neither demanded nor expected to see big changes reflecting their interests; rather, it was the case that life was okay and football far more important than politics. This is a bit of an oversimplification, of course, but not as much as one might think. There were periodic issues that caught the minds and hearts of the masses; reforms were made and reforms were reversed. Things happened. But things were pretty much stable. This was less true of the city than the countryside, as, for example, the educated youth of the city responded to international events and trends. The city-based vote of the Colorados, while usually larger than that of the Blancos, was a little less stable. The landed power of the Blancos was sometimes considerably less than fully democratic; that is, the rural peasantry tended to vote the way they were told to vote by their traditional masters. But the key factor in the whole set-up, as far as democracy was concerned, was not corruption, though that existed, but rather apathy. People, if not exactly content, were not sufficiently disturbed to demand change or even complain very loudly. When the economy took a severe downturn, all that began to change.

Though they represented slightly different interests nationally, the Colorados and Blancos were not so different; one could say that *together* they ruled the country for most of its democratic history. They formed the center of the Uruguayan political spectrum, and Uruguay's politics were dominated by the center. Again, this is similar to the US. Perhaps the right wing of the Republicans and left wing of the Democrats are outside the political center consensus of its uniformed, unthinking, politically apathetic populace, but the major political power that rules the land is a choice between Tweedledum and Tweedledee. Bush the Second and his gang were perhaps the only power grouping where one could say they were possibly outside this "democratic consensus." But even they are argued to be too liberal on any number of issues for the real Far Right. When Uruguay's economic troubles began, though, the center also began to fold; the previously too Far Right and too Far Left began to grow in power. The Far Right and Far Left fed each other's rise to power.

A largely Montevideo-based group of revolutionaries, the Tupamaros (Movimiento de Liberacion Nacional), formed up and began to undertake spectacular "terrorist" actions. These urban-living, mainly young, well-educated political activists had a keen sense of drama. There was usually evidence of artistry and imagination in their political actions. For example, they collected a large body of evidence demonstrating corruption of the legal system, but arguably, at least, the legal procedures of their "illegal trial" (many Tupamoros were legally trained) of the country's attorney general who they kidnapped, were actually more in accord with the country's constitution and the laws of the land than many, many cases actually handled by the state's legal system (of which the attorney general was the nominal head). They also had a creative flare for publicity. Uruguayans are mad about football and have the custom of listening to radio coverage of the event while at the match itself. The Tupamoros took over the most popular of the radio stations during an important match. Then, with much of the whole country listening, they played a tape of their trial of the attorney general. The tape played for hours and hours; it played all the way through a few times before the police finally gained entrance to the station and stopped it. It took such a long time for them to gain entrance because the Tupamoros had left a note saying they had mined the radio station even though they had not actually done so (their use of violence in general was quite minimal). The next morning the attorney general was found bound and gagged on the Montevideo courthouse steps. Beside him was a mountain of documentary evidence of his crimes against the country and the people.

The Tupamoros were, of course, only a small minority of the population. But they increasingly found favor with a larger and larger section of the population as time went on and economic hardship increased. The Right responded to both the Tupamoros actions and the growing political restlessness of other groups in society (organized labour for example) in an increasingly repressive fashion. The security apparatus of the state frequently broke its own laws and codes of conduct; more and more progressive legislation was repealed, and more repressive legislation passed. The military's power grew, and it became ever more involved in the governance of the country.

It was believed by some at the time, not only by the Tupamaros themselves but by some on all sides of the political spectrum, that a left-wing socialist revolution was a real possibility. It was believed by many *more* others that a democratic transition to a more socialist leaning, as well as more democratic, government was also possible. A new political party grouping was a formed to represent the newly emergent force of middle-class liberals and a revitalized trade union movement. The potential power of both the Tupamoros and this new movement were overestimated. The military was very clumsy, (particularly near the beginning of the struggle) in their pursuit of the Tupamoros and in their repressive use of power. For this reason, they were perhaps underestimated as a force.

Uruguay is a small country, and Montevideo is not only its largest city, it is really its *only* city. If the election had been held only in Montevideo, the Frente Amplio (Broad Front) coalition of left-wing groups[17] may well have won. But Montevideo is not the whole country, and the peaceful reform "revolution" was *not* supported in the rural areas. The new right-wing government committed itself to crushing the Tupamoros . . . and by extension, using that justification and their new mandate, the military was actually able to crush the entirety of the Left. A whole generation of trade union leadership was imprisoned, tortured and killed in the new wave of oppression.

The easily controlled rural poor not only effectively stopped the evolution in democracy that emanated in the city but they were also the raw recruits for the War on Terror, or rather the recruits for the new army of torturers. Those that experienced their actions and lived to tell about it describe a terrifying mix of ferocity and a certain robot-like quality in their tormentors. Such a perception was not an illusion, and the odd combination not a matter of accident. It was a result of the process by which the torturer is manufactured.

First, those who directly participated in the torturing were from a rural background and usually had absolutely no prior experience of the city. One could go so far as to say, in a sense, that these people were recruited from a time capsule. Their previous life experience connected in some ways more with an earlier time than to the modernized Montevideo. The Tupamoros and later the trade union leaders, university professors and suchlike came from entirely different backgrounds and likely appeared incredibly alien to the inexperienced peasantry. But it was not that these peasant torturers had no knowledge of the people they were torturing; they had been told many things about them . . . evil things, preposterous things, things that made these poor prisoners seem less than human. Finally, of course, a not insignificant element in the training of these torturers was the fact that their training was so brutal that one could say they were

---

[17] A revival of this grouping later obtained power after years of an oppressive military dictatorship during which it was a banned illegal organization. It won the 2004 elections for both chambers (Deputies and Senate) as well as the presidency.

effectively tortured themselves. This is the dynamic that molds torturers, a dehumanizing of the torturer, accompanied by a well-taught perception of a less than fully human victim.

Uruguay is only one story, but the process is more or less the same all over. It is one story of the structural forces of the past that produced monsters. It is a warning cautionary tale of the growing structural forces of the present that will produce the monstrosities of the future. And, of course, according to the dystopia thesis, it is a tale forces are at work to keep from being be heeded.

Conclusion: No Lifeboats

> *The essential fact which emerges . . . is that*
> *the three smallest and most active reservoirs*
> *(of carbon in the global carbon cycle), the*
> *atmosphere, the plants and the soil, are*
> *all of roughly the same size. This means*
> *that large human disturbance of any one*
> *of these reservoirs will have large effects*
> *on all three. We cannot hope either to*
> *understand or to manage the carbon in the*
> *atmosphere unless we understand and*
> *manage the trees and the soil too.*
>   Dyson Freeman

Space tourism was mentioned earlier but another aspect of "space" connects us with our final example from the past. This, unlike the first two examples, is not in the far past; nor is it, to use Jared Diamond's term, an example of a societal "collapse." Like the My Lai example, it crucially illustrates some elements of structural force and causality. In this case, the structures are to do with science and economy and ecology. It is relevant to a societal collapse – our own – but strictly speaking, the ecological failure that we will be looking at is less a society and more of an experiment. I am speaking here of Biosphere II.

There are a great many inspiring and lofty motivations for the human interest in space exploration, and I do not wish to downplay them. There are also some quite crass commercial considerations. But among the more interesting motivations for space science and space adventure is the notion of off-world colonization. Yes, I mean colonies on Mars or our moon or one of the moons of Jupiter, perhaps even a distant (they are all incredibly distant!) star and new planetary system. Colonization, as well as exploration, has its inspirational side and its commercial side too. But there is still another side to it. It connects up with a "survivalist" mentality.

I, of course, see nothing wrong with wishing to either personally survive or caring for a prolongation of the life of the species. Indeed, that latter motivation is one of the motivations for writing this book; I am hoping that the act of articulating a distressing and depressing argument about our future prospects might contribute in some small way to the argument being proved wrong. The "survivalist" mentality to which I refer, however, is rather different. Life is spent in preparation for the personal survival of Armageddon (in whatever imagined form), and a mentality develops that positively embraces it, that waits impatiently for the mega-disaster to occur. There are many versions of survivalism, but one of its versions is the notion of an "escape pod" from the earth. We (some of us, a few of us, a very, very tiny select few of us) will leave behind this degraded, stinking, irrevocably doomed earth and start again on Mars . . . or somewhere in the great new space frontier . . . a more high-tech modernized version of the American West.

I do not wish to assert that the Biosphere II experiment was principally driven by a survivalist mentality. But it was tinged with it. Some of the hype surrounding it derived from it. And lastly, some of what could have been a far more scientific experiment was distorted by it.

Present era space projects are burdened with the need for virtually everything to be sent up from earth. There is some utilization of solar energy, but principally everything from food and water to the air breathed by the astronauts needs be imported from the earth. If the lengthy journeys and extremely hostile site conditions of any other worldly colonization are ever to be made possible, a certain level of self-sufficiency and longer-term sustainability would be required. Early European settlers in North America brought tools and seeds and a limited number of other useful materials with them to the New World; they still need to mainly provide their own means of long-term livelihood through agriculture and hunting. Any space colonization effort must be able to do something similar. Indeed, they must do much more – they must succeed in a process of continual renewal for both water and breathable air.

Biosphere I, that is to say, the earth, does this (in spite of our best efforts to wreck it) very successfully in its complex interdependent and interacting ecosystem. Water is recycled through a complex hydrological cycle involving our oceans, rivers, underground aquifers, evaporation, snow, ice, rainfall, hot and cold, dry winds, wet winds and high and low barometric pressure change. Our breathable atmosphere is maintained through an equally complex system involving not only the cycle of life and death for the larger plants and animals but also an even more complicated set of microbial interactions. This was the basic idea of Biosphere II: to, albeit in simplified form, replicate this process. The initial conditions would be provided from the "outside," so to speak, but once set up, Biosphere II would be completely self-sustaining, relying only upon the sun to energize the system.

Biosphere II mimicked the earth's system in miniature. It was divided into compartments consisting (in addition to human living quarters and a laboratory) of a rainforest, a savannah, an ocean, a marsh, a desert etc. that as closely as possible reflected the real conditions of Biosphere I (i.e., the earth); for example, there is a coral reef in the "ocean." On September 26, 1991, the eight "Biospherian" pioneers entered this earth ecologically modeled glass-dome enclosure for a two-year stay.

The idea was that they were to be entirely self-sustaining for this period. They did, in fact, succeed in staying inside Biosphere II for the two-year period, not counting a five-hour release to undergo surgery by one of them who had severely injured her finger in an accident with a threshing machine. But it is not at all to do with this tiny "cheat" that is why I have called the experiment a failure. It was in some ways also immensely successful. Actually its greatest success lies in how its failures were and are instructive. Its greatest success derives from its scientific utility[18] . . . in spite of the failure of much of its science.

The goal, as I have said, was to be self-sustaining with respect to water and air, as well as food. In this it failed. Oxygen levels quickly began falling, reaching at one point the equivalent of a 4,550-meter elevation with respect to breathing, and thus, endangering the Biospherians' lives. From that point, some three months into the experimental stay, oxygen had to be pumped in from the outside to retain a breathable atmosphere.

The reason for the decline in Biosphere II's human-friendly atmosphere is interesting on many levels. First, there is the very specific question of why the oxygen levels declined. This took some time to discover. Two principal factors were discovered. The microbial soil composition and the carbon absorption qualities of the cement in the structure were largely responsible for the carbon dioxide/oxygen imbalance of the atmosphere. The glass dome itself acted as a further contributing factor; the glass weakened the photosynthesis process of the plants.

This brings us to the instructiveness of failure. The earth's ecosystem is highly complex. We are still learning about many of the complications of its interactive systems. The Biospherians had a respect for biodiversity and put a great deal of thought into the "biomes" they designed. But as one scientist put it: they put a lot of thought into it but still perhaps not enough. The complexity of Biosphere I is so complicated, involving so many relationships in such delicate balance, that perfectly reproducing them may well be beyond human capability. The failure of Biosphere II illustrates the dangers of human hubris with respect to unanticipated consequences regarding these complicated ecological interconnections.

For example, many of the primary food crops that the "biomes" were specifically designed to make flourish did poorly

---

[18] Much has been written about the Biosphere II experiment of both a journalistic and scientific nature. For a good example of the latter, see B.D.V. Marino and H.T. Odum (eds.), *Biosphere 2: Research Past and Present*, Elseveir, 1999.

or failed entirely, while many unpredicted weeds spread at an alarming rate. This result should perhaps give us some caution when introducing genetically modified organisms into the wild. More generally, the Biosphere II experiment should suggest extreme caution concerning any and all human activity in terms of causing unexpected effects upon the ecosystem.

I stated earlier that reproducing in a closed system a complex self-sustaining cyclical ecology may be beyond human powers. However, we do not know that from the results of the two-year living experiment of Biosphere II. Science is humanity's best knowledge-producing instrument. But there is science and science; there is good science and bad science; and the science of Biosphere II was sadly lacking in many respects. I was amazed to learn, for example, that the eight Biospherians were enthusiastic amateurs rather than trained scientists.[19] Their rainforest soil (one of the key problems of the experiment) did not mimic the soil of any rainforest on earth in its chemical composition or microbial content. The role of microbial organisms in the soil in the carbon-dioxide-oxygen cycle was not appreciated. The dearth of good microbiological science on the part of the Biospherians was thus one of the immediate causes of the experiment's failure. But this lack of good scientific practice was not entirely accidental. And it is here that we have our principal dystopian lesson.

The Biosphere II project was undertaken by enthusiastic amateurs with a severely circumscribed scientific advisory panel. It was funded primarily by a somewhat eccentric, though by no means crazy, businessman. Its parameters, in other words, were defined through American capitalism. The rich can indulge their whims, even altruistic whims, even scientific whims. So, we have the science of the project taking a back seat to the media focus on

---

[19] The experiment suffered from problems possibly unrelated (though, on the other hand, possibly it is) to the dystopia thesis. They split into two hostile factions. An interesting (though biased, of course) account of this was written by one of the participants. See Poynter, Jayne (2006), *The Human Experiment: Two Years and Twenty Minutes inside Biosphere Two*, Thunders Mouth Press: New York.

self-contained prototype of an earth escape pod aspect of it. We have scientific experimentation burdened by notions of secrecy and the proprietary rights of future applicability and profitability.[20] This, of course, is not restricted to the Biosphere II project. The whole scientific endeavor is burdened with it to some degree. Thus, humanity's best hope for understanding our ecological problems is distorted through the bottom-line priorities of investment and control. This is one of the central arguments of the dystopia thesis.

Chapter 6 explains the concept of structural mystification, a crucial portion of the dystopia thesis. Knowledge is needed to have any chance of avoiding the dystopian horrors of the future. It needs to be not only produced but widely distributed in order to first of all conceive of the strategies for change that would save us, and secondly create the requisite collective political will to implement these strategies. Remember the dystopia argument is not that our doomed future is outside any potential human control. Rather, it is that the necessary knowledge will not be achieved; the measures that could be taken, will not be taken. The Biosphere II project suggests that even science operates within the structural constraints of political economy and can be ideologically corrupted. Perhaps the most chilling lesson of the Biosphere II experiment in comparison with our earth, Biosphere I, comes from their most fundamental difference. Biosphere II was an experiment whose lessons could be learned from and then repeated.[21] The "human experiment" on planet earth allows for no

---

[20] The Wikipedia entry on Biosphere II asks "Is Biosphere II a scientific experiment or a business venture?"

[21] A second experiment was initiated. While some technical lessons were learned from the first experiment's failure, most of the overall lessons we have been discussing were not. This experiment was also unsuccessful. The mission that was planned to last ten months was abandoned prematurely after only three months. However, lack of success in obtaining the hoped for objectives was obvious long before that. In the course of a managerial dispute the doors to the dome were deliberately opened by the crew, thus compromising the experiment.

repetition. The next chapter focuses upon the relation between political economy and ecology. It shows the mistakes that have been made already and the ones that we are on track for making Biosphere I a failure as well.

Perhaps, a number of the Easter Islanders escaped their societal collapse. Perhaps, when they got down to a few hundred trees, they could see the writing on the wall. Perhaps, before their society began to tear itself apart, perhaps while there was still wood available for the building of ocean-going canoes, some of them built themselves a couple and quietly stole away to search out a new world. But it seems apparent that the "lifeboat strategy" for escaping the dystopian fate of planet earth will not succeed. Among the other things the Biosphere II project has shown us is that the lifeboat almost certainly would sink.

For a brief account of this, see the Wikipedia entry: http://en.wikipedia.org/wiki/Biosphere_2

Chapter 3

The Global Environment: A Catalogue of Problems

*We are biological beings, as dependent on the
biosphere as any other life form, and we forget
our animal nature at our peril. As we undermine
clean air, water, soil and energy; as we burn
fossil fuels beyond the capacity of the earth to
absorb the greenhouse molecules thus created;
as we use our surroundings as dumping grounds
for toxic effluents; and as we degrade pristine
areas once teeming with other life and resources,
I believe we are embarking on a suicidal path.*
David Suzuki and Holly Dressel

Introduction: Earth, Air, Fire and Water

*Water can create canyons and nurture the land.
Fire can destroy yet set the stage for renewal.
Wind can scour the earth or scatter seeds. The
Earth can shelter or heave and expose. Fire,
Air, Earth and Water act together to create the
the world that we inhabit.*
Website intro to the art show *Elemental* (2005)

The Ancient Greek philosopher Empedocles classified the four elements of the universe: earth, air, fire and water. That this schema bears little resemblance to our current scientific understanding of physical reality is irrelevant; it works well enough metaphorically as a differentiating tool for a system that ultimately is too interlinked to really be conceptually divided at all. It has thus been chosen as the organizing schema for this chapter.

All of the elements have serious environmental problems. The analysis of each of them demonstrates different aspects of present environmental degradation and possible future catastrophic accelerations of such. But there are a number of themes to this chapter aside from a simple enumeration of alarming facts and trends. They concern the human understanding of these problems, of their causes and of the hope for their potential rectification. Consistent with the dystopia thesis of this book, the prognosis for the latter is gloomy. We begin with earth.

The Salt of the Earth: People and Planning in Capitalist Communism

*Under capitalism, man exploits man. Under
communism, it's just the opposite.*
John Kenneth Galbraith

*There is nothing in which the birds differ more
from man than the way in which they can build
and yet leave a landscape as it was before.*
Robert Lynd

As we begin this survey of the four elements of Biosphere I, we should remember the key role that soil played in the failure of Biosphere II (see chapter 2): a microbial imbalance left the air-sealed dome gradually starving of oxygen. We should recall, as well, the catastrophic effects of soil erosion upon Easter Island and many other early societal collapses (again, see chapter 2). Fertile soil is crucial to human survival. From the mass emigration provoked by the Oklahoma dust bowl in the thirties, to the African famines of today, one can see the results of bad, indeed virtually suicidal, agricultural management. We see throughout the globe over-farming, overgrazing, inappropriate crop choice, foolish irrigation schemes and generally bad land use management. Deforestation and desertification take place simultaneously in a causal weave of interconnectivity.

We cut down forests to clear land for agriculture. We replace native plants with a specialized monoculture. We replace vegetation well adapted to arid climates with water-guzzling cash crops. We build dams and divert rivers with a careless short-sighted abandon. Rich top soils wash away. Rich top soils are blown away. In both rich countries and poor, farms fail. In the poor countries, farmers become refugees or starve. In the rich countries, they fail to pay their mortgages and the banks repossess their land. Or even worse, in both rich and poor countries, they prosper. That is they reap some short-term benefits at the cost of long-term *catastrophe*. Such is the logic of capitalist agriculture.

In many cases, our salt-of-the-earth farmers are defeated quite literally by just that: salt. Increased soil salinization of agricultural lands is part of the larger complex of problems of land and water management in a capitalist economy. Australia can be used as an example to show that such problems are not restricted to the poorer nations of the world. Australia is a desert. Australia is a desert with an enormous reservoir of salt beneath the surface of the land. Native Australian vegetation evolved to be salt-tolerant. Not only were the forests cleared, but agribusiness replaced the salt-tolerant vegetation with more commercially viable commodities such as wheat. The woodland species of plants with their deep roots left the salt beneath the soil undisturbed. The shorter-rooted new plants let the water soak down to the salt and gradually raise the salt to the surface. The result is land with ever-greater salinity levels. Australian farmlands are degrading at an ever-accelerating rate. Dr Tom Hatton, of the CSIRO Division of Land and Water argues to his fellow citizens that "without question this is the largest environmental crisis we face, and if people don't believe me now, they soon will." He is beginning to be believed, but it may already be too late because "arresting the salinity crisis over large tracts of the Australian wheat belt will be akin to trying to turn around a supertanker."[1]

What Hatton and other Australian scientists are calling for is "industrial-strength" land care. Such scientists argue that the structure of rural communities will have to change and the economics of regional Australia will have to shift radically. The traditional family farm may disappear, with people being paid to

---

[1] Hatton, Tom (1999), Environment News Network: Australia. http://www.geocities.com/RainForest/Andes/4996/env-news.htm#Salinity

stop cropping and start the long-term investment of tree planting. Justin Murphy, an Australian journalist, while accepting the foregoing, goes on to state: "But how the banks and large agribusiness firms will respond is uncertain."[2] Our dystopia thesis can relieve his uncertainty, though he will not be happy with the answer. The banks will behave towards the small Australian farmers in their "salt bowl" just as they behaved toward the dirt farmers of Oklahoma in the 1830s "dust bowl". Yes, indeed the traditional family farm will disappear, but it is unlikely they will be paid to stop cropping and invest in tree farms. This is beyond the planning time frame of both government and corporations. Farms both small and large will continue to the end; that is, they will continue their unsustainable practices until they *absolutely* can no longer be sustained. The government will do some bailouts from these disasters, but it will be the big agribusinesses they will bail out *not* the small farmer.

It should be noted that this is a global rather than merely an Australian problem. A few years ago, I was puzzled as I drove across the entire prairie length of the Trans-Canada Highway. There was all this white beside the golden wheat fields. It was summer time; it couldn't be snow, though that is what it looked like. Finally, I stopped the car for a closer look. It was salt. Poor agricultural land-use decisions have created a salinity problem in many parts of the world. Most often it is complicated by other problems such as drought and erosion. Frequently increased salinity is accompanied by other more poisonous substances that have infected the water table. And of course, the source of these poisons is almost always the chemicals and pesticides of industrial agriculture, that is to say, capitalist agriculture. The logic of capitalism demands a maximization of short-term individual profit and gain at the expense of longer-term planning for collective benefit . . . even if that "benefit" is only the most basic of survival needs.

---

[2] Murphy, Justin (1999) *Australian Broadcasting Corporation 7:30 Report*, May 13.

I am arguing here that the capitalist decision-making logic is the driving force of environmental catastrophe. But my critics will surely point out that it is not capitalism that is responsible for such; indeed, they will assert the most dramatic case of such disaster that can be pointed to was a result of the "logic of communism." So let us examine that case; let us examine that logic.

The story of the Aral Sea not only illustrates the logic of what I would call "communist capitalism," it illustrates the interconnection of environmental problems. Wind and fire transform the land; they fertilize or denude it. Land-use policies are perhaps most significantly water-use policies. Our ancient elements in the earth, air, fire, water categorization, while useful as an organizing principal for this chapter, are not merely completely outmoded in scientific terms but actually illustrate something else through their sheer categorical inadequacy: the *multi-faceted, mutual interpenetration of causes and effects across an ecology whose most significant feature is its holistic inter-relation of elements.* Even the particularity of an issue such as land degradation because of soil salinity cannot be separated from "salinity" more generally; that is, we cannot think of soil salinization without considering water salinization. Most, in statistical terms nearly all, of the earth's water is salty to varying degrees. The interpenetration of salt and fresh water (or the lack thereof) has significant consequences. We shall see later (ironically in the "air" rather than the "water" section of this chapter) how the fresh water melt will interact with global warming to possibly produce a new ice age. The opposite salinity problem does not have consequences quite so severe. Still they are dramatic enough.

Indeed, the story of the Aral Sea is perhaps the very icon of environmental catastrophe. It belongs to the "dystopia of the present" rather than the future. The environmental disaster has already occurred, and there is little to predict about the future concerning it. The inland sea and its surrounding environment are *already completely ruined.* We can only predict for the future that they won't get better. We can only predict that, as long as land-use policies, water diversion and dam-building policies are driven by the insane short-term logic of the world economic market, there will be many more Aral Sea disasters.

In 1956, Muynak was a fishing village located on an island in the Amu Darya Delta. By 1962, the island had become a peninsula, but fishing was still possible. But by 1970, the sea was 10 kilometers away; by 1980, 40 kilometers away; and by 1998, 75 kilometers.[3] But even if the Muynak fishermen were still close to the water, they would not be able to fish. The world's oceans are saltwater bodies, but how salty is a matter of degree that varies. Some salinity levels are too high even for fish to live in . . . particularly if the salt is mixed with poison. Concentrations of pesticides and other chemicals are high in the three small saline lakes that this once-great inland sea now comprises.

But water destruction is also *land destruction*. What was once seabed is now *desert*. It is a salty desert with a poisonous topsoil. The salt and the chemical pollutants are blown by the wind for hundreds, sometimes even thousands, of miles damaging or completely destroying agricultural land. The shrinkage of the Aral had other rather surprising negative effects as well. It forced a localized climate change. It once was large enough to cut off extremes of temperature in the surrounding area. It acted as a coolant in summer and a heat sink in winter. As it shrank, the weather became more properly continental and appropriate to its latitude. The growing season shrank to only 170 days, as opposed to the 200 needed for cotton. Thus, local farmers switched from cotton to rice . . . which only exacerbated the problems as rice needs more water.[4] However, cotton was the original source of the problem. Or rather the *world market demand for cotton* and the *political economy of the Soviet Union* was the problem.

The waters flowing into the Aral Sea were all diverted into the gigantic projects that turned the Uzbek and Kazakh deserts into rich agricultural lands . . . or so it seemed for a time. Why did

---

[3] de Villiers, Marq (2003) *Water*, McClelland & Stewart, Toronto, p. 117.

[4] Ibid., p. 118.

they do this? Well, American economists, political ideologues and the average brainwashed man on the street would all have a quick and easy answer: not only is totalitarian communism evil, its centralized planning is inefficient to the point of foolishness. Everyone of the baby boomer generation, at least, has heard of the Soviet right-boot factory surpluses and the left-boot shortages. However, three points need to be considered with respect to the Aral Sea ecological-economic disaster and the Soviet economic disaster more generally. First, whatever the Soviet system was, it was certainly *not communist* (regardless if they chose to call themselves such). Second, I do not understand *why bad central planning decisions should discredit all planning* that is not simply a response to markets. Third, the market is precisely what dictated the Soviets' plans for water diversion. They needed a cash crop for export. As we will see when analyzing the world system in more detail in chapter 6, most significantly it is just that: a *world* system. And the world system is capitalist!

The Soviet decisions concerning water diversion and irrigation were short-sighted from an ecological perspective. But they were quite unremarkable from a capitalist economic point of view. What is an inappropriate land use from a longer-term ecological perspective (indeed inappropriate to the point of insanity) can be quite good business. It can be actually quite profitable, from the point of view of short-term, market-driven economic policy. Indeed, such decisions are the norm. The logic behind them is actually a key component of the dystopia thesis. In attempting to make the deserts green with dollars, the Soviets were only doing the same as the Americans, the Israelis, the Libyans and many others. There was nothing "socialist" about it. The world may now be purged from the evils of Soviet "socialism," but the forces that produced the Aral Sea ecological destruction are all still present. We can expect to see many more such results in the years to come.

Hot Air and a Bad Atmosphere

> *The answer, my friend, is blowing in the wind . . .*
> Bob Dylan

Pollution is the environmental problem most people are most familiar with. Partially this is because many billions of people, myself included, live where they can actually see it. We can look out over our cities and see the dirty grey brown haze settled onto them. Again, for many millions of people, their media and meteorologists decided a good many years ago to include a local "air quality" as part of the weather report. So most people are well-aware that industry and the automobile are seriously polluting the air we must breathe.

The "salinization" of pollution is a result not merely of these factors but also of "biomass burning," that is, from the cooking fires of kerosene or cow dung, from forests being slashed and burned, as well as accidental forest fires. CNN reported[5] that the two-mile-thick cloud that in the dry season hangs over much of South Asia and the Indian Ocean is said to be responsible for hundreds of thousands of respiratory deaths each year. The less gargantuan clouds of pollution we find in the First World are also responsible for many, many illnesses and deaths.

If we include the widespread awareness of the threat posed to crops and trees by acid rain as a consequence of industrial pollution and smog, then we see the predominant awareness the general public has of the dangers to our air and atmosphere. I do not wish to trivialize the millions of air-quality-related illnesses and other problems, but simply thinking about air pollution, about smog *per se,* is to fail to grasp the true scale of the dystopian disasters to come. One would not be wrong to imagine dirtier, uglier, more widespread pollution clouds and an urban life of gas masks and oxygen stations. Many of the residents of the world's mega-cities are already living that lifestyle. No, the pretty sunsets that air pollution facilitates are not the icons of dystopia. We have much greater atmospheric problems than mere smog, even greater than the super smog of the Asian Brown Cloud. The Brown Cloud is already significantly affecting the climate on a local level and bringing with such change the extreme weather instability that

---

[5] *CNN News*, August 12, 2002.

causes floods and droughts. But it is merely a single contributor among many responsible for our most serious environmental problem: *global warming.*

Perhaps most significant about the present state of global warming with respect to the dystopia thesis is its delicate balance between the solid knowledge we have of it and the greater realm of the unknown concerning it. Considerable speculation and scientifically educated guesses populate the latter, but it is neither of these things that make the issue of knowledge with respect to global warming such a key exemplar of the dystopia thesis. We need remember that the dystopia thesis is *not* simply that bad things are happening now and that more will occur in the future to the point of absolute hell on earth; though the roasting heat aspect of the problem perhaps makes it quite apt metaphorically. No, the dystopia thesis consists of three further aspects. With respect to the present pervasive suffering endured by people, the dystopia thesis predicts that it *will not be alleviated* significantly. Second, it argues that not only will such problems as we have now get worse but that they will be conjoined with new ones to move the level of human suffering onto *a whole new level of misery.* Third, however, it propounds an explanation as to *why we will not solve these problems* and puts forward *the imbrication of power relations with knowledge* as a significant causal element in this.

That which is only in the realm of speculation with respect to global warming is *not* the question of whether it is occurring. The knowledge that the phenomenon is at least in part significantly induced by human activities is *not* a part of the reasoned scientific debate upon the subject either. This is a matter of consensus in the scientific community at least since the publication by the Intergovernmental Panel on Climate Change's (IPCC) *Third Assessment Report: Climate Change 2001* and further solidified by IPCC Four that was publicly released in the fall of 2006. Of course, there is considerably more evidence available for *the fact of climate change occurring* than there is with respect to the question of whether human causation is significantly involved with it. The existence of global warming is inherently less controversial than the question of human inducement. By their very nature, discussion of such causal connections evokes parallel issues of blame and responsibility; questions concerning response immediately arise. In short, the question of human responsibility for climate change is inherently political, while a question solely concerned with a natural process is less so. Nonetheless, the existence of global warming *and* the significant causal role of human activity exacerbating the process are now *both* accepted as *facts* by the world scientific establishment.[6] That debate *still* surrounds the subject is wholly a matter of structural mystification.

True, there are scientists who continue to question both these consensuses of facticity. True, there are corporate entities and politicians who press forward the notion that the very existence of global warming is subject to scientific doubt. But it is here that one can clearly see the effects of vested financial interests obscuring the production of knowledge. Exon-Mobil, for example, has now emerged as the primary funder of the prominent "greenhouse skeptics."[7] It is here that we can see the political functioning of mystification in the service of political ideology. But there is *no true scientific doubt* that global warming is occurring.

One can observe, for example, the rapid retreat of many glaciers. Great chunks of Arctic and Antarctic ice have been witnessed breaking off. Photos of 20 years ago can be compared with the contemporary views that show miles of glacial retreat. Behavioral effects upon wildlife have been observed. Polar bears, for example, are drowning with increased frequency as the ice shelves upon which they depend for their seal hunting are either broken up or absent entirely for a much greater portion of the year. We have air and sea temperature records and much else to empirically support the warming hypothesis.

---

[6] IPCC, *Climate Change 2007: The Physical Science Basis, Summary for Policymakers.*

[7] People such as S. Fred Singer, Patrick Michaels, Robert Balling and Sherwood Idso were traditionally funded by the coal industry.

The question of human inducement of global warming is a little bit trickier to prove absolutely. There are, indeed, quite natural processes that contribute to warming. The earth has experienced great swings of hot and cold climate change in the past. However, though the causes are multiple, overall the causation forces are reasonably well understood scientifically. The greenhouse warming effect occurs because of changing concentrations of certain gases in the atmosphere. And human beings are significantly contributing to the buildup of those gases. We know the main culprit in this: the burning of fossil fuels for energy. On the one hand, we know that some of this is virtually unavoidable. We need power to run our modern economies. On the other hand, however, some of our gas-emission-producing activities are from an environmental point of view entirely frivolous.

What do I mean by "frivolous"? I mean the enormous consumption of aviation fuel spent transporting people and goods from one place on the globe to another. South-central Ontario, a producer of some extremely good apples, nonetheless imports apples from not only another Canadian province thousands of miles away (British Columbia) but also from Australia . . . about as far away from Ontario as exists on the earth. People who live in Florida vacation in Hawaii. Well, it can certainly be argued that the free trade in produce and tourism are built into the global economy. I would not disagree. Such, indeed, is part of my point. We will not solve a very great many environmental problems precisely because the activities that cause them are part of the global economic system.

The United States government's subsidy of the purchase of high-fuel-consumption vehicles over others is frivolous from a different point of view. Surely, gas-guzzling SUVs are *not absolutely essential* to the world economic system? But yet again, such governmental involvement in the economy *is fundamental* to its operation. As we shall see in chapter 6, the economy is global, but it has certainly never been run on a free-trade basis in spite of all the ideology trumpeting it. The US automobile industry was taking a beating at the hands of the Japanese. Classifying SUVs as light trucks, and thus not subjecting them to the much more stringent fuel-emission and efficiency standards for cars, gave these mega-consuming vehicles a significant market advantage. That is the political economic logic in a globalized but still nation-state world. But what about global warming and the environment? The public is increasingly aware of the global warming problem and the relation of poor-gas-mileage vehicles in relation to it. But public concern is to some extent mollified by the belief that if the government is perhaps not doing enough to prevent global warming, they at least are beginning to take some moderate measures. And indeed, as of 2003, the Bush administration made some tax changes with respect to SUVs.

> So now a chiropractor in Sausalito can buy a top of the line Hummer for that $102,581 and then claim a $75,000 deduction for capital equipment, an $8,274 post-Sep. 11 bonus capital equipment deduction and a first-year depreciation allowance of $3,861. The total deduction: $87,135. Assuming the driver is in the top income bracket, the federal tax savings for buying a Hummer is $33,634.[8]

We can put this in today's context of solving a critical environmental problem: total average fuel-economy improvement for the US vehicle fleet peaked in 1988, and has since declined. This is substantially due to the tax legislation favoring the manufacture, marketing, sale and purchase of the fuel-inefficient SUVs. We can contrast the voluntary ethical decision-making consumer forces in support of the environment, with the structural economic forces hurting it. While one might have hope for the former, the dystopia thesis emphasizes the latter.

Those who would dispute the dystopia thesis from the perspective of political optimism and respect for our current rulers would do well to reflect upon the facts. Not only are the politicians failing to take the crucial steps to preventively engage with global warming – the US failure to sign the Kyoto accord for

---

[8] (2003) "The SUV War: Dumb And Dumber", *CBS News*, January 23. http://www.cbsnews.com/stories/2003/01/23/opinion/meyer/main537649.shtml

example – they are actually engaged in the legislative promotion of harmful actions.

Where scientific knowledge begins to thin and speculation begins to abound is with respect to the consequences of global warming, the severity of those consequences and the timeline for their manifestation. For example, the internationally renowned Canadian journalist Gwyne Dyer, in a public lecture on the dire consequences of global warming, gave, in addition to quite a number of alarming truths about the situation, presented as an alleged fact that British agriculture would be largely unaffected. He correctly asserted that the IPCC estimated (very conservatively) a twenty-five percent loss in world food production in association with a two degree increase in average world temperature.[9] But the assertions concerning the UK are a typical journalistic (even among good journalists such as Dyer) mistranslation of qualified scientific hypothesis into certainties.

The global climate is a complex ecosystem with multiple feedback causal loops. Wind and cloud and ocean currents, the rain forest and iceberg creation, these are all interlinked in a fashion that contains frightening possibilities of positive feedback accelerations of change. The British and Western Europeans mainly moderate climates are entirely the product of a powerful warm ocean current: the Atlantic Conveyor (also known as the Atlantic thermohaline circulation or THC). The meltdown and breakup of the polar ice caps dramatically affect this system of ocean currents (and other ones as well, of course). The melting process itself is affected by the ice shrinkage. As there is less white ice to reflect the sun, the more the ocean absorbs the heat of the sun's rays, thus accelerating the melting process: ergo a positive feedback loop.

It is not that this general warming of the ocean would *directly* affect the British and European climate. No, the warming one might expect would likely *not* be the effect. Indeed, it would likely be quite the opposite. The polar ice melt and general ocean

---

[9] Dyer, Gwyne (2007) "Climate Wars," lecture given at the University of Waterloo, March 21.

warming could alter or even halt the flow of the warm surface current that provides the higher temperatures and greater precipitation for the English weather that an otherwise freezing and dry northern latitude would prevent. This is the basis for Dyer's assertion that the UK would be all right. The warming and cooling would balance each other out. This is *possibly* true. But ascertaining how likely this is, is actually beyond all scientific certainty or consensus. Extreme agriculture-destroying cold is as least as likely.

How quickly *could* such a dramatic change occur? Well, if the Atlantic conveyor's speed in bringing the warmer sea surface temperatures from below the tropics even slowed down a little, the effects *could be* immense – Canadian winters for the UK and cold drought for North America's Eastern seaboard. Such could happen in as short a time period as ten years! Ironically, one of the effects of global warming *could* be a new ice age.

The key word in the last couple of paragraphs was "could." It is a matter of probabilities, on one level, and a matter of too great a complexity to go much beyond total uncertainty, on another. We know that global warming will have powerful effects upon the world's weather. But we do not know *how* powerful. We know that global warming will make some currently dry regions of the world wetter . . . and vice versa. We know that the same will occur with respect to temperatures. We know that the effect upon human life in a few places will be beneficial. But we also know that the very high probability *for almost everywhere* will be the opposite.

We do not know just how profound an effect this could be. The previously cited estimate of a 25 percent loss of food production does not take into account all the possibly intersecting and mutually reinforcing causal variables. At the far end of the danger spectrum would be *a threat to the very survival of the human species*! The earth's climate has changed dramatically over time with respect to both warmth and cooling. The complexity of the process is part of the reason it took so long for a scientific consensus about global warming to emerge. Though we know that it is happening, it is still a process about which there is *much we do not know*. We do know that the grimmer scenarios are more likely than the less so. Ergo, the incredible sale of mass starvation that a twenty-five percent loss of world food output is the best we can hope for if global warming is not significantly checked.

Effects become causes that interact with the original complex of multi-causes to accelerate the process of change. We have quite powerful positive feedback loops at work. For example, the maybe gradual, maybe not so gradual melting of the polar ice caps that is an effect of global warming in turn produces two other effects, which in their turn become causes. First, the injection of a large freshwater melt into the earth's ocean system, in addition to raising sea levels profoundly, also affects the pattern of currents and thus wind. Secondly, the shrinkage of ice-white polar caps to reflect the sun further intensifies the warming of the waters . . . which further melts the ice which further warms the water . . . and so on and so on. As the permafrost melts both carbon dioxide and methane, a much more potent (23 times the effect of CO_2) contributor to global warming, is released into the atmosphere. The more permafrost melted, the more greenhouse gases released, the warmer it becomes and thus the more permafrost melted; we do not know, but it seems possible that this positive feedback loop could reach a critical tipping point in which the entire process gathers a momentum beyond anything we can predict or even potentially control. The polar caps and the glaciers entirely melt. The warming accelerates in a runaway set of interactions to a point where human life becomes impossible.

However, that is in the realm of the unknown. It is a result of a global spectrum of possibility that is almost unthinkable . . . yet still possible. At the near end of the spectrum of possible effects, there is considerably more certainty. This end of the spectrum of possible negative effects is a certainty because we are experiencing them already: a proliferation of extreme weather events – of droughts, of floods, of hurricanes. How great a proliferation? We do not know for sure; but we know it has been increasing significantly. The number of Category 4 and 5 hurricanes has increased eighty percent in the past thirty years, and climate models of tropical seas temperature increase show that substantial increase in hurricane prevalence and intensity will occur.[10]

Once again it needs to be said that the most significant aspect of the global warming phenomenon from the dystopia thesis's perspective is to do with knowledge and action. Even the *chance* that a phenomenon *might* lead to the extinction of the human species *should* provoke large-scale dramatic action to stave off the possibility . . . even if it is "only" a possibility. But even with respect to less horrendous outcomes, even a mere minor increase in drought, flood and hurricane frequency *should* trigger a significant global attempt to avert such crises. It *should.* But the problem is that, for example, in the case of Hurricane Katrina, we do not know that global warming played a causal role in the destruction it wreaked. We know that global warming will tend to increase the intensity of hurricanes. But we do not know *specifically* that this was the case for Katrina . . . or any other *specific* event.

A small coastal village or a huge swathe of Bangladeshi countryside is flooded. Such things happen. Such things have always happened . . . to Bangladesh in particular. We *do not know for sure* that this year's death, disease and destruction effects of the super-flood were most significantly caused by the global rise in sea level, which might have occurred as a result of the carbon emissions causing the earth to warm a little more. We do not know for sure; but we do know there is *a high degree of probability* that this was a causal factor. And we *do know for sure* that there will be a strong tendency for a greater frequency of floods and droughts in the future, and thus for famine and disease as well.

---

[10] Webster, P. J., Holland, G. J., Curry, J. A. and Chang, H. R. (2005), "Changes in Tropical Cyclone Number, Duration, and Intensity in a Warming Environment," *Science*, Vol. 309, no. 5742. It should be noted that their argument and evidence have been challenged. See, for example, John A. Knaff and Raymond M. Zehr (2007), "Reexamination of Tropical Cyclone Wind-Pressure Relationships," *Weather and Forecasting*, Volume 22, Issue 1.

There have always been hurricanes and droughts and flooding. But this is a key part of the dystopia thesis with respect to knowledge: the lack of simplistic certainty with respect to consequences in a complex system appears to be enough of a wedge to destroy the necessary consensus to act. The economic interests of the powerful few that might be hurt by strong preventative actions can all the more easily subvert the knowledge dissemination process to prevent the necessary collective accord for such action to be taken. We shall look at this phenomenon quite closely in Chapter 7.

The situation with respect to global warming can thus be summarized. It is presently affecting human well-being in the form of its causal input into extreme weather events. We do not know how much fossil-fuel burning has so far causally contributed to the human suffering resulting from these events. We do know that the effects will be multiplied significantly in the future. We do know, that as a *minimum,* there will be more floods and droughts. We know that storms will be stronger and more frequent. We even know that significantly greater disease outbreaks will occur (see chapter 4). Even if there is only a small global change in temperature, the vectors for many contagious diseases – several species of mosquitoes, rats, fleas and other carriers – will extend their ranges both northward and to higher altitudes. But, of course, we do not know for sure just how significant a facilitating factor this might be towards a future global pandemic. We know that climate warming and its drought-causing effects upon rainfall patterns will significantly reduce the world's food supply, even as our population and need dramatically increases. We do not know whether there will be sufficient climate change so as to threaten the possibility of human life itself. We only know that human action is causing global warming to accelerate. We only know that the scale of human suffering will be significant. We only know that we are not going to do what we could to prevent it. We only know that it seems likely we are not going to do very much about it at all.

My earth, air, fire and water categorization should emphasize the fact that environmental problems are certainly not easily compartmentalized. Thus, we shall include in our section on "air", a problem whose least-known and possibly profoundest effects, are actually upon the smallest creatures of the ocean. I am referring here to ozone depletion and damage to the ozone layer.

The ozone layer, among other things, protects us against damaging ultraviolet (UV) radiation coming from the sun. This portion of the atmosphere has been seriously damaged as a result of a number of specialized air pollution practices. In this context, people are most aware of the negative effects of CFCs (chlorofluorocarbons). The (First World educated) public is generally aware that common refrigeration coolants strongly contributed to ozone depletion, and most people have likely heard of the Antarctic "hole" in the ozone layer. Probably what most people were most aware of was that CFCs were found in aerosol sprays. I can remember a drink-muddled association in the minds of myself and a group of friends as we basked one spring in uncharacteristic English warmth and sunshine: "If aerosol sprays are causing global warming" someone said, "then let's get spraying!" It was only a joke of course. But it was a joke that depended upon considerable misunderstanding. First, while ozone depletion is connected with global warming, the connection was *not* what we thought. Ozone level *replenishment* will likely actually warm the stratosphere. And more relevantly, we were in England at the time, and as said earlier, global warming's effects upon ocean currents is far more likely to produce an ice age Britain than anything else. Still, we were aware of the ozone problem to some degree.

Some of us were even aware of the Montreal Protocol, an international (non-binding!) treaty that called upon countries to dramatically change their industrial and consumer behavior with respect to ODCs (ozone-depleting compounds). But as most of us shifted from aerosol-spray deodorants to roll-ons, we kind of assumed the problem was solved. And it *might be* to some extent. That is, strict adherence to the Montreal Protocol *could* stabilize the ozone levels. However, a report commissioned by the US Department of Commerce,[11] asserts that, while CFCs in the

---

[11] US Department of Commerce Chemical Sciences Division, *The Scientific Assessment of Ozone Depletion: 2002.*

atmosphere have declined, tropospheric *bromine levels have increased*. The problem is ongoing.

But as with public awareness of atmospheric problems generally, there is a misplaced anthropogenic focus. That is, when people think of ozone depletion, they think of skin cancer and other "sunburn-related" problems. Again, I do not wish to downplay the significance of UV radiation as a carcinogen. Nor am I in general opposed to a human-centered focus of attention. But as I have been at great pains to make clear, ecological problems are very interconnected, and sometimes the greatest threats to humanity are *indirect in nature*. The increases in UV radiation associated with ozone depletion are much more dangerous with respect to the ocean's food chain rather than simply as a human carcinogen!

Enhanced levels of UV radiation result from the diminution of the earth's protective ozone layer, which filters out some of this spectrum of light. Plankton are not able to filter out ultraviolet B radiation and are seriously harmed by it when not outright killed. Plankton are, as it were, at the *bottom of the food-chain*. Our attention is generally directed toward the top. Problems besetting the top predators in the food chain act as a warning indicator that there are problems in the ecosystem. But though we often most closely identify with these higher-level creatures (perhaps because we are *the* top predator in the global system), they are not actually as important as those at the other end of the food chain spectrum. The tiny creatures at the bottom perform the first steps of transforming light and energy into life . . . the energy and food that all else feeds upon, that ultimately *all else depends upon*. A plankton failure of any serious proportion could quickly become *the eco-failure of the entire system*. Yes, not only more serious than sunburn, but in the longer term perhaps, even more serious than cancer. And there is also an ozone connection with disease. Ultraviolet radiation has a profound effect upon algae production, and algae spread is the perfect microbial disease vector.[12]

---

[12] See chapter 4.

It shows how much our ecological problems are interlinked that we should next engage in an extended discussion of the problem of deforestation in the middle of our section on the air and the atmosphere. But deforestation has a clear cut (pardon the pun) connection to global warming. It is one of its causes. The process of deforestation releases approximately 1.6 billion metric tons of carbon into the atmosphere per year. The carbon combines with oxygen to produce carbon dioxide, a major greenhouse-effect producing gas. By way of comparison, fossil-fuel burning (coal, oil and gas) releases about six billion metric tons per year,[13] so it is clear that deforestation makes a significant contribution to the increasing CO_2 in the atmosphere. In addition, deforestation affects the hydrological cycle. Trees draw groundwater up through their roots and release it into the atmosphere (transpiration). In Amazonia, over half of all the water circulating through the region's ecosystem remains within the plants. With removal of part of the forest, the region cannot hold as much water. The effect of this could be a drier climate. A much drier climate! The effects of this would not only be local to the Amazon but could affect the American Southwest as well. Ergo, we have one of the many links between deforestation and desertification.

Tropical rain forests, like many other complex yet ultimately fragile ecosystems, are suspected by scientists to have a "death threshold." That is, once deforestation has passed a certain point, the remaining rain forest becomes increasingly degraded through a disastrous positive feedback loop that finally results in the forest's extinction. The reason for this is that much of the rainfall that sustains the forest is recycled; i.e., it is water absorbed by the trees and returned to the atmosphere "evapo-transpiration." An estimated seven trillion[14] tons of water are recycled that way and help to cool the atmosphere immediately above the forests. The

---

[13] (1998) "Tropical Deforestation," *The Earth Science Enterprise Series*, National Aeronautics and Space Administration (NASA), p. 3.

[14] http://www.biofuelwatch.org.uk

water cycle, which allows not just the Amazon but all agriculture in the region to thrive, appears to be a self-sustaining cycle. If enough trees are removed from the ecosystem, it could thus break down. Scientists have not yet identified the crucial threshold at which such a cataclysmic event would occur. This is all in the realm of speculation. But it is speculation about an incredible environmental danger based upon known facts and reasoned analysis.

It is thus clear that among the global warming and climate change prevention measures that humanity ought to be taking now is to slow, if not stop entirely, the rate of deforestation in the world. But "we" (some of us, anyway) have been aware of this need for quite some time; and yet the rate of deforestation has actually *increased* through the nineties and the first few years of the new millennium. Brazil's highest-ever amount of deforestation occurred in 1995 (29,059) and second highest in 2004 (26,129 square kilometers). [15]

Global climate change, though the most alarming of the possible consequences of deforestation, is not the only serious effect. There is also the loss of biodiversity. We can shrug off one aspect of this problem: the aesthetic. A growing number of people feel that our quality of life will be threatened and that the world would just be a much poorer place generally if there were to be no more polar bears or great white sharks or horned owls or tigers . . . or, or, the list goes on and on. But this is truly a pseudo-problem. The spiritual/aesthetic care about the existence of animals is a product of a certain level of wealth, and as we shall see in later chapters (especially chapter 6), the First World, middle-class, affluent lifestyle will likely be extinct long before the tiger. While Discovery Channel watchers appreciate and marvel at the degree of human-like qualities found in chimpanzees, the Congolese poor hunt them for food! No, the loss of biodiversity will have other much more *practical effects* upon humanity.

---

[15] National Institute of Space Research estimates.
http://www.mongabay.com/brazil.html

Each day more plant and animal species disappear forever as the tropical forests are cleared. The film *Medicine Man* (1992, Sean Connery, Lorraine Bracco) illustrates in dramatic fictional form the most serious loss to humanity. A cure for cancer is found in the forest only to be immediately destroyed by commercial logging. This example was fictional, but yet it could well have been real. Who knows if several plants that might have had the potential for a cheap simple cure for AIDS have not already been destroyed in the deforestation-species-extinction process? There is much that we will never know about what has already been destroyed.

Loss of an important benefit is not the only negative aspect of the loss of biodiversity either. As forests are replaced with ranches, farms or simply wasteland, as human reforesting projects fail to replace the complex ecosystems that have been destroyed, human life becomes much more vulnerable to disease and parasitic plagues. Plant life too is vulnerable; and the lack of diversity of agribusiness makes it possible for a catastrophe to hit the plantations upon which our food supply depends! This is yet another reason why the previously cited twenty-five percent loss of food production figure is such an unrealistically conservative figure.

We have throughout the Third World an ever-increasing impoverished urban population of displaced peasants. They came to the city seeking a better life but had their hopes rapidly dashed. Their dream then becomes to return to the country. Many, many of them do so. In Brazil, for example, this problem is acute. It is a problem for the rich owners of the land who have other more selfish plans for it. It is a problem for the police who fight for the landowners to try and attempt to stop the poverty-driven tide of land invasion. But most seriously of all, it is a problem for humanity. The land is permanently (well, permanently, given the context of the human existence time frame) degraded! Unlike forests of the Northern hemisphere, tropical rain forests hold most of their nutrients in the plants themselves rather than the soil. When the forests are slashed and burned to be cleared for agriculture, the nutrient-rich soil is quite rapidly washed away in the intense rainfall. The farms are abandoned, and new forest areas are cleared. Or the farms fail, and the peasant squatter returns to his life of urban misery.

The peasant seizure and agricultural development of forested land is, however, definitely not the most significant cause of deforestation. The principal cause is either commercial logging or, as in Brazil, large-scale land-clearance for either ranching or commercial-scale sugar cane production. As we shall continue to see throughout this book, not only does one problem frequently feed into another but attempted solutions into new or old problems can become problems themselves. Sugar-cane-made ethanol fuel has been Brazil's answer to past, present and future problems of oil supply. Forty percent of Brazil's transport fuel comes from ethanol made from sugar cane. In chapter 6, I shall show why such solutions are not globally viable. But suffice it to say here that the Brazilian solution to the oil crisis is greatly exacerbating an already severe deforestation problem. Sugar cane encroaches on the Amazon, but much more so on the Atlantic forest and the Cerrado, a very bio-diverse and unique savannah-type ecosystem. But two-thirds of the Cerrado has already been destroyed or degraded.[16]

Commercial logging is the greatest cause of deforestation in the Southeast Asian rain forests, though only second in Brazil. Logging illustrates a crucial aspect of the dystopia thesis. It illustrates how, even with good scientific understanding of a problem and a plethora of NGOs (non-governmental organizations) devoted to disseminating that knowledge and advocating resolution strategies, the problem will still fail to be solved. One NGO is the Forest Stewardship Council (FSC). They are an organization that if one has any concern for the environment, for the future of our children and humanity as a whole, one only applauds them. They, and other such organizations, presently represent what hope there is for the avoidance of environmental catastrophe and future nightmare. The FSC has developed a creative approach for ensuring sensible forest management . . . within the existing economic system.

---

[16] http://www.biofuelwatch.org.uk

That last qualification is why their scheme, excellent in every other way, will largely fail to achieve its intended result. In cooperation with many governments and corporations, the FSC has implemented a forest certification scheme.

The FSC promotes responsible management of the world's forests. First, it has set international standards for such. Second, it accredits independent third-party organizations who can certify forest managers and forest product producers as adhering to these international standards. The two types of certification are a Forest Management Certificate (FM) and a Chain of Custody Certificate (COC). Obtaining the first involves an inspection to ensure that the forestry company is in fact complying with the standards set. The second certificate is designed to check that the final product being offered consumers after the frequently complex series of wholesale sales and re-sales did in fact originate in a "responsibly managed" forestry operation.

Readers at this point must surely be asking themselves just what could possibly be wrong with this? The scheme seems eminently sensible in every respect save for one: *it conflicts with the deepest logic of the capitalist system*! It is not merely that significant motivation and practical potential for fraud exists. The profits underpinning the irresponsible, and frequently illegal, logging operations are vast in comparison with the relatively tiny resources of the FSC and its sister organizations. Their true policing (with the only actual penalty being loss of their certification) potential for retraining unpleasant corporate practices is really quite limited and relies more upon corporate "good citizenship" than anything else. But serious as fraudulent forest certification and "illegal" logging are, they are not the real problem. The real problem is that behind all such schemes is a notion of the responsible consumer.

Consumer "good citizenship" is usually as flawed and hypocritical as corporate "good citizenship." What the marketplace provides us with is a choice (the be-all and end-all of the system's ideological justification). On the one hand, we have "fair trade" coffee; on the other, we have "unfair trade" (though obviously it is not ever advertised this way) coffee. The first costs considerably more than the second. Though there is a proven market for "fair trade" products, nonetheless *it is a minority taste market.* The majority of people are scarcely aware of its existence, as it is nowhere distributed or advertised to the same extent as the "unfair trade" coffee. When the fair trade coffee is available to compete, the cheaper "we get the best beans," "we are the most trendy" coffee usually wins the consumer pound, yen, euro or dollar. I am sure many hosts proudly inform their guests that their new furniture was *FSC certified.* But many, many more simply say their table is *mahogany* . . . without mentioning the destruction of the rain forest to which they are contributing.

As we proceed through this catalogue of global problems, their interconnectivity should become clearer and clearer. The complicated weave of connections between environmental problems will be the first to emerge as, of course, the biosphere is a total system. But as we proceed, we shall see common themes of causality for a quite disparate set of problems; we shall see the manner in which war and terrorism and political repression are connected to the environmental problems. Our next section again takes us to the forest ecosystem, but it illustrates not merely environmental interconnections but connections between economics and human psychology.

Fire and Insanity

> *Now the Lord can make you tumble*
> *And the Lord can make you turn*
> *And the Lord can make you overflow*
> *But the Lord can't make you burn*
> *Burn on, big river, burn on.*
> Randy Newman

Fire contains within its category what are perhaps the least serious of our environmental problems (at least the way this chapter is organized). Fires destroy millions of dollars worth of property each year in Canada and the US. In Southeast Asia, the human-initiated burn created a forest fire so large its smoke reached cities across an ocean and over 1,000 miles away. Many lives of both humans and animals are lost through fire.

Ecosystems are sometimes permanently destroyed. So it is not that fire problems are slight and insignificant; it is merely that they are dwarfed the scale of many others.

Forest fires, whether they were human started or a result of natural causes, are, of course, not locally self-contained. They contribute to climate change both in their extended locality and globally. Fires as a result of human activity have their dramatic side as icons of human filth and folly. The Cuyahoga River in Cleveland was so polluted that in 1969 it apparently spontaneously ignited.[17] The napalming of the jungle and people of Vietnam gave the baby boomer generation a badly burned child as an iconic image of the horrors of war. The satellite TV images of the burning of the Kuwait oil fields similarly can similarly be construed as an icon of America's "new world order."

However, we wish to emphasize something quite different. We wish to emphasize the capitalist system's *degradation of human nature* as symbolized by a firefighter. Dystopia has a variety of manifestations. Environmental problems cause some unexpected human ones.

In 2002, Arizona experienced its largest-ever out-of-control forest fire. Millions of acres of trees were destroyed. Arson was the cause of the fire. The arsonist was a Forest Service firefighter! The arsonist was an Aboriginal American, an Apache native of the Arizona locality of the fire. His motive was *money*! Quite simply, he needed the work.[18]

Such at least was the story. It is possible that this father of six had serious mental health problems. Nonetheless, even if his understanding of the situation owed a great deal to mental imbalance, the story still says a great deal about the desperation of the poor. The story says something about the manner in which the human spirit may be deformed by capitalist socialization. The

---

[17] Or so says urban myth and the famous Randy Newman song. But whether spontaneous or not, polluted rivers catching fire have actually been a relatively common events.

[18] (2002) *Indian Country Today*, July 19.

story says something about our First World treatment of the "Fourth World" of aboriginal peoples. Carey N. Vicenti rightly suggests that "Leonard Gregg could be a man who represents a nexus between the federal mismanagement of forestlands and the federal neglect of tribal economies."[19] The dystopia thesis suggests he represents a nexus between the profit-driven, short-sighted destruction of the environment upon which all human life depends, as well as its destruction of older systems of collective values, with simultaneous distortions of the human psyche.

Native peoples (as well as anthropologists) tell us that they have a special bond with nature and a deep spiritual respect for the earth. It is not that this is without any truth, but frequently the romanticization of Native spirituality impairs some of the more prosaic unpleasantness of their political-economic situation. In Canada, for example, the Innu tribe forcibly situated in Davis Inlet developed a suicide rate that was twelve times the Canadian average.[20] Nearly twenty-five percent of the population tried to kill themselves in one year alone.[21] If such misery as that can be found as a colonial inheritance, is it any wonder that we might find an individual desperate enough to start a forest fire?

As it turns out, vandalism is actually one of the *major causes of forest fires*. As it turns out, it is *not rare for Forest Service workers to be the arsonists* (though rarely Native Americans). In fact, it is common enough that Pennsylvania initiated a Firefighters Arson Task Force in the year 2000. The FBI has profiled firefighter arsonists;[22] they tend to be white males

---

[19] Ibid.

[20] (1999) *Canada's Tibet: The Killing of the Innu*, Survival International.

[21] Partridge, Bill (1993) local addiction counselor quoted in *Time Magazine*, February 22.

[22] (2003) US Fire Administration, *Firefighter Arson Special Report*, January.

between seventeen and twenty-five from dysfunctional homes, alcoholic, with homosexual and suicidal tendencies, have average to higher intelligence but bad academic performances, bad jobs and bad marriages. Regardless, of the healthy skepticism one might justifiably feel concerning such FBI profiling, it says quite a lot about American society simply that they have such a category as "criminal firefighters."

A principal motivation for firefighter vandals apparently is "excitement." They are looking for glamour. They are looking to be heroes in the aftermath of the calamity they caused themselves. This actually tells us something about the degree of alienation to be found in contemporary society. A lot of people who would fit that FBI profile. This perverted desire to be a hero demonstrates a distortion of an ethos of social responsibility on an enormous scale! If we think enough about capitalism's alienating propensity, it is thus actually quite unremarkable that we might find people attempting to purge their personal inadequacies through fire.

The dystopia thesis does not merely predict a greater degree of human and property loss, as well as serious future environmental harm due to the economic-ecological trends of mutual causality; no, it also predicts an exponential expansion of the socio-economically induced insanity symbolized by the "firefighter arsonist."

Water: When the "Trickle Down" Dries Up

Water, water everywhere, so let's all have a drink.
Homer Simpson (adrift on the ocean)

The water problem that is most in the news at the moment is the grotesque pollution of the Gulf of Mexico caused by the BP oil-drilling platform explosion catastrophe. At the time of writing, the cap put on the wellhead is apparently holding and tropical storm Bonnie had just passed by without causing much further damage. But enormous quantities of oil — estimates range from an initial BP guesstimate of 5,000 barrels a day to 100,000 barrels[23] (that is 4,200,000 gallons!) — have been leaking for 86 days! And there apparently are still some small subsidiary leakages. The oil slick covers some 2,500 square miles.[24] The oil blown ashore is ruining the delicate wetlands of Louisiana and seeping into Lake Pontchartrain, yet another blow to the New Orleans region. The coastlines of Florida, Alabama and Mississippi are all significantly affected.

This is not the first oil spill, nor will it be the last. Capitalism will pit economics and the increasing need for oil against ecology. In such cases ecology usually loses. Oil exploration is going on in environmentally sensitive and what are currently legislatively protected areas. But the drilling will almost certainly begin soon . . . to be surely followed by new environmental catastrophes.

Oil spills are, of course, not the only, or even the main, form of water pollution. All the world's water resources are increasingly becoming filthy and diseased. Our lakes, rivers and oceans are being filled with agricultural and industrial effluent. We are contaminating our drinking water with our own shit.

There is also the destruction of the delicate, living coral reef ecosystems. These fragile systems perform enormous services to the 54 countries whose coastlines they are found off. Coral reefs provide coastal protection as well as economic benefits through fishing and tourism. They are also a source of medicine from their enormous diversity of plant and animal life, containing one-quarter of the world's marine species of fish. But the reefs are dying owing to pollution, the gradual warming of seas where they live and through other human-caused damage. Fifty-eight percent of the total world's coral reef systems have been severely damaged by human activity.[25] Eighty-two percent of Indonesia's

---

[23] http://en.wikipedia.org/wiki/Deepwater_Horizon_oil_spill

[24] http://en.wikipedia.org/wiki/Deepwater_Horizon_oil_spill

[25] *The World Atlas of Coral Reefs,* United Nations Environment Program World Conservation Monitoring Centre, 2001, http://coral.unep.ch/atlaspr.htm

reefs are at risk, largely do to dynamite fishing. All this, of course, is related to a significant loss of biodiversity, as these reef systems are the most life prolific and complex of the oceans' ecosystems.

We can live without pretty fish or coral, I suppose. We can probably live without any fish at all. In the future, we probably will have to. Fishing is perhaps the world's prime example of the human failure to sensibly manage a renewable resource. We have a knack for transforming forever-renewable resources into never-to-be-renewed resources. The dystopia thesis suggests Newfoundland's Grand Banks fishery collapse (as discussed in Chapter 1) as the blueprint for the earth's future in this respect. Ecological disasters will almost certainly be repeated if no lessons are learned from them. And no lessons have been learned apparently. Incredibly wasteful "industrial" fishing practices are engaged in more and more. Huge swathes of the ocean floor are dredged; and the non-commercially targeted fish of the operation simply discarded.

Conservationists are concerned about the populations of the whales and the great white shark. I applaud their efforts on behalf of the whale, if less thrilled about the shark. I feel a bond of sorts with all the higher-order mammals. But, once again, with respect to the dystopia thesis, it is possibly not so significant. If we can live without fish, we can certainly live without whales. Once again, I would argue that while top predators, of course, fulfill important functions in complex ecosystems, their role is not as crucial as that of those lower down the food chain. The extinction of higher-order animals merely *symbolizes* our failures, rather than being a principal cause of the disasters to come. If the polar bears perish from the effects of human-caused global warming, we can see this perhaps as a great shame. But rather than mourning the polar bears' fate, we should see their difficulties as a warning, as a portent of our own grim future.

The natural diversity of water ecosystems is likely to be greatly diminished as mono-aquaculture increases to offset the natural fishing decline. The injection of genetic modification into this enterprise may well also have calamitous results. Just as is the case for mono-agriculture, the humanly induced reduction in biodiversity leaves both our crops and our seafood stocks dangerously vulnerable. The result of such industrial-scale, narrowly focused food-producing enterprises ironically may well be famine!

Tsunamis, and flooding more generally, take a great toll upon human life, not the least as a result of the epidemics, which frequently follow these natural disasters. The dystopia thesis is fairly simple with respect to such. Expect much, much more of the same. Global warming is raising sea levels so that coastal cities may well be inundated. The great mega-disaster floods of places like Bangladesh, which in 1999 displaced two million people,[26] can be expected to be repeated annually in the future. Flooding will occur not merely because of tidal waves, unusually heavy rains and other "natural" occurrences but also because of unsustainable agricultural practices and soil erosion. We can expect many, many more New Orleans disasters with the same causes of suffering: a lack of heed to warnings, inadequate preventive measures and poor emergency responses.

In the First World, this will occur due to shady contracting and construction practices, governmental incompetence and a virtually criminal short-sightedness and inability to learn from previous disasters. In the Third World, the disasters will be felt even more harshly, the loss of life will be that much greater and the preventative measures never taken. This is simply because such measures simply cannot be afforded from their position in the global "free" enterprise system. The fatalistic outlook developed by many in the Third World is not irrational; rather, it is a reasonable response to a quite realistic assessment of their potential for averting what frequently are horrific fates. In the First World too, a kind of fatalism will soon develop as a political philosophy; though in this case, one is tempted to simply call it a callousness toward the suffering of others.

The most alarming elements of the dystopia thesis are the questions concerning shortages of *clean* water and the systemic response to them. It is estimated that by 2015 three billion people

---

[26] (1999) *CNN News*, July 24.

(about 40 percent of the population) will live in countries where it is difficult or impossible to get enough water to satisfy basic human needs.[27] The world's aquifers are rapidly shrinking just as the human population is rapidly increasing. There are also globally related geographical distribution problems: we have too little water in one place and too much of it in another; literally, we have water frequently in the wrong place, at the wrong time.

Our clean water supply is crucial to us. We are speaking of basic animal needs here. We need not only to drink but also to clean ourselves and our food. We need water for sanitation. It is terribly important that our agricultural runoff, our industrial discharge and our human sewage systems be prevented from contaminating our clean water supplies. Yet such a separation is certainly not happening. A survey of the world's rivers found *only two fit for drinking without chemical treatment!*[28]

The world's waters are not only contaminated with industrial chemicals, arsenic and DDT but are infested with bacteria, viruses and other disease-causing parasites. Diarrhea is now chronic for most of the children of the Third World. It is a leading cause of death for children and infants. We can expect the infant mortality rate everywhere to multiply enormously.

Some of the problems of water stress and scarcity are quite natural in origin. Much of the land surface of the world is arid or semi-arid. People who live in such regions have perhaps always had to marshal their limited water resources carefully and walk long distances to acquire them. But today and tomorrow, as demand exponentially increases, we can expect both longer walks and deeper wells. We can expect for millions of people the wells to quite literally run dry. We can expect long waits and long queues in the Third World cities as their erratically functioning water infrastructure leaks from its poorly maintained pipes. We can expect similar problems in First World cities too, as the love affair with neo-liberal policies leaves cities with few resources to

---

[27] Marq de Villiers, *Water*, p. 12.

[28] Ibid.

update what in some cases are now ancient systems. This is because, exacerbating all the "natural" difficulties of maintaining adequate water in places naturally quite dry, a long-running series of very *unnatural* decisions and actions were undertaken.

The much vaunted "green revolution" that did so much to feed the increasing numbers of people in the world took place in a context of massive damn building, irrigation and river-diversion projects. While some of the newly irrigated land did grow much-needed food, most of it was given over to the production of cash crops for the luxury consumption lifestyles of the First World middle classes. While this has been all very nice for them (us!), the industrial agricultural system's benefits have a heavy water price tag attached to them, which we (them!) are only just beginning to pay. Some of the places that grew rice or cotton should not have been developed at all! Their development occurred at the price of shortages elsewhere; their development occurred at the price of future food and water shortages.

Water is distributed very unequally in the world. As with other aspects of inequality, dystopian problems are both created, and existing ones exacerbated, by it. One could say that, with respect to water inequality, a great deal of it is simply geographical. With the earth's diverse collection of ecosystems ranging from desert to rain forest, one could say that inequality with respect to water resources is "only natural." One *could* say that; but it isn't true! This is part of the problem: deserts bloom with fruit trees, cotton plantations and bright green golf courses. But even in the same desert, there is tremendous inequality. The Israelis control the Palestinian water dispensation. They give themselves four times as much. The Palestinians are extremely water-stressed while the Israelis water their lawns and golf courses. Meanwhile the Dead Sea is becoming truly dead, and the River Jordan is transforming itself into a desultory trickle.

Problems to do with the distribution of water have led to problems in the past. Problems to do with the distribution of water have led to war. It has been famously predicted that if the wars of 20th century have revolved around oil, the wars of the twenty-first will derive from conflicts over water. This both is and is not true. It *is not true* insofar as warfare seldom results from a single cause. It *is not true* insofar as latent conflicts over oil, so far from diminishing in importance, are likely to be multiplied many times over in intensity as we pass the world's oil production peak (see Chapter 6). But it *is true* insofar as increased competition over an increasingly scarce resource will intensify. Further, the possibilities for frameworks for any agreed-upon equitable distribution are increasingly corrupted by the powerful corporate forces of commoditization. It *is true* insofar as the world's contemporary epicenter of political turmoil – the Middle East – is not only the geographical site of world's major oil-producing countries but also an increasingly water-stressed desert. Both the politically disputed entities of Israel and Palestine may not have oil, but they are at the heart of the political conflict that determines the political-economy of oil production. The conflicts of interests over water are *conjoined* with the complex politics of oil and ideology (see Chapter 7).

The ongoing Arab-Israeli conflicts of interest over water are not the only significant water conflicts of interest in the world that have the potential for sparking wars. Many of the major rivers of the world cross borders with significant disputes of usage. There is the Tigris-Euphrates system, the Nile, the Mekong, the Ganges and Brahmaputra systems to name only those with the greatest history of past conflict and the greatest potential for the future. We have, for example, water-usage issues complicating the very frontlines of America's War on Terror. The Turks continue to plan huge dams and irrigation schemes as they also continue to persecute the Kurds, even as Saddam Hussein was given a show trial and hung for gassing them. Turkish water mega-projects, of course, add existing tensions to not only religious and ethnic political issues but complications to America's geo-political agenda. What is a commonality with respect to most water issues is their political economic effects: as one group increases its take of a shared resource, another usually loses out. The Kurds have the unhappy fate to have their hereditary ethnic homeland sited within three nations that have complicated cross-border religious-ethnic alliances and conflicts with one another: Iran, Iraq and Turkey. Once again, issues with respect to water intersect with the issues to do with oil, religion, ideology and nationalism.

Another of the early cradles of civilization, the Nile, passes through many countries. It is the world's longest river (6,800 kilometers) and taking into account both the Blue Nile and the White Nile, the Nile basin includes Sudan, Ethiopia, Tanzania, Rwanda, Kenya, Burundi, Uganda, the Democratic Republic of the Congo (DRC) and, of course, Egypt.

All of the others are upstream from Egypt. This is another of the geographical constants of water conflicts of interest. Anything done to the water by the upstream riparian nations will have a profound effect upon those living downstream. Pollution, dam building and diversions, irrigation intake, all this will affect the quality and quantity of potentially usable water for the downstream nation. There are many unresolved issues with respect to the Nile's usage. There have to date been no agreed-upon mechanisms for resolving them, save for one: Egypt has made it very clear that *it will go to war* if anything is done to damage its water supply (again see Chapter 7). Of course, they have, through rather unwise mega-projects, done exactly that themselves.

The Ganges is India's most sacred river. It is a Hindu religious belief that the river has its source in the heavens and thus is a sacred crossing place to the divine. Unfortunately, the river's source is to be found not only in the "heaven" of the Indian Himalayas but also in China and Nepal. Unfortunately, part of its sacred length forms the border with Bangladesh. And Indian water diversions lead to *tremendous shortages* in Bangladesh. The pain of nearly all of Bangladesh's entire poverty-stricken existence comes from water. It either has too much (floods) or too little (drought). India is involved with water problems for Bangladesh that are based upon control of and rights to the Ganges and also with the water problems for Pakistan based upon the Indus. Tensions accelerate to dangerous levels[29] but *never fully diminish*. Both these nations possess nuclear weapons.

---

[29] See chapter 7 for some speculation as to how this tensions might result in a disastrous war.

Vandana Shiva, in her book *Water Wars*,[30] argues that there are not only *material conflicts* over water but also *a conflict of ideas*, a "paradigm war," as she calls it. In using the term "paradigm," she is drawing from a very powerful idea in the history and philosophy of science.[31] Within any particular scientific discipline, "paradigms" are sets of agreed-upon criteria of judgment, as well as agreement as to what are interesting questions with a broad methodological consensus as to how to go about answering them. Within the paradigm, considerable consensus also exists as to what constitutes contemporary knowledge within the area at any given time. Knowledge does, of course, build upon knowledge within the scientific enterprise, but it is by no means a linear accumulation of such. Rather it proceeds in fits and starts with periodic "revolutions"[32] or paradigm shifts. The revolutions occur when an older paradigm is found to be inadequate by some practitioners, and a whole new perspective is utilized then. This is not mere scientific disagreement; rather, it involves more basic issues. The problems being investigated, as well as criteria of judgment, are changed. This sometimes results in scientists "talking past one another" as deep issues of understanding and perspective are involved. Issues seemingly cannot be decisively resolved by some single key experiment or set of data.

A prime example in the history of science, which can be used to illustrate the notion of competing paradigms, is that of the Copernican revolution. The world, everything, looked so very much different after the notion that the earth was center of it was dethroned. It changed everything! It was this fundamental change

---

[30] Vandana Shiva (2002), *Water Wars: Privatization, Pollution and Profit*, Southend Press, Cambridge, MA.

[31] See Thomas Kuhn (1996) [1962], *The Structure of Scientific Revolutions,* 3rd edition, University Of Chicago Press.

[32] This too is one of Kuhn's terms.

in mindset more than any of the specifics of it that enabled the scientific progress that later followed.

This notion of paradigm as applied to water can be used to clearly distinguish the dystopia perspective from all others, including Shiva's. Shiva sets up the oppositional older idea of water as a "commons," as against the notion of it as a commodity. It is a naturally existing substance that is a common good for all because of its universal need by all members of the human (and animal) species. It is, has been and would be in the future best managed on a local community level in some kind of communitarian democratic fashion. Though perhaps a little less enthralled than she with the fairness and sense of the past history of water management by local communities, I too would be in favor of some such arrangements for the future. But this is where Shiva and I would disagree; this is where the dystopian perspective upon both capitalism and water rights is distinctive. Hope and preferences do not make actuality!

One could say that the dystopian perspective is operating from within a different "paradigm" from that of both Shiva's and that of the giant water corporations and their ideologues that are her targets. Shiva presents it, just as they often do, as a question of good, better, best . . . of values, of morality, of choices and understanding. Arguments are made for neo-liberal economics and the market with respect to water management. They conclude that the water market will eventually act in the best interests of all; that in this case, the benefits of "trickle-down" economics will be quite literal. Shiva presents both logic and empirical evidence to strongly suggest otherwise. She is, of course, quite correct in this. Yet she, too, is missing the main point.

Arguments for the utility and collective benefits of a global free market in water are simply part of the constant ideological mystification accompaniment to a material reality. Shiva is herself inadvertently contributing to this mystification, insofar as she agrees to debate the question in moralistic terms . . . *as though water could be anything else other than a commodity* in a capitalist system. Shiva presents the "paradigm war" as though we could simply *choose to understand* water as a common good to be managed collectively for the benefit of all as opposed to seeing it as a commodity to be exploited for profit. Well, we certainly can choose to understand it as something that *ought* to be a common good and managed for the benefit of all. But this does not make it so. It simply *is* a commodity. For things to be otherwise would involve changes far deeper and widespread than merely changing corporate water policies.

Water was, of course, managed quite differently in the past. It did not become a commodity until capitalism was fully developed; it did not become a global commodity until capitalism was fully globalized. But now it is! This is not a question of morality or values or choices or preferences. It is simply a fact. The question of paradigm arises not with respect to whether it should be understood as a commodity or not; that is a question of power, not understanding; no, the question of paradigms exists with respect to the understanding not of water *but of capitalism*. Both market-worshiping neo-liberal ideologues and Shiva speak about water as if it could be something else other than a commodity within a capitalist system.

I agree with her when she argues that "[for the] company, sustainable development is the conversion of an ecological crisis into a market of scarce resources."[33] I agree with her, except that I have taken her slightly out of context. She was speaking about a particular company (Monsanto) in a particular situation. I would make the assertion *as a general condition of the world economy.*

Of course, water has become increasingly commodified. Of course, this does not result in the collective good. Of course, it results in fountains and swimming pools for a few and drought-driven agricultural failure and famine for many. But the commodification of *everything* is simply a part of the impersonal remorseless logic of the world economic system. Perhaps if *that fact* could be more widely understood and acted upon, then we might have a chance. Perhaps. But it is certain that perpetuating our existing system will result in human misery on a scale never before even contemplated. This, of course, is precisely the

---

[33] Shiva, *Water Wars,* p. 88.

dystopia thesis. Our "trickle-down" economy will ensure that, with respect to water, even the "trickle" will dry up.

Conclusion: New Catastrophes and Ancient Pestilence

> *For they covered the face of the whole earth,*
> *so that the land was darkened; and they did eat*
> *every herb of the land, and all the fruit of the trees*
> *which the hail had left: and there remained not any*
> *green thing in the trees, or in the herbs of the field,*
> *through all the land of Egypt.*
>   Revelations, The Bible

There is ever-increasing awareness of environmental problems. More and more people are aware of the complexity of inter-linkages between one problem and another. There is widespread understanding that the earth's natural environment is a "total system" and that effects upon one aspect of it will surely have indirect but nonetheless substantial impacts upon others. There is an emerging awareness that ecology is intimately bound up with economy. However, in most cases, this awareness is rather flawed. The poverty-driven alienation that produces forestry arsonists is only the dramatic flip side to an environmentalism that is produced by privilege and whose principal perspective upon nature is an aesthetic spiritualism that is ultimately mystifying with respect to that economic component. The relentless market forces culling the natural world are not likely to be substantially curbed by "deep ecology." The beauty of the shark or the cuddliness of baby seals is fine for the focus of those with enough to eat. But most people do not give a damn about sharks or seals or tigers. Nor should they. The problems do not lie at the top of the food chain. And in one sense at least, that includes us: the problem is not "man"; the problem is not anthropocentrism, and the problem is not one of spiritual orientation or attitude to nature.

The problem is the way political economy is bound up with biology. The things that threaten us for the future are not the fates of the polar bear or other beautiful creatures but rather the life at the bottom of the food chain. I have no aesthetic, spiritual or any other kind of affinity with the micro-organisms to be found in land or water; and quite frankly, even the idea of the (necessary) micro-organisms found in the human body quite disgusts me. But it is the fate of these small living things that will cause us to die of thirst or starve . . . or maybe just cost us a lot of money.

> Damage and control measures for the estimated 7,000 species of invasive plants, mammals, birds, amphibians, reptiles, arthropods and mollusks now established in the United States cost tens of billions of dollars annually.[34]

It is not merely that the environment is in peril from new threats. Long-existing enemies of our health and harvests interact with the new problems. Locusts are an ancient pestilence and a cause of famine in the present. Locusts live for years as a dormant threat to human farming. The swarming behavior where billions of them flock together and ravenously devour all before them covering millions of square kilometers usually requires substantial rainfall to get it started. Some twenty-five countries were affected by the 2004 swarms.[35] West African food security (never good at the best of times) goes into immediate crisis when there is a locust outbreak. Global warming causally interacts yet again with a pre-existing problem and will likely do so more in the future when rainfall patterns change even more significantly. But already it has had an unprecedented effect. Already it demonstrates that, while it is the poor and the South who are affected first and hardest by dystopian events, eventually the wealthier people and countries are affected as well. The locusts combined with severe drought to cause millions of francs damage

---

[34] "Invasive Species," *Sound Science Initiative*, Union of Concerned Scientists, http://www.ucsusa.org/ssi/invasive_species/

[35] FAQ Desert Locust Information Service. http://www.fao.org/ag/locusts/.

to the French agriculture in 2005.[36] The locusts had never been that far north before.

Our mutually interacting environmental problems thus are set to stage famines on a scale never before seen in human history. The ugly creatures at the bottom of the food chain will assert themselves, and locusts are not the only ancient plague that will be given a revitalization by humanity's insane political economy. As we will see in the next chapter, the plague itself is among the horrors of dystopia. We shall see the interaction of children, poverty and the micro-organisms of disease.

---

[36] (2005) "Plague of Locusts Invades France," *The Observer International*, July 17.

Chapter 4

Children, Poverty and Disease: A Catalogue of Horror

> *The horror, the horror!*
> Kurtz, from Joseph Conrad's *Heart of Darkness*

Introduction: An Imagined Vision of the Future or Facts of the Present?

> *Reality is that which, when you stop believing in it, doesn't go away.*
> Philip K. Dick

> *We are not concerned with the very poor. They are unthinkable, and only to be approached by the statistician or the poet.*
> E. M. Forster

It is almost perfect. You are sitting on an underwater stool at the "swim-up" pool bar. Just past the beautifully manicured tropical garden with its brightly colored parrots is the ocean. You can see the gentle blue surf roll in from where you sit. Your drink is cold, and the sun is hot. But not too hot; it is almost perfect. The live band playing in the garden is very good. They are dancing and smiling, and you can't quite make out the lyrics because of their accent. But it is reggae, and they are singing something about slavery and rebellion.

The music covers the sound of the cries from the other side of the hotel wall. It is actually the wall surrounding the resort-like compound that aesthetically detracts from what would otherwise be hedonistic perfection. The high walls all have jagged glass embedded on top. This security measure makes you uneasy. It is suggestive of what is on the other side of the wall. The walls extend beyond the beach out into the ocean becoming a steel fence as it touches the water – to protect swimmers from sharks, you've been told – but you know what it is really for. It is not sharks from which you require protection. You need to be protected from the . . . the . . . the people outside the wall. The poor people. The resort-like compound is somehow, through magic or science, protected even from mosquitoes, the mosquitoes that are biting the poor people outside the wall and making them ill. A huge proportion of these people are ill, crying out from the terrible pain of hemorrhagic fevers or consumptively coughing up blood.

They are so young, most of these poor people, and they are treating each other so brutally. The children are especially vicious. You feel you really need the security guards, the Rottweillers and that jagged glass on the top of the wall. But you don't like to think about it. Outside the wall the . . . people . . . scare you. These poor people, their squalor and disease, their violence, their lives that you cannot see as being worth living, are they really even human?

Yet you feel you are not *completely* shielded from the danger. You need some of the people outside. You need them to cook for you, to clean for you, even to provide the muscle for security. You pay them for sex and entertainment. And so the disease sneaks in. The violence sneaks in. The suffering sneaks in. It is very unequally spread, the suffering. But there is so much of it, some of it is bound to seep into your world. These people outside, they hate you and they want your money. Sometimes they murder you. And they carry disease into your world. But most of all, they spoil your pleasure with their pain. Their cries are ever getting louder and harder to ignore.

Is this some paranoid vision of a future condition that will never arrive? Or is it simply a factual picture of the inequity and suffering of the present human condition? Well, this next story is certainly based upon fact. Diego and Rafael died from bullets to their brains. This does not at all mark them out as unusual. The world has many conflicts. It is a very violent place. Many, many people throughout the world die from bullets both from accident and intent. In Diego and Rafael's case, it was through intent. They were murdered. But this does not mark their deaths as unusual either.

Diego and Rafael were killed the same night. They were hunted down and killed by a death squad. This in itself is also unremarkable. Assassinations, death squads, vigilante groups, these things are not unusual. Even outside of war, organized murder is a commonplace fact of the contemporary human condition. But yet there was something "special" about these killings that is especially horrifying, even in this terrible world. Diego was eleven years old. Rafael was only nine.

But, then again, perhaps even the fact of their young age is not really remarkable. Child murders are certainly not a rare occurrence. It is estimated that in Brazil five to six children a day die this way.[1]

There are many aspects of dystopia that seem insane. There are many aspects of it that seem wholly evil. And certainly, on one level at least, that is exactly the case. However, such labels do little to explain anything; and most all of even very bizarre and nasty human behavior is explicable. Diego and Rafael were part of a problem. They were street children. Of course, from a First World middle-class liberal perspective, their very existence as street children is a problem. Their illiteracy, their poor nutrition, their exploitation, their abused and suffering lives are the problem. How to care for them is the practical issue. But this is not the only perspective.

Diego and Rafael were tough little guys. They fought and struggled to survive. They joined a gang to look after one another, for security, for psychological comfort. They roamed the streets in packs. They used all their intelligence, all their creativity and what came to be a kind of ruthlessness, to manage to stay alive . . . for eleven and nine years respectively. They foraged through rubbish; they begged; they stole. For local merchants, they were a different kind of problem than for the aid agencies who bemoaned their plight. They were robbing them; they were driving their

---

[1] *Brazil's Street Children Report* for Jubilee Action UK. This report was compiled in the 1990s, but NGOs like Human Rights Watch assert that such killings continue to go on.
http://www.jubileeaction.co.uk/reports/Brazilian%20Street%20Children .pdf

customers away. Some were frightened of them; some were simply annoyed by them. But for many Sao Paulo or Rio merchants, they were a problem well beyond simply being a nuisance. And the government seemed unable or unwilling to solve this problem.

So, a number of very respectable citizens formed vigilante groups. So a number of "respectable" citizens began hunting down and killing children.

These people are, of course, morally culpable. But the dystopia thesis is not about "bad people." That there are many, many such people in the world is not the point of the dystopia thesis. The dystopia thesis is about *causality*. It is about understanding causal responsibility rather than moral responsibility. The "bad people" are a part of a system. They are merely the human face of *structural* violence: that is what this chapter is about. It is about systemic poverty. It is about guns and soldiers, but it is also about the violence of failing health and welfare systems and exploited labor. Or, rather, it is about the institutions that fail to provide health and welfare but instead aid in the systematic manufacture of inequality. We may wish to see the people who murdered Diego and Rafael as monsters. What sort of people could hunt down and murder children? But we should also be able to see the context in which such takes place. We should be able to understand the motivations of the murderers. We should understand that the rationale for such motivations takes place in a context whereby the richest one percent of Brazil's population control fifty percent of its income, while the poorest half of the people have only ten percent.[2] The struggle for survival, the struggle for a share of that ten percent is, *of course*, going to be brutal.

We should also note as well that though Brazilian inequality, pretty much exactly like most of the Third World, is extreme, the wealth disparity between them and a rich country is also extreme. The GDP (Gross Domestic Product) per capita figure provided by the Central Intelligence Agency's *The World Fact Book* is essentially the average income in a country adjusted to US

[2] Ibid.

dollars. In Brazil (for 2005), it was $8,400. That year in the US, it was $41,800. However, while this disparity is indeed extreme, it is nothing compared to the gap between the rich countries and the *really* poor countries. It is estimated that about one billion people live in truly desperate poverty. Bangladesh's GDP per capita was $2,100, and for the Democratic Republic of the Congo, it was only $700 (both again 2005 estimates).[3] Perhaps it is not altogether coincidental that it is this last country where we find the largest number of child soldiers.

In this chapter, we are only going to look at the more extreme effects of the structural violence of poverty. We shall look at war and disease. We shall look too at the grinding down of the human soul through the poorly paid work that is simultaneously monotonous and dangerous. But though these conditions affect people of all ages and sometimes are particularly painful for the old, we shall instead focus on children. If we brutalize them, they shall in turn be brutal. How we treat our children is a measure of our civilization. Or rather, it is not how we treat *our* children but rather how we treat the children of the world! The dystopia thesis concerning this is of a present-day horror that is almost beyond comprehension. But it is also a thesis concerning the future. Children are the future!

The War on Children

> *It is poverty to decide that a child must die so that you may live as you wish.*
> Mother Teresa

> *What's done to children, they will do to society.*
> Karl Menninger

Child soldiers are being used in more than thirty countries around the world. Human Rights Watch estimates that some

---

[3] All of these figures come from *The World Fact Book*, United States Central Intelligence Agency.
https://www.cia.gov/cia/publications/factbook/index.html

300,000 children are serving as soldiers in current conflicts. Most of these, *but not all,* are boys. Girls, too, kill and get killed. In addition to having combat duties, girls are often subject to sexual abuse and may be taken as "wives" by adult commanders in some countries. *Human Rights Watch* interviewed girls who had been impregnated by rebel commanders and then forced to strap their babies on their backs and take up arms against the Ugandan security forces.

Boys and girls make very good soldiers. This may seem surprising to those who take our media culture of muscled machismo daredevil warriors or patriotic heroism too seriously. Today's weaponry (and even yesterday's) does not require either acrobatics or Schwarzenegger musculature. Children can use it to kill quite easily. No, putting our hero-warrior cultural myths aside, what makes a good soldier is simply obedience: obedience to orders to risk their lives, acceptance of harsh unpleasant conditions, obedience to orders to maim and kill. Children's lack of maturity makes them very easily manipulated. In most of the arenas where children are involved in combat, they have the highest casualty rates. Children's innocence can live hand in hand with cruelty, and they can be quickly conditioned to brutality . . . particularly when they have known little else. The perfect soldier in vicious and often senseless conflict is not a Hollywood action hero, she is a 15-year-old girl.

Children usually do need to be first forced into violence. It is only after time passes that they become inured to it. The title of the 2003 Human Rights Watch report on child combat in Columbia is instructive in this regard: *You'll Learn Not To Cry.* The quotation from an interview with a child soldier that their report derives its title is even more so.

> I had a friend, Juanita, who got into trouble for sleeping around. We had been friends in civilian life, and we shared a tent together. The commander said that it didn't matter that she was my friend. She had committed an error and had to be killed. I closed my eyes and fired the gun, but I didn't hit her. So I shot again. The grave was right nearby. I had to bury her and put dirt on top of her. The Commander said, "You did very well. Even

though you started to cry, you did well. You'll have to do this again many more times, and you'll have to learn not to cry.[4]

Such brutalization of children achieves the desired results. They frequently become cold-blooded killers. The following selection of fighting nicknames for Liberian child combatants is suggestive: Laughing and Killing, Castrator, Captain No Mercy and Nut Bag Mechanic.[5]

Organizations such as Human Rights Watch have many sensible recommendations for governments and international organizations to begin to eliminate child combat. They address deeper concerns than merely the immediate violence and danger experienced by the children. They see them as likely scarred for life even if they manage to avoid serious physical harm. It is believed that the exposure of these children to such horrific scenes of violence and suffering, to the deaths and injuries of friends and family members and above all to their own participation in acts of brutality will leave deep long-term psychological disturbances. A number of programs have been set up to aid the child "veterans" who were fortunate enough to escape the fighting or allowed to go home. They try to give the children some skills other than those of combat. They try to address the psychological wounds through counseling. These are all worthy objectives. However, the scale of the amelioration does not match the scale of the problem. The dystopia thesis is that the situation will get worse. There will be even more child soldiers in the future. There will be even more brutal adults as these children grow to adulthood (the ones lucky enough to survive that long). The children brutalized today will be the adults brutalizing children tomorrow . . . because children are the future.

---

[4] (2003) *"You'll Learn Not To Cry": Child Combatants in Colombia,* Human Rights Watch.
http://www.hrw.org

[5] Ibid.

Child Labor

> *Children's talent to endure stems from their*
> *ignorance of alternatives.*
> Maya Angelou

Soldiering is by far not the only dangerous job that children do. Indeed, their participation in other sorts of unhealthy and dangerous employment quite dwarfs the child soldier problem. There are approximately 250 million child laborers in the world today, a number is likely to grow rather than shrink in the future, efforts of well intentioned liberals notwithstanding. Some of these jobs can be classified as "light labor" . . . but not most of them. UNICEF estimates that of the 246 million children engaged in child labor (their figure), almost three-quarters (171 million) work in hazardous situations. Children, even quite young children, work in mines. They work in factories and operate dangerous machinery without supervision. They work with toxic chemicals and pesticides in agriculture. Indeed, the majority work in agriculture. Millions of girls work as domestic servants, some of them sold into bondage by their parents. UNICEF estimates that there are 5.7 million children living in what can only be described literally as conditions of slavery. Perhaps not surprisingly in such situations, they are frequently sexually abused. Besides the 300,000 child soldiers we have already spoken of, there are believed to be another 600,000 involved in criminal activities.[6]

Let us try and understand this dystopian condition. What drives the exploitation of children? Perhaps this is an answer: gold. The glamour of gold. The irresistible lure of gold. Yet there is nothing glamorous in the life of 15-year-old Abdou Adamou, even though his life is completely controlled by the power of gold. He spends his working days 50 to 80 meters below the earth, crushing and carrying rocks. Nor was he irresistibly lured by dreams of riches, as were the prospectors of the North American "gold rushes." No his "lure" to the mines was much more mundane. He was brought there by his parents because they

---

[6] http://www.unicef.org/protection/index_childlabour.html

had no one to leave him with when they were driven by poverty to seek out work in the Komabangou mines in Niger. It seemed only natural that their son should work there too. Though Niger has laws requiring a minimum age of eighteen for such work, they are not enforced, and many other children, some much younger than Abdou, work in the mine.[7] In other parts of the world, children as young as five are found doing chores in the mines.[8]

When we think of the horrors of child labor in the mines, we tend to think of the 19th century. We conjure up images of the skinny bodies and blackened faces of child coal miners. But we like to think such days are very long over in our modern civilized world. But the International Labor Office estimates that there are approximately *one million children* worldwide working in small-scale mining operations.[9] This is out of an estimated 246 million children forced to do some kind of work.[10]

However bad the situations of such children can be, there are still worse. Though children may be young, impressionable and easily taken advantage of, most of those working in some sense or another entered their work situation "voluntarily." Most child laborers are "free laborers." Though, of course, such freedom and its choices are always severely curtailed by circumstances of desperation. But there are other child laborers whose situation is not free in any possible sense of the word. They work in forced labor, they have been sold into bondage . . . most usually by their

---

[7] Ousseini, Issa (2005), *Gold Miners Exploit Children* Global Policy Forum.
http://www.globalpolicy.org/socecon/inequal/labor/2005/0826amadou.htm

[8] *A Load Too Heavy: Children in Mining and Quarrying* (2005), International Labor Office.
http://www.ilo.org/public/english/b   ...
u/inf/download/child/childmining.pdf

[9] Lisa Schlein (12-06-05), *Child Labor Report for Voice of America.*
http://www.voanews.com

[10] Ibid.

own families. The families were paying off debt. Their "choice" to sell a child into the slavery of bonded labor is usually the sort of choice one makes with a gun to one's head. A nine-year-old beedi (cigarette) roller in Tamil Nadu India explains about his sister.

> My sister is ten years old. Every morning at seven, she goes to the bonded labor man, and every night at nine, she comes home. He treats her badly; he hits her if he thinks she is working slowly or if she talks to the other children, he yells at her, he comes looking for her if she is sick and cannot go to work. I feel this is very difficult for her. I don't care . . . about school or playing. I don't care about any of that. All I want is to bring my sister home from the bonded labor man. For 600 rupees, I can bring her home – that is our only chance to get her back. We don't have 600 rupees . . . we will never have 600 rupees.[11]

Bonded child labor is a long standing tradition in India. Indeed, "tradition" has disgustingly even been used as a rationalization by an Indian government minister for its extraordinary prevalence in his country.[12] Understandably he was trying to deflect product boycotts and the like from concerned Westerners. Less forgivably, he was attempting to justify his own government's failings in enforcing its laws, funding education and living up to its alleged commitment to protect children from exploitation. Bonded child labor is the practice whereby children work in conditions of servitude in order to pay off a debt, usually one incurred by their parents or guardians. The creditors-cum-employers offer these "loans" to destitute parents in an effort to secure the labor of a child, which is always cheap, *but even cheaper under a situation of bondage*. This is where "tradition" meets the exigencies of contemporary capitalism. In India, these

---

[11] Human Rights Watch, September 1996.
http://www.hrw.org/reports/1996/India3.htm#P159_9339

[12] *Frontline*, Vol.15, No. 2, 1998.
http://www.ashanet.org/library/articles/frontline.199801.html

debts tend to be very modest. The all important 600 rupees that the young boy in the story above thought they would never get is only *seventeen dollars* American.

The working of the system is clearly explained in *The Small Hands of Slavery: Bonded Child Labor in India.*

> The children who are sold to these bond masters work long hours over many years in an attempt to pay off these debts. Due to the astronomically high rates of interest charged and the abysmally low wages paid, they are usually unsuccessful. As they reach maturity, some of them may be released by the employer in favor of a newly indebted and younger child. Many others will pass the debt on, intact or even higher, to a younger sibling, back to a parent, or on to their own children. [13]

Child Prostitution

> *If we don't stand up for children, then we don't stand up for much.*
> Marion Wright Edelman

The young girl knocked on the door. She was surprised and a little frightened by the big dog with the man who answered the door. She looked at him and the dog with a question in her eyes. "I don't do animals" she said. "You do now," the man said and pulled her into the apartment.

Whatever else there is involved in the working conditions of prostitution, danger is a constant feature of it. It is particularly dangerous for children. The younger the child, the smaller and weaker, the more vulnerable she . . . or he, is. One might think from the apparent intensity of the perception of risk that those most at risk for potential assaults would be elderly widows in the middle-class suburbs. In chapter 6, we will discuss this disjuncture between risk perception and true risk probabilities. However, the actual risk for assaults, rapes or indeed any form of

---

[13] Human Rights Watch, September 1996,
http://www.hrw.org/reports/1996/India3.htm#P159_9339

violence being directed at one is highest for the young. As far as occupations go, prostitution is likely considerably more dangerous than police work.

The intrinsic disgrace, indignity and degradation of prostitutes is perhaps over-exaggerated. The prostitute provides a service in turn for which he or she receives payment. In some ways, this is just like any job and possibly less unpleasant than many, cleaning toilets for example. The degree to which the "moral disgrace" of the occupation is felt is mainly to do with the degree of internalization of religious morality. True, the social status of the job is generally low but then so too is that of toilet cleaners. The point I am leading to here is one to do with the conditions of work and pay. In this regard, prostitution *is* just like any other occupation. The very highest-class "call girls" can make a great deal of money indeed. They can afford to have some autonomy and control of their own lives and also, of course, over their working conditions. They can afford, financially and psychologically, to thumb their noses at the hypocritical prissy moral judgments of society. However, this is a very, very small proportion of sex workers. The pay and working conditions for the rest range from pretty bad to abysmal.

One might think that the best-paid prostitutes would be the best-looking or the best practitioners of sex. One might think that, if one had not thought much about it. In fact, the price of sexual services has very little to do with that . . . and how much money the prostitute actually receives, even less. Indeed, though both adult women and men are frequently exploited by others, and extravagant shares of their earnings are taken from them through trickery or force, it is the child sex prostitute who has the greatest discrepancy between money charged and money received.

Children are seldom independent operators. Some may have entered the sex trade voluntarily, in the sense described above of making a choice with an economic gun to their heads. But once involved, they usually lose all autonomy and are at the mercy of unscrupulous adults. Then, of course, there are those that did not enter the sex trade at all voluntarily in any sense of the word. Many children are violently taken and forced into pornography or prostitution. Many? How many? One million eight-hundred thousand the International Labor Organization estimates for the year 2000.[14] One million two-hundred thousand children were what are labeled "trafficked".[15] According to the *UN Protocol to Prevent, Suppress and Punish Trafficking in Persons, Especially Women and Children,* child trafficking can be defined as "the recruitment, transportation, transfer, harboring or receipt of a girl or boy of less than eighteen years of age for the purpose of exploitation." The above figure for child trafficking by the International Labor Organization is much narrower. Their figure is limited to those children trafficked for prostitution and other forms of sexual exploitation, such as the use of children for pornography or forced labor *under conditions similar to slavery and servitude.*

The dystopia thesis here bears no relation to the tut-tutting of the moral judgments of the affluent. The dystopia thesis is about suffering. The dystopia thesis is about a world in which there is a positive moral hysteria about sex and children on the one hand, yet a tolerance to the point of encouragement of their slavery and abuse on the other. Am I arguing here that there is little knowledge of the problem or nothing being done to address it? No, not at all. There are myriad academics researching the issue and a plethora of NGOs, charities, national and international governmental agencies involved in addressing the problem. Yet in spite of these worthy efforts, the numbers of those suffering abuse continues to increase. Why? The organizations and academics studying the problem all seem to agree upon one thing: the issue is complex. Perhaps that is part of the problem. Perhaps that consensus upon complexity is part of the reason for the persistence of a problem that is in fact not complicated all. Perhaps the sexual exploitation of children issue is in fact very simple.

---

[14] *Every Child Counts: New Global Estimates on Child Labor,* International Labor Organization, Statistical Information and Monitoring Program on Child Labor, p. 25.

[15] Ibid.

The dystopia thesis suggests that while, of course, there are all kinds of related law enforcement problems, national and international legal issues, cultural and religious subtleties and so on, the ever-increasing commercial exploitation of children (not just sexually but in every way) has a few basic causes. The child sexual tourism trade is a case in point. It has expanded with capitalism's increasingly globalized market *for everything*.

Capitalism, as even Marx conceded, is not all bad. The capitalist organization of the production of goods and services has produced an astonishing abundance of both. It continues to do so. Thus, there is an ever-increasing number of First World middle-class people, and even working-class people, able to indulge their tastes for snow and surf and sunshine in exotic locales. It also provides them with an income to afford to indulge their more "exotic" sexual tastes. And just as capitalist development in the developed world has made such expenditures possible for the ordinary citizen, so too has its corollary of underdevelopment and inequality (that is to say, poverty) provided an ever-increasing number of seriously desperate people. Ergo, the poor provide for the tastes of the tourists, whether such tastes for adventure happen to be mountain climbing, hang gliding or the sexual molestation of young boys.

The primary cause for the pain and suffering associated with child prostitution derives from the structural violence of the capitalist system. It is very simple. There is both ample money to pay for sexual services and money to be made from providing them. The poor, young, old and in-between all have a desperate need for money. It is about survival. The dystopia thesis suggests this struggle for survival will intensify as world social inequality intensifies. The amount of money required to buy the body of another for sexual purposes is becoming less and less. That is, its cost in terms of relative income and purchasing power to the affluent is declining, at the same time as the desperation of the poor for even miniscule sums of money (again in terms of relative income and purchasing power) is growing. The following extract of a bargaining discussion, one of millions that take place daily, should make this point clear. The conversation takes place in Cameroon.[16]

> **Man:** *Okay, how much do you take?*

> **Girl:** *How much do you have first?*

> **Man:** *Tell me your price first.*

> **Girl:** *Okay, say 2000 Frs* (USD 3.84).

> **Man:** *2000, but you are expensive! Let's say 500* Frs (USD 0.96).

> **Girl:** *What? 500 Frs? No, it cannot work! And my sister will not accept that I go with a man for only 500 Frs If you have 1500 Frs* (USD2.88), *let's go.*

> **Man:** *No, it is too much. Let's say 1000 Frs* (USD 1.92).

> **Girl:** *1000 Frs? But you won't be long, eh? Because I don't want my sister to meet me with a man who pays only 1500 Frs (USD 2.88) and wastes my time.*

So, as the quotation makes clear, the long-standing couple of poverty and prostitution is very seriously connected to an increasing number of suffering children. However callous the attitude, though, the general First World perception of this problem is that of something very remote from their lives. It is another one of those "drop in the ocean," "contribute just two dollars a month to better the life of an abused child" . . . an abused child who lives very far away in another world entirely. Even the fact that child prostitution is an increasing problem for every wealthy country as well does not really dispel this distance of

---

[16] The conversation was actually between a child prostitute and a researcher into child sexual abuse in Cameroon. *Report Child Sexual Exploitation in Cameroon*, compiled for ECPAT International by Marie Thérèse, p. 33, 2006.
http://www.ecpat.net/eng/index.asp

vague unreality. The runaways, the street children, the child
prostitutes of Birmingham (whether Birmingham, UK or
Birmingham, Alabama does not matter), while geographically
close to the First World suburban reality, they actually belong to
that other world, that world of desperation and suffering, *the
Third World within the First*, the world of dystopia.

But though the two worlds have an incredible distance
between them in terms of probabilities for pain and probabilities
for violence, suburban reality is now being penetrated
nonetheless. What has brought this about has been the arrival of a
new sexy dystopian guest. Poverty and prostitution are a long-
time couple, but the couple is now frequently a threesome.
Disease has joined the party!

Sex workers are quite naturally at increased risk of HIV and
AIDS. This is a quite obvious connection to make with respect to
probabilities for any STD (sexually transmitted disease). But
child prostitutes have even higher probabilities of infection than
their older "colleagues." Why is this so? The mechanism for
transmission is a matter of chance and probabilities, blood and
other bodily fluids. A single sexual encounter with an infected
person does not guarantee contracting the HIV infection. Just as a
single blindfolded walk across a busy street does not guarantee
being hit by a car . . . though it certainly increases one's chances.
No, small abrasions, tiny cuts to the skin, greatly enhance the
probability of infection. Children being small make such more
likely; the penetration of children by adults can cause such
abrasions. Children being weak make them unable to fend off
more-violent attempts at penetration. The fact of children being
small and weak, of children simply being children, gives them
less power to negotiate the terms of their sexual encounters. Even
if they are aware of the dangers of unprotected sex, it is harder for
them to insist upon the use of condoms, for example.

There is a trend now for child prostitutes to be younger and
younger. This is also related to sexually transmitted disease. A

United Nations Commission on Human Rights report[17] suggests that demand for child prostitutes has grown beyond the pedophile market. There is an increased demand for virgins. There is an increased demand for unprotected sex with perceived to be cleaner (read here younger) prostitutes. But, as said earlier, though demand will drive prices up, there is usually a severe disjuncture between the price of services and the "wage" actually received by the sex worker. This, as also was said earlier, is even more so in the case of the child prostitute. No, the fear of AIDS has driven the demand for younger children, but it has not increased their earning power. No, it has simply led to younger and younger prostitutes and more and more of them . . . precisely the dystopia thesis about humanity's future. Remember, as the politicians say: "Children *are* the future." And the future holds a "sick" partnership between children, poverty and disease.

Infectious Disease (1): Malaria, Cholera, Diarrhea and the Flu

> *True, it's not enough money to eradicate malaria*
> *in the Dano region, but it is enough to keep some*
> *children alive who might otherwise die.*
> Andy Johnson

> *In Mozambique there has been a problem with*
> *payment – and there are problems there like*
> *malaria and high taxes. It's not friendly for us.*
> Mike Lomas

The two worlds may be divided in terms of disease. One world faces sudden severe acute outbreaks of contagious diseases. The other world principally faces chronic conditions that manifest themselves in terms of mortality mainly amongst those that are older. For example, the figure for years of life lost to

---

[17]   Office of the High Commissioner for Human Rights, *Special Rapporteur on the Sale of Children, Child Prostitution and Child Pornography.*
http://www.unhchr.ch/children/hiv.htm

communicable diseases in Canada was 5.7 in 2002, while the figure for years of life lost to non-communicable diseases in that year was 79.6. For Burundi, in the same year, it was exactly the opposite: 80.9 years of life lost to communicable diseases and only 7.2 years of life lost to non-communicable diseases.[18] The wealthy world tends to die of heart diseases, strokes and cancer. The "other world," while of course having some who experience such things, tends not to live long enough for cholesterol to become a problem.

Most cases of serious and fatal infectious diseases occur within the poor world. It could be said that there is "an ecology of disease," a realm of what can be called the "bio-social." Geography, human social conditions, human economic conditions facilitate or inhibit the pathological power of the microbial world. Poverty is the single most-crucial of the factors with respect to this. Capitalism facilitates the spread of disease; capitalism blocks effective modes of prevention; capitalism condemns millions to untreated or ineffectively treated conditions of suffering and death. Capitalism condemns ever increasing numbers to death from *treatable conditions*!

But we are ahead of ourselves. Let us begin with a sad story from the past that has become a nightmare in the present that is continuing to grow. Let us talk of the causal mechanisms of infectious disease and the causal mechanisms of political economy. Let us talk of malaria.

Malaria is a horrendous endemic chronic condition for millions of people, on the one hand, and a lethally acute condition, on the other. It is estimated[19] that there are 300 to 500 million clinical cases of malaria each year resulting in 1.5 to 2.7

---

[18] YLL (years of life lost) are calculated from the number of deaths multiplied by a standard life expectancy at the age at which death occurs. The standard life expectancy used for YLL at each age is the same for deaths in all regions of the world.
World Health Organization Statistics (2006) *Core health Indicators.* http://www3.who.int/whosis/core/core_select_process.cfm

[19] World Health Organization figures.

million deaths annually. Malaria is responsible for as many as half the deaths of African children under the age of five. About forty percent of the world's population (about two billion people) is at risk in about ninety countries and territories.

The importance of malaria for the dystopia thesis is not simply because of such horrifying statistics but also because it illustrates an important part of the relationship between disease and political economy. In 1980, the World Health Assembly declared the complete eradication of smallpox.[20] It was widely believed that malaria could be similarly eradicated from the world. There had been early success with its control. Near the beginning of the 20th century, the US Army Medical Corps largely succeeded in controlling both yellow fever and malaria in Panama. But there are more malaria cases in the world now than ever before.

The dystopia thesis is not simply that this situation or that one is a terrible problem. The dystopia thesis is an argument about why the most serious problems we face *will not be solved.* The dystopia thesis gives an explanation as to why that is so. The explanation for the successful malaria and yellow fever effort in Panama is very simple. The economic facts of the Panama Canal's importance to world trade are sufficient explanation. The economic stakes for building the canal were enormous. Malarial disease was perhaps the principal obstacle. Ergo, sufficient political will and economic resources were committed to ensure the disease's eradication. The same economic factors were not the case more generally in the world.

The success of the world smallpox eradication campaign and the success of malaria and yellow fever control in Panama illustrate two rather optimistic things concerning disease prevention. First, smallpox eradication illustrates the power and potential of properly financed medical science. Secondly, the Panama example illustrates this potential in a capitalist context of serious economic motivation. But the *failure* of the worldwide eradication of malaria campaign illustrates the short-term planning focus of capitalist political economy. The combination

---

[20] Institute of Medicine, S.C. Oates et al. (eds.), *Malaria: Obstacles and Opportunities*, National Academic Press: Washington, 1991.

of that *political* failure with some of the facts of microbial and insect ecology illustrates a dystopian tragedy of unnecessary suffering and death on a global pandemic scale. Though the consequences of the failure almost beggar belief, the reasons for the failure are clear and simple.

Mosquitoes are the prime vector (agent of transmission) for malaria. The mosquito sucks the parasites out of infected humans through its proboscis (its kind of needle-like nose) and allows them to reproduce within its gut; it later injects them back into another human being, who then gets the disease. Malaria, at that time (we will later explain why that is no longer the case) was most often relatively easily treatable with drugs of the quinine family. Thus, the strategy for defeating malaria is fairly simple in theory – treat the infected people directly and kill the malarial parasite and also attack its vector: the mosquito. Since the beginning of the latter half of the 20th century, human beings have possessed a powerful weapon for destroying the breeding populations of mosquitoes: DDT. Though this chemical toxin was, and is, problematic with respect to the environment, it was extremely effective against mosquitoes. Not only would it kill one generation, but because of its lack of biodegradability (part of the problem with respect to the environment) and the persistence of its toxicity, it would continue to be lethal to subsequent generations of mosquitoes.

In 1958, the worldwide effort to eradicate malaria began in earnest. It was led by Paul Russell from Harvard's School of Public Health. The United States Congress directly allocated $23 million a year towards the battle. It also provided 90 percent of the World Health Organization's anti-malaria budget and a significant proportion of the budgets of the Pan-American Health Organization and UNICEF (United Nations Children's Education Foundation). This constituted a financial commitment in the order of *billions* in today's dollars.

It was a serious commitment to eradicate a serious collective human problem. It also was an effort with a definite time limit to it. Paul Russell in his *International Development Advisory Board Report* had emphasized the time line of malaria eradication: four years of DDT spraying and four years of monitoring that there are three consecutive years of no mosquito transmission in an area. He also emphasized the dangers of failing to complete the program of eradication: DDT resistance, renewed disease pandemics and a virtual economic impossibility of having another attempt in the future be successful. However, this aspect of his report was apparently not as persuasive as the four-year figure. A four-year commitment was made, and four years of funding was what was given[21].

Four years were *nearly* enough. In 1955, Sri Lanka had a million cases of malaria. In 1963, it had only 18. Only another two or three years of concerted effort and financial commitment would have given the world the same success with malaria as it had had with smallpox. But the funding was cut off.

The result, of course, was not merely the failure to eradicate something that was eradicable. The result was to make the problem worse, much worse. The insects developed resistance to DDT and other pesticides. The malarial parasites developed resistances to quinine, chloroquine and other drugs. Most importantly, in areas where the mosquitoes and disease would almost certainly make a comeback, many millions of people now lacked *all resistance to the disease*. By cutting off funding to the eradication efforts, Congress and the other "money people" were condemning millions of people to death in the future. Such is the relationship between the time frame for capitalist political economic planning and future calamity.

Part, though only part, of the problem was the lack of understanding of the science connected to the disease's eradication program by those most crucial to its success, that is, the politicians, the people with the money. In chapter 7, we will be analyzing just this sort of problem as an effect of structural mystification. Structural mystification is an important aspect of the dystopia thesis. It is the negative side of the relationship between power and knowledge.

---

[21] This tragic saga is well narrated by Laurie Garrett. *The Coming Plague: Newly Emerging Diseases in a World out of Balance*, Penguin: New York, 1995, pp. 48-52.

Cholera is another ailment of humanity going back to pre-biblical times. It is even long-standing in terms of the present day. Today's cholera pandemic began in 1961. Even if the disease has not yet been, or perhaps cannot ever be, eradicated, we still can ask at least why has the present pandemic not been stopped. Can it ever be? Actually these questions are all closely related and have a simple answer.

Cholera, in comparison to malaria or AIDS or tuberculosis, does not cause so many deaths or sick people even in its present pandemic conditions. In 2005, "only" 101,383 cases and 2,345 deaths were reported to the World Heath Organization.[22] These figures, however, as the WHO acknowledges, are almost certainly extreme underestimates. The principal symptom is a watery diarrhea with the resultant serious dehydration being the cause of death in fatal cases. Thus, cholera is often under-diagnosed because of its similarity with other diseases with this symptom. Diarrhea more generally is the principal cause of death for young children in Africa. Some of the other causes for under-reporting of the disease are the same as those which contribute to the continuation of the pandemic. It is the socio-economic conditions of the countries that are experiencing the continuing outbreaks. This, rather than the sheer numbers of cholera victims, is why we are discussing it as part of the dystopia thesis. Cholera outbreaks occur essentially because of poor sanitation infrastructures. Cholera occurs because of a lack of clean water. So too, we might add do most of the other forms of diarrhea commonly found sickening and killing the poor.

There are effective vaccines against cholera. Improved sanitation virtually eradicated it from Europe and North America. So what is the prognosis for the future? Is there any hope of eliminating the cholera and diarrhea plaguing the old and young amongst the poor? Virtually none, the dystopia argument would assert. Oversimplifying only slightly, one could say that poverty causes cholera and poverty does not appear to be on the way out.

---

[22]World Health Organization, *Weekly Epidemiological Record*, No. 31, August 5, 2005,
http://www.who.int/wer

This is only an oversimplification because this and myriad other health problems could be solved without such a drastic long-term solution as the elimination of poverty being enacted. That is, we could simply help the poor. We could provide them with medical treatment for treatable diseases. We could . . . in theory. We could and do . . . but only to a limited degree. The response to cholera, just like the response to many of the crises of suffering amongst the poor is reactive. We need to see a lot of television pictures of suffering and dying people before our charity gives them a "band-aid."

The dystopia perspective is not one from which to chastise liberal altruistic concern for its lack of charity. Rather, the dystopia perspective bemoans the structurally produced *lack of enlightened self-interest*. If we recall one of the "lessons from the past" from chapter 3, we know that the wealthy among the Greenland Norse were only able to purchase for themselves the privilege of being the last to die. The dystopia argument is that the problems of the poor will also eventually impact the rich. The dystopia argument is that Third World problems *are* First World problems. Some "bio-social conditions" of disease make this point more clearly than others. The avian and swine flu pandemic worry is such a bio-social condition.

The last serious flu pandemic of the 20th century was in 1968, and it killed relatively few people. In the 1980s and early 1990s, few people were very aware of the terrible history of the 1918 flu pandemic. However, in recent years, people have become widely aware of the awful statistical fact of life that the 1918 flu killed more people than did World War I. People have become aware of the way the 1918 flu differed from the more familiar flu varieties that attack us each year. Some people die of these "ordinary" flu outbreaks. But these people are usually old or young or weakened by other afflictions. But the 1918 virus was different. It killed indiscriminately. Healthy people in the prime of life were as likely to die as the old. It killed quickly, too. People could feel the first slight tinges of fever at lunch time and be dead before dinner.

The reason for the public's renewed interest and knowledge of that terrible history is because of the recent scientific concern that a new and potentially even more lethal global pandemic flu may soon emerge. The concern has been sufficiently great that the media have given the matter considerable attention. Scientists suggest there is a risk that the avian flu virus H5N1 (which is infecting millions of birds in countries worldwide) will "recombine" genetically so as to become a virus not only frequently fatal to humans but easily transmissible between humans. The present lack of human-to-human communicability is only the last in the microbial evolutionary steps necessary for a global pandemic. And for a time, it seemed to the public that the scientific community's worst fears were coming true with the swine flu of 2009. A pandemic was declared by the WHO.[23]

This could have made the eighteen million deaths of the 1918 pandemic seem mild by comparison. It could have but didn't. It didn't but still could. The public was very scared for a time. But then many, many people got the flu and got over it after only suffering marginally more on average than they might have with a case coming from a "normal" flu season. Most of the public got over the flu, and they got over the fear too. Unfortunately the danger has not passed.

Factory farming of domestic birds, particularly poultry, facilitates bird-to-bird contagion. The globalization of trade, and most particularly the enormous scale of human travel throughout the world, would greatly facilitate the spread of the virus should it once emerge in a human-to-human transmissible form. The 1918 virus spread to virtually the whole world before it was over. The new avian-originated disease would do so much, much more quickly, as actually did the swine flu.

We are fortunate that two common characteristics of viruses are rare in combination: virulence and contagion. Flu viruses that are easily transmissible are not usually as severe as others less contagious. The 2009 pandemic was a pandemic of relatively mild illness and few fatalities, unlike the death toll of 1918, probably because a great many people had already been exposed to a very similar virus and thus had an at least partial immunity.

---

[23] On June 29, 2009, the World Health Organization officially declared the swine flu a pandemic.

This is the prime fear with respect to any strain of flu that originates outside the human species; it will be wholly new to us; we will have no immune system protection from it. A new variation of swine or bird flu might have very different mortality rates that that of 2009 pandemic. People are widely aware (to various degrees of knowledge and ignorance) of this possibility. People are concerned and expecting their governments and international organizations to do something about it.

So, what are they doing? There is a lot of scientific work. There are a lot of conferences. There are a lot of pronouncements by politicians. The WHO has an emergency preparedness plan. Many governments also have such plans. Individual local government and public institutions have such plans. My own university had such a plan, which seemed to consist primarily of reminding us to be careful how we cough and to frequently wash our hands. I was not greatly reassured by this.

The first section title of the WHO 2005 risk assessment report[24] asserts: "The risk of a pandemic is great." This has not changed. But we have had a pandemic, not birds but swine, and we seem to be fine. The world media performed its role of scaring us. But the fear evaporated with the lack of a significant death toll. The danger is not over, yet people seem to believe that it is. Should we be frightened? The dystopia thesis says yes: "be afraid, be very afraid".

But why should we be frightened? Why should we be concerned if the scientific community, governments and all the relevant international organizations are well-aware of the problem and trying to address it? The reason is not difficult to ascertain. It is the priorities of capitalist political economy that are the problem. It is the wealth-centric (read misguidedly self-centered) focus of the richer country governments. In a word, it is money!

In some respects, what needs to be done to globally and nationally prepare for potential new pandemic is obvious. We see the same themes running through the WHO's report, the US National Preparedness Plan, the Canadian National Preparedness

---

[24] WHO Report 2005, *Responding to the Avian Influenza Pandemic Threat: Recommended Strategic Actions*, p. 3.

Plan and that of many other countries. They all stress surveillance, reporting and communication, as well as containment at the site(s) of first emergence. They argue for an aggressive policy of poultry and other problem livestock (such as pigs) culling. As said before, the strategy and steps to be taken are fairly obvious. Though at the later stages of the situation, i.e., when a fully-fledged pandemic is already underway, developing, globally stockpiling and selectively administering a vaccine, would be perhaps the highest priority (the problems that emerged with this with respect to the swine flu are a whole story in themselves). But in the early stages, what is required is careful monitoring, treatment and investigation of such cases as they emerge and widespread culling of the bird populations found to be infected. But this is where things break down. It is not that the world experts don't know what should be done; it is that they are not doing it. The problem is factory farming and the facilitation of the conditions for viral outbreak. The problem is money.

Most of the H5N1 bird flu cases have thus far emerged in countries with a considerable amount of rural subsistence agriculture. Such countries are experiencing enormous agricultural losses.

> [The losses] are presently estimated at more than *USD $10 billion*. They are being asked to sustain – if not intensify – resource-intensive activities needed to safeguard international public health while struggling to cope with many other competing health and infectious disease priorities.[25] [my italics]

So, the problem is money. Those countries being asked to pay it are those who can least afford to. But surely the international community is contributing? After all, it is in everyone's interest that a new flu pandemic is stopped in its tracks before decimating the world's population of rich and poor alike. Well, a donors' conference of rich nations pledged some *$1.9 billion* (US) to aid developing countries in their fight against the avian flu. Canada

---

[25] Ibid.

has committed $15 million (over five years!) to strengthen the capacity of public health systems in Southeast Asia and China to respond to infectious diseases.[26] Let's see, on the one hand, there is the $10 billion in costs to the poor countries, and on the other hand there is $1.9 billion in aid coming from the rich, including Canada's "generous" 15 million.

What is the real cost of failing to aid these countries? Early detection, investigation, treatment of people and culling of animals is crucial. But the discrepancies in money are not merely between countries but between people in countries. Who does it cost the most for aggressive culling actions? It is the small farmer who owns the flock. At a stroke, he is expected to wipe out his family's sole means of support . . . usually without any compensation. Rural poverty causes further problems; for example, it perpetuates high-risk behaviors, including the traditional home-slaughter and consumption of diseased birds.[27]

The WHO argues that a general lack of funding impedes the whole pandemic prevention effort.

> Detection of human cases is impeded by patchy surveillance in these areas. Diagnosis of human cases is impeded by weak laboratory support and the complexity and high costs of testing. Few affected countries have the staff and resources needed to thoroughly investigate human cases and, most importantly, to detect and investigate clusters of cases – an essential warning signal. In virtually all affected countries, antiviral drugs are in very short supply.[28]

---

[26] *Embassy: Canada's Foreign Policy Newspaper*, May 24, 2006, http://www.embassymag.ca/html/index.php?display=story&full_path=/2006/may/24

[27] WHO Report 2005, *Responding to the Avian Influenza Pandemic Threat: Recommended Strategic Actions*, p. 3.

[28] Ibid.

By comparison the US government has committed $7 billion to its own pandemic plan.[29] Most of this will be spent within its own borders. So America, do you feel safe? Do you think you have your priorities straight?

Infectious Diseases (2) New Hemorrhagic Fevers and the Old Black Death

> *Father abandoned child, wife, husband, one*
> *brother another . . . And I, Agnolo di Tura . . .*
> *buried my five children with my own hands. . .*
> *So many died that all believed that it was the*
> *end of the world.*
> Agnolo di Tura (Italy, 1348)

Plague! The very name provokes terror. Over one-third of the population of Europe was struck dead by this dreadful disease in the Middle Ages. In some places, it was said that there were so many deaths that there were not enough of the living to bury the dead. It has thus far been the most potent microbial scourge to "plague" humankind. But surely that is simply history and the plague is no more? Try suggesting that to India's tourism bureau. The plague has decimated it. The collective reaction that there has been to plague illustrates well our most common pattern of risk perception. A long-standing complacency both of disinterest and ignorance is suddenly shattered and replaced by a hysteria whereby the fear is disproportionate to the threat. Still there are dystopian lessons to be learned from a consideration of the plague's most recent large outbreak – 1994 in India – and more recent smaller occurrences both in India and other countries.

First, the plague has never really gone away and likely never will. It occurs quite naturally among rodents and other small animals in the wild. Bubonic plague (the most common form of the disease) occurs among humans through fleas from these animals biting us. Each year, there are a number of occurrences of

---

[29] *Embassy: Canada's Foreign Policy Newspaper*, May 24th 2006.

plague in a number of countries, including the United States. Plague, however, can be both cured and controlled. The thirty or so cases that are contracted in Southwestern United States seldom result in secondary infection, i.e., the people are infected directly from the flea-borne disease directly from the rodents, and further transmission usually does not occur. Plague is contagious. Pneumonic plague (transmitted in airborne form) is the most infectious. However, its degree of contagion is generally exaggerated in people's fear-derived perception. You have to get very close to an infected coughing person to catch the airborne bacterium from them. No, the causes of plague epidemic are basically simple: they almost all derive from poverty.

Let us briefly examine the 1994 outbreak in Surat, India. Correct (WHO-prescribed) measures for both treatment and containment were taken. The antibiotic drugs Gentamicin, Streptomycin sulfate and others are effective against *Yersinia pestis*, the plague bacillus. Untreated, the plague fatality rate ranges from sixty percent to one-hundred percent. Early treatment with antibiotics (hopefully within twenty-four hours of the first symptoms appearing) lowers this rate to fifteen percent or even lower in some situations. Containment measures principally involve three things. First, an insecticide attack upon the fleas is required. Second, an extermination effort must be directed at the rats or other rodent populations in the outbreak areas. It is important that these two steps be sequential. Killing the rats before the fleas results in the fleas frequently jumping to human hosts. Quarantine is perhaps the most important step in keeping the disease from spreading. This step has a local, a national and an international dimension to it.

All of these steps were taken in the 1994 outbreak, and ultimately the disease *was* contained. But many more people died than was necessary, and the rest of India and the world were actually very *lucky* that so little of the plague escaped to the outside world. We have already given the general cause for this result – poverty – but let us break this down to understand how it works as a causal mechanism. Imagine *yourself* and *your family* visiting Surat just as information of the plague comes out. What are you going to want to do? The answer is obvious: you're going to try and get your family the hell away from there as fast as possible. You might turn to the Internet and quickly brush up on facts about the disease. You would learn of its one-to-six day symptom-less incubation period. You would learn the imperative of early antibiotic treatment and what these antibiotics were. When you found out that you needed no prescription to buy them locally, you would stock up and perhaps immediately begin taking them as a preventative measure. And when you reached the military checkpoint enforcing the public health quarantine order to stop all travel in or out of the city, you would note that, notwithstanding this absolute travel crackdown, some people were somehow allowed through. It was as though a powerful magic token protected them. The magic token was money.

So, if one thinks of it this way, you can probably imagine yourself doing just what the wealthier segment of Surat's population did, what even many doctors did. The plague outbreak stretched local and national public health resources. The poor did not all receive prompt medical attention and antibiotics. Their overcrowded rat- and flea-infested slum conditions and poor sanitation facilitated the disease's spread amongst them. This is the ecosystem of choice for plague: amongst the poor. Ironically, the principal effect upon the rich of the richer countries is to make a poor country such as India even poorer by spending their tourist dollars elsewhere.

Perhaps, not at all ironically, the greatest source of research funding for investigations into the disease is directed towards examining the possibilities for its use as a bio-weapon. As such, perhaps, the old terror concerning it is warranted.

The Office of Rare Diseases (ORD) of the National Institute of Health (NIH) lists Marburg virus as a "rare disease." This means that Marburg virus, or a subtype of it, affects less than 200,000 people in the US. It actually affects (so far!) nearly no one in the First World, even though its name comes from the town of Marburg, Germany, the site of the first outbreak. It was brought to Marburg from Africa by infected health workers transported there for treatment. It is the same story for its genetic cousin Ebola, a disease with an even higher mortality rate. The fatality rate for Ebola is eighty percent and Marburg thirty percent. That is, it is their fatality rate with the best intensive care treatment being provided. Without such care, the fatality rate is virtually one-hundred percent. Ebola hemorrhagic fever has thus far killed 793 of its 1,100 known victims.[30] The most recent Marburg outbreak in Angola in 2005 killed sixty-three people.[31] The Ebola family of diseases thus truly *is* "rare," even notwithstanding the ethnocentric bias of the US NIH. The reader may well wonder why they are being discussed in my presentation of the dystopia thesis.

Well, the first point to be made is that, while the present nightmare elucidated and the future nightmare predicted by the dystopia thesis is quantitative in nature, it is not wholly so. We are usually discussing prevalence and incidence of suffering. The dystopia thesis points to a massive scale of woe deriving from structural features of the system. But of course, there is a qualitative aspect of pain as well. Many are suffering in the world today. Many more will suffer in the future. But some will suffer on a scale of pain that is beyond imagination.

The progression of Marburg hemorrhagic fever symptoms is as follows. For a couple of days, you might think you had the flu. You would have muscle aches and be somewhat feverish. Then you would notice tender lymph nodes along your throat and perhaps inflammation elsewhere. It could still be flu, you could tell yourself and make yourself believe it. But then a few days later, your body would gradually become covered with a rash that made it absolutely unbearable to be touched. By this time, you would of course be hospitalized, which is just as well because now your throat would be so painfully inflamed you would find it impossible to eat and would need to be fed intravenously. Soon you would be suffering from acute diarrhea. Inside your body, there would be microscopic blockages to your capillaries. This

---

[30] WHO statistics cited by *Bellwether:* 48, Winter, 2001 (The newsmagazine of the University of Pennsylvania School of Veterinary Medicine).

[31] WHO, *Marburg Haemorrhagic Fever in Angola – Update 26*, November 7, 2005.

would manifest itself in a transformation of your rashes into an excruciatingly painful reddening of your entire body. You would actually have a kind of reddish glow to you. Your nerve endings would respond to the oxygen deprivation caused by the capillary and other red blood cell blockages by producing ever-greater pain. By your tenth day of suffering this viral disease, you would be frequently vomiting blood. After about two to three weeks with no improvement or easing of the pain of your already existing symptoms, all your skin would begin to peel off, giving you yet a new level of pain, as well as psychological distress and horror. Blood would be leaking from all your orifices. By this time, the constant pain would have likely driven you close to insanity, and you would begin to exhibit symptoms of dementia. Perhaps fortunately at this point, you would likely go into a coma from which you would never regain consciousness. There is no cure.

However, as was said earlier, the numbers of people affected in the world remain small. Marburg and Ebola outbreaks are rare occurrences. Do *you* need to be worried about these diseases? I mean you as a First World reader. If you live in West Africa, they are perhaps only the most terrifying of the health hazards you face. But my answer to the question for even the First World reader is yes!

The Ebola family of viruses is not very well understood. It is widely suspected that they are zoonotic. This means the virus is carried by animals and transmitted to humans through insect vectors, such as mosquitoes or fleas, or else through direct contact with the animal. But it is not known which animal is the source. Speculation has focused upon the fruit-fly-bat and primates. No matter, the problem is that there is a vast worldwide trade in wild animals of almost every description. The illegal trade in wild animals alone is estimated at $15 billion dollars a year.[32] A great many people from specialized animal handlers to ordinary transport employees come into contact with these animals. So a First World disease outbreak *could* occur. However, this is not the real reason to worry. This is not the reason these viruses have

---

[32] *Pravda*, November 17, 2003.

been included in this chapter. They are there to point the way to a later chapter. Chapter 7 will deal with terrorism and warfare.

The Ebola family of viruses is not very well understood. They, like most infectious diseases, in terms of time and money spent upon them, reflect the two-world structure of power, money and risk perception. That this wealth-centric focus is misguided in a globalized world where microbes need no security clearances or passports is, of course, part of the dystopia argument. However, it is not our point here. Because there has been and is currently quite a lot of research being done. Most of it is classified. Most of it is secret. But Marburg and Ebola can be turned into weapons of terrible mass destruction. That such should be *the* principal priority of research into such terrifying diseases in terms of time, money and expertise, is itself a part of the dystopia of the present.

The eradication of smallpox was perhaps the greatest triumph of modern medicine and world public health campaigns. It is ironic *that it is now being combined with Ebola*! Ebola has been genetically combined with smallpox and other microorganisms to create a chimeric weapon. A chimeric organism is one that contains genes from a foreign species. The genetic basis for desired traits is identified and then recombined into another organism, adding novel characteristics in a useful way. Chimeric weapons are a product where "useful" is defined in terms of either increased lethality or ease of contagion. This last characteristic makes the weapon rather more difficult to control than a nuclear bomb.

There is yet another element of potential danger related to chimeras. A genetic combination of the common cold and the polio virus has been shown to be effective in treating brain cancer. Such research is, of course, done by people with both enormous expertise and the best of intentions. But one wonders:

> Although it may not seem particularly wise to combine lethal pathogens with the common cold, a sufferer of some terminal condition which might be cured by a chimera might see the situation a bit differently.[33]

---

[33] *ZKea News.*

We can certainly see the point made by ZKea News, but the phrase *"not seem particularly wise"* in relation to combining "lethal pathogens with the common cold" is a *massive* understatement. And though this is only rumor, some believe that amongst the other great achievements of the Cold War, the Soviet program in bio-weaponry may have succeeded in *combining the common cold with Ebola*! Such a weapon demonstrates utter insanity. If unleashed it could well result in the extinction of the human species. In chapter 7, we will discuss whether we can take comfort in the sanity of those who control such weaponry and question who are the real terrorists.

Tuberculosis and AIDS

> *Decay and disease are often beautiful, like the pearly tear of the shellfish and the hectic glow of consumption.*
> Henry David Thoreau

> *The effort to discourage HIV infection is laudable, but the campaign against sex parties is completely misguided.*
> Keith Boykin

For some of the fortunate people of the world, the principal experience of some aspects of reality is literary. Tuberculosis, or consumption as it was known in the past, had tragic-glamorous representations in the literary works that were set in the times when the disease was most prevalent in Europe. According to Dostoevsky, the disease would cause people to literally bloom with life and beauty shortly before the inevitable fatal end of the course of the illness's progression. His consumptive heroines were always exquisitely beautiful in their fragility and extraordinary paleness. The latter would be caused by the anemia accompanying their coughing up blood. But upon getting close to death, their cheeks would flush and their eyes would burn with an intensity of life. Dostoevsky's characters would always then remark upon this fusion of life and beauty and the irony of it being an icon of approaching death.

Tuberculosis in its present-day setting has no glamour to it. Instead it has a terrible mundane aspect to it. People suffer a slowly debilitating condition with sudden acute flare-ups and small improvements and regressions. Their suffering is usually in dreary surroundings and conditioned by everyday practicalities – the price of corn in relation to the price of medication, or the cost of a bus journey calculated in the relational terms of a family's food expenditure versus the exhaustion of a weakened condition and a difficult walk of many miles to a clinic. There is no beauty to this and certainly no glamour. Tuberculosis, like most of the diseases we have reflected upon so far, is very largely a disease of the poor. It has much to teach us about the contours of present-day dystopia. However, it also has much to teach us about the shaping up of future "death control" of the human population beyond the simple reality of its association with poverty.

One of the principal dystopian facts about tuberculosis is its dreadful symbiosis with AIDS. They form, as it were, the perfect dystopia partnership. HIV infection is the most potent risk factor for converting latent TB into active transmissible TB – accelerating the spread of the disease – while TB bacteria help accelerate the progress of the AIDS infection in the patient. HIV and TB form a lethal combination, each speeding the other's progress. HIV weakens the immune system. Someone who is HIV-positive and infected with TB bacilli is many times more likely to become sick with TB than someone infected with TB bacilli who is HIV-negative. Today TB is the leading cause of death in persons who are HIV-positive. Here are the central facts of the dystopia disease partnership.[34]

- One in three HIV-infected people worldwide are co-infected with the TB bacterium.

---

[34] Source: The Global Alliance for TB Drug Development.
http://www.tballiance.org/2_1_1_TBandHIV.asp

• TB is responsible for the death of one out of every three people with HIV/AIDS worldwide.

• People who are HIV-positive and infected with TB are 30 times more likely to develop active TB than people who are HIV-negative.

• The TB bacterium enhances HIV replication and might accelerate the natural progression of HIV infection.

• Because of the increased spread of HIV in sub-Saharan Africa, the number of TB cases in that region will double to 4 million new cases per year soon after 2005.

• Almost half of HIV patients in sub-Saharan Africa develop active TB, whereas only 5% to 10% of individuals infected with TB and not infected with HIV develop active TB.

The full horror of these statistical facts about TB's association with AIDS cannot be grasped until we have the central AIDS statistics. It is estimated that 4.9 million people are newly infected with HIV in 2005 bringing the numbers to a total of 40.3 million people living with HIV/AIDS in that year[35]. It is estimated that 3.1 million people died from AIDS during 2005[36] and that more than twenty-five million people have died of AIDS since 1981.[37] Despite massive amounts of money invested in the fight against

---

[35] Joint World Health Organization United Nations Program on HIV/AIDS (UNAIDS) AIDS Epidemic Update 2005. Note: precise figures are very difficult to arrive at and these are estimates. The 40.3 million figure, for example, actually derives from a range estimate of between 36.7 million to 45.3 million people.

[36] Ibid.

[37] AVERT UK (international AIDS charity) http://www.avert.org/

the disease, despite scientific breakthroughs in therapeutic drugs to treat it, despite global education programs, these figures represent a trajectory of expansion for the future. The number of HIV infections has continued to rise year after year since the disease was first detected.

There are a few more salient dystopian facts concerning AIDS to list before commencing our analysis. The social inequalities of the disease's incidence and treatment are the most obvious. The graph shows the degree to which it is an African disease, but it does not show how the African dimension carries over into America. Estimates of the number of HIV-positive people living in the US range from 900,000 to 1,200,000. There are approximately 415,000 people living with full-blown AIDS. Since 1981, it has killed over 500,000 Americans.

But some of the ways that these numbers break down according to ethnic grouping is interesting. Non-Hispanic whites account for sixty-nine percent of the total population and twenty-eight percent of AIDS diagnoses in 2004. While African-Americans constitute only thirteen percent of the population, they accounted for forty-nine percent of AIDS diagnoses in the same year.[38] This statistic is interesting because there are no physiological propensities for AIDS among the African-American population that would account for this enormous difference. Once again, it is most significantly an issue of poverty and relative wealth . . . of the Third World peoples living within the First World and right next to its affluence.

The absence of a proper universal public health care system in the United States is likely the major causal feature of the disease's disproportionate incidence. The most up-to-date and effective treatment regimes are expensive, and many amongst the poor of the world's richest country simply cannot afford it. Perhaps for the dystopia thesis the most salient AIDS statistic is that, in "developing countries," 6.8 million people are in immediate need

---

[38] http://www.avert.org/america.htm

of life-saving AIDS drugs; of these, only 1.65 million are receiving the drugs.[39]

There is, of course, both in the US and worldwide, help for the poor with treatment. Indeed, a fair proportion of those 1.65 million receiving AIDS drugs are financially aided by charities and governments. But in many ways, the internal logic of capitalist political economy interferes with the fight against AIDS and TB that altruism and enlightened self-interest inspires.

First, there is an ongoing battle between the public health efforts of the most severely afflicted countries in the world and the structural adjustment programs (SAPs) imposed upon them by capitalism's world banking and trade control institutions (e.g., the General Agreement on Tariffs and Trade – GATT). Government-subsidized health care systems are forced into either full or partial privatization. So the poor are forced to spend their meager savings or perhaps sell the small plots of land that they depend on for a living. They are forced into choices between food and medication. Or perhaps they receive no treatment at all.

The running down of Britain's National Health Service and the country's increasing privatization of health care has been hotly debated over the years. Proponents argue that health care privatization promotes efficiency. It allows the market to better direct resources than the "fat" bureaucracy of the public sector. Against this argument, opponents of privatization insist that it promotes a "two-tier" health care system, whereby those who can afford proper health insurance receive the best of state-of-the-art medical treatment, while those who cannot languish in long queues to receive the best treatment the increasingly over-stretched and under-resourced system can provide. But these arguments have an entirely different level of resonance of extremes in the Third World.

Zambia, for example, is a poor country that has rigorously followed International Monetary Fund prescriptions. Its health care system is very significantly privatized. Just as in Britain, this has caused strains on the resources available to public health care. It has created some small "problems."

---

[39] http://www.avert.org/

The problem with taking a blood sample for your malaria test is that the cockroaches may eat it in the night," announced the nurse. "Ants are an even worse problem. The place is infested with them." Siavonga Hospital, on the shores of Lake Karibe in southern Zambia, is suffering. "We have to put patients with TB in the same room as women who are giving birth," says one of the four Cuban doctors who battle to run the place. They also have to charge fees for their health care, and patients have to provide their own medicines, syringes and clean needles. What if they can't afford to pay? The doctor shrugs. "What do you think? They die".[40]

The comparative statistics underlying the human suffering are illuminating.

In 1980, under the former socialist government of Kenneth Kaunda, the under-5 mortality rate was 162 deaths per 1,000 births. It's now 202 per 1,000. That means one in five children in Zambia dies before reaching the age of 5. The average life expectancy has fallen from 54 in the mid-80s to 40 now.[41]

Secondly, the development and utilization of much-cheaper generic drugs is fought on every level by the major drug companies and their governmental allies. In the spring of 2005, India's parliament voted to restrict production of low-cost generic medicines. This decision is likely to have profoundly unfortunate consequences for the battle against HIV and AIDS in the poorer countries, as India is the largest supplier of generic, as opposed to brand named, drugs to these countries. What is the difference between generic and brand name products of the multinational drug companies? It is entirely a difference in costs: between $15,000 per patient per year and $200 per patient per year. But

---

[40] Mark Lynasp, "Letter from Zambia," *The Nation Magazine*, February 14, 2000.
http://www.thirdworldtraveler.com/Africa/Letter_Zambia.html

[41] Ibid.

why would they do such a thing? The new law will encourage further outsourcing from the West. According to the New Delhi-based newspaper *Financial Express*, more than 30 agreements between Indian and multinational drug companies have already been signed, including deals with Cipla and Ranbaxy, the two largest AIDS drug manufacturers in India.[42]

From the point of view of the public good, both of these policies seem rather unwise, to say the least. Though AIDS and TB, indeed all infectious diseases, disproportionately afflict the poor, they do not *exclusively* affect them. The international policies that force curtailment of public services in Third World countries, and the national policies that force public health care cutbacks in the richer ones, actually facilitate the spread of disease. That poor people are unable to access generic drugs and cannot afford the more-expensive treatments available ultimately increases the chances of infection of the world's rich. In protecting their markets and their money, they are not protecting health.

But this is not all. Ignorance of the way poverty interacts with disease can be an exacerbating force in its causality. Ignorance more generally can have pernicious effects. Both TB and AIDS have an unfortunate history of such ignorance. We shall deal with AIDS first. The medical science attempting to understand AIDS faced an enormous hurdle at the very beginning, deriving simply from an accident. Well no, that is not quite correct; it was the prejudices afflicting many of the scientists concerning the accident of the American male homosexual community being the first in North America to experience the infection. They became obsessed with finding a cause for the disease in the "male homosexual lifestyle" or, worse, seeking a gay genetics explanation.

Sexually transmitted diseases run through groups sharing lifestyle and contact with one another. Gays gave other gays the disease. That is all there is to it. That a disproportionate number

---

[42] Meredith Dearborn, "India Restricts Generic Drugs," *YES! Magazine*, Summer 2005.
  http://www.yesmagazine.org/article.asp?ID=1295

of gay people (in relation to the general population) were initially infected in North America perhaps makes it understandable that first attention should be directed toward the *possibility* of some degree of "gay causality." However, as we clearly know now, there is nothing about the "male homosexual lifestyle" or genetic makeup, that makes this group any more susceptible than any other group. That HIV is sexually transmitted and that male homosexuals most frequently have sex with other male homosexuals ensured in North America a disproportionate number of infections among such people. It is as simple as that.

In most of the rest of the world, it is predominantly a *heterosexual disease* and increasingly non-gendered. By the end of 2005, women accounted for forty-eight percent of all adults living with HIV worldwide.[43] Our point here is not simply that the now very well-known facts concerning AIDS were not known as soon as medical scientists became aware there was an outbreak of some kind of infectious disease that affected our immune systems. Rather, the point is just how very long many scientists remained blinded by their preconceptions and ignorance and continued to ignore a plethora of mounting evidence.[44]

The blinders seem to now be lifted from most of the scientific and medical community, but the politics of sexuality have not yet left the issue. An enormous amount of American money is now being poured into efforts aimed at containment of the African super-pandemic. But there are restrictions upon the use of this money. Abstinence rather than condoms is the American money-tied message . . . in spite of an abundance of evidence that "abstinence education" simply does not work as a public health tactic for limiting the spread of infection, while safe sex does.

We mention the homosexuality/ignorance/scientific incompetence/politics of AIDS here merely as a lead into the way an ignorance of poverty as a causal mechanism for an enhanced

---

[43] Ibid.

[44] The misguided scientific resistance to abandoning the "homosexuality causal thesis" is documented by Laurie Garret in chapters 10 and 11 of *The Coming Plague*.

disease ecology can work as a causal mechanism itself. I need to be clear here. I am not asserting that an awareness of the linkage between TB incidence and poverty was long lacking. No, quite the contrary, Robert Koch, the discoverer of the tubercle bacillus in 1882, asserted:

> One has been accustomed up until now to regard tuberculosis as the outcome of social misery and to hope by relief of distress to diminish the disease. But in the future struggles against this dreadful plague of the human race, one will no longer have to contend with an indefinite something but with an actual parasite.[45]

Though often twisted into racist and other untenable assumptions about the socially disadvantaged, a perception of TB's association with poverty continues to the present – as indeed it should. However, what the "experts" are ignorant of is how poverty affects the lives of the poor. What medical doctors are unaware of is the way poverty is manifest as structural violence. What they are unaware of is that some of their own blinkered assumptions are causing errors of medical judgment affecting not merely their patients' unfortunate experiences in their care but also causing a facilitation of the further development of multi-drug resistant tuberculosis (MDR-TB).

> Drug-resistant TB is caused by inconsistent or partial treatment, when patients do not take all their medicines regularly for the required period because they start to feel better, because doctors and health workers prescribe the wrong treatment regimens, or because the drug supply is unreliable. A particularly dangerous form of drug-resistant TB is multi-drug-resistant TB (MDR-TB), which is defined as the disease caused by TB bacilli

---

[45] Robert Koch, quoted in *Infections and Inequalities: The Modern Plague*, Paul Farmer, University of California Press: Berkeley, 2001, p. 202.

resistant to at least isoniazid and rifampicin, the two most powerful anti-TB drugs.[46]

One part of the dystopia thesis concerns structural violence. Another part of the thesis concerns structural mystification. The manner in which many doctors and social scientists understand poor patients' reasons for not completing their courses of medication and the consequences of that understanding is where the thesis of structural mystification meets the thesis of structural violence.

Understanding the manner in which human agency exists within a context of structural causality is perhaps difficult conceptually. Certainly many of my students have found it so when I discussed the issue with them in social theory classes. However, the erroneous assumptions of both health professionals and social scientists in this regard go beyond a failure to grasp difficult abstractions. In their case, the failure is far more basic. They fail to understand the life conditions that cause their patients to fail to complete their courses of medication.

The mutation and evolution of TB bacterium drug resistance, as is also the case for the resistance of other pathological organisms, has a very simple dynamic. It does indeed derive from patients' failures to complete antibiotic regimes and their infection of others with the new form of the disease. This does, of course, suggest patient agency, that is their actions (in this case, a lack of action), as causally responsible for disease evolution in this particularly unfortunate manner. But structural causality makes some "choices," some "actions" virtually inevitable. Thus, though individual patients may well be the proximate causes of parasitic evolutionary success against the drugs used to combat them, more critical awareness suggests the structural context determining choices and actions as bearing a greater causal responsibility. To put this in a simpler form: if the social context issues are not addressed, then the patients will continue to perform the same way.

---

[46] WHO, *Tuberculosis Fact Sheet.*
http://www.who.int/mediacentre/factsheets/fs104/en/index.html

Jesus and Mary: Non-compliant Patients

> *The good physician treats the disease; the great*
> *physician treats the patient who has the disease.*
>   William Osler

Jesus is infected with "normal bacilli," that is, bacilli that are not resistant to the usual first-line treatment course of drugs. He is prescribed them, and they begin to work. But he was a poor man living in a poor country. It was very difficult for him to afford these drugs even though they were being partially subsidized by the government. When the government (in line with the "harsh economic medicine" of structural adjustment programs) cut its drug subsidy program for the poor, he could no longer afford to buy the medication. The disease had been responding to treatment, and Jesus was experiencing a partial remission of symptoms. But the bacilli began making a comeback once the medication regime was suspended.

If the treatment regime had been completed, all that would have been left would have been a very few of the mutant drug-resistant bacilli. These would have been quickly mopped up by Jesus's immune system. But now both they and the normal ones proliferate. The disease begins to progress again, this time until Jesus is too weak to work any longer. The disease further flourishes in the environment of his weakened immune system. This was caused by malnutrition. The proportion of the normal to mutant bacilli tilts toward the latter because of the earlier heavy mortality of the former, from when Jesus was taking his medication. Eventually, of course, Jesus dies. But this does not occur before he infects a large number of people . . . with the new mutant drug-resistant strain of bacteria.

Among the people infected by Jesus is Mary. She is infected with MDR-TB. She has a little more money than Jesus and can afford to pay for the drugs prescribed to her, though this is only with enormous difficulty and through considerable sacrifice by relatives who help her. Unfortunately, the drugs prescribed are the same first-line drugs as prescribed for Jesus. While they would've worked for him, they will not work for her. The bacilli strain of her infection has evolved to be drug resistant . . . or at least resistant to *these* drugs. Mary has a daughter who is also infected and a young son who they think might be. But the appointments at the clinic are never scheduled at the same time. Mary's job, the difficulties of finding babysitters and the long journey across town on an inefficient public transit system makes it very difficult to make all her appointments.

The drugs seem to be making her condition worse if anything. At any rate, she is certainly not getting better. Nor will she on such a drug regime. But the clinic insists upon a full six-month compliance with it, even though the resistant nature of Mary's tubercle bacilli should be apparent after she fails to show any response to treatment after the first few weeks. Not only is Mary finding it difficult to make appointments for herself and her children and to afford all the drugs, she is skeptical about the potency of these drugs. Her uncle and her nephew took the same drugs for the full six months. They both died. So she stops taking the drugs and only returns to the clinic when her condition worsens.

Mary is aware of other drugs – the second-line much more-costly drugs used to treat MDR-TB. She asks for them to be given her. She is refused. Mary has been labeled a "non-compliant patient." And of course, we know that patient non-compliance is the principal cause for drug resistance to evolve. It is feared that, some day, resistances will develop to even those few drugs that are now still effective against MDR-TB. It is also believed that only a targeted utilization of these drugs is really cost-effective. So Mary wanders off and infects more people, thus spreading further MDR tuberculosis. So Mary wanders off and dies.[47]

---

[47] The hypothetical cases of Jesus and Mary are derived from composites of the real cases and situations narrated in Paul Farmer's book *Infections and Inequalities*.

Social Science, Medicine and Ignorance

> *I observe the physician with the same diligence*
> *as he the disease.*
>   John Donne

> *It would be nice if the poor were to get even*
> *half of the money that is spent in studying them.*
>   Bill Vaughan

Soon MDR-TB will be the dominant form of TB. Such, at least, is the dystopia thesis concerning it. Paul Farmer writes:

> It is difficult to be optimistic. The arrival of strains of *M. tuberculosis* that are resistant to all first-line and many second-line drugs is surely a harbinger of pan-resistant strains to come. And HIV looms: ever-increasing numbers of co-infected individuals, most of them poor, promise millions of cases of reactivation tuberculosis. These "excess cases" will in turn infect tens of millions. In failing to curb tuberculosis before the advent of these truly novel problems, it seems clear that a window of opportunity has been slammed shut.[48]

But how was the opportunity missed? First of all, it was government health services penny-pinching. This is a claim that will not only be disputed but dismissed as absurd by those that know the financially over-stretched conditions of Third World health services. It will be argued that the price of second-line TB drugs is so exorbitantly expensive as to make my assertions of penny-pinching doubly absurd. But I am making the assertion not in the context of contemporary economic cost accountancy but in the value terms of the future welfare of individual human beings as well as the species as a whole. The world political economy not only actively impoverishes the Third World through a manipulation of the market but insists upon policies of health privation. The word "privation" was not a mistake. International

---

[48] Farmer, (2001) *Infections and Inequalities*, p. 207.

agencies force the privatization of services upon poor countries, and the dystopia thesis insists that *privatization equals privation* for the poor.

It would be in the long-term future interests of the wealthy to help the poor with health care costs. Such help as is presently given is pitifully inadequate and badly directed. The price of second-line drugs would be greatly reduced if the production of generic equivalents in Third World countries was facilitated rather than frustrated. The sum of these complex political-economic legal realities for curbing a future HIV-MDR-TB co-infection: a penny pinching investment in serious disease prevention. It is the story of malaria all over again.

Secondly, as the story of Jesus and Mary should make clear, an opportunity to control MDR-TB continues to be missed because of ignorance concerning how poverty affects people's lives. As Farmer observes, "even modest interventions can produce drastic changes in outcome."[49] But the interventions have to be directed according to sound epidemiological understanding. Blaming the patients' different cultural values or their lack of understanding concerning the disease and its treatment, or blaming their irresponsibility, laziness or other moral culpabilities is medically misguided. Structural mystification becomes structural violence through such practices.

Farmer, who spent many years running a clinic in Haiti, describes the manner in which the "voodoo" and "witchcraft" belief system and cultural practices of Haitians were blamed for the frequent failure of patients to complete their courses of drug treatment. He points out that, while many Haitians do retain such beliefs and frequently seek the alternative therapies that go along with them, they tend do so either in *addition* to Western medical care or only when they cannot afford it. In spite of the popularity of the "voodoo thesis" for patient non-compliance with medical treatment regimes, no statistical correlations support it. The "voodoo thesis" of patient non-compliance appears to be as much

---

[49] Ibid.

inspired by culturally promulgated false beliefs and prejudices of the scientists as by science.

Farmer has a stock phrase to describe a good deal of the medical and particularly *social scientific* work on the issues surrounding patient non-compliance with drug treatment regimes. In his book *Infections and Inequalities*,[50] he repeatedly uses the phrase: "immodest claims of causality." Indeed, it is one of his chapter titles. He uses it to refer to such theories unsubstantiated by evidence as that described above concerning cultural reasons for not completing drug regimes. It applies as well to the popularly believed yet equally unsubstantiated "patient ignorance thesis." Whatever other beliefs people may have about HIV and AIDS, they are generally well-aware that the disease is sexually transmitted and that safe sex would be desirable. The failure of sex workers to practice safe sex is as much because of the force or bribery of clients as any lack of awareness concerning the possibility of infection. There is no evidence that TB patients who do not complete their courses of drug treatment fail to do so because of an ignorance of the consequences of such behavior. Indeed, there is a fair degree of evidence that many of those infected with MDR-TB quit clinical treatment when their condition fails to respond to first-line medication *because they are aware that what they need is not the first-line drugs but the second-line medications* . . . which they are refused. There is even evidence to suggest that many patients would complete their treatment with what they know to be useless drugs for their condition simply to get the second-line drugs . . . if both sets of drugs were not so prohibitively expensive.[51]

Farmer's "immodest claims of causality" phrase is perhaps the right sort to use in a measured and serious scholarly forum. But it is deficient in terms of outrage. Both science and social science

---

[50] Farmer, (2001) *Infections and Inequalities*.

[51] Ibid. Chapter 9 in this book details the above argument with a measured critique of many case studies in which the conclusions of these social scientists seem to be dictated more by their preconceived notions than their own data.

are crucially important to humanity's well-being and even survival. Indeed, the dystopia thesis is in part predicated upon their failures. The flip side to these "immodest claims of causality" concerning beliefs, culture, patient ignorance, irresponsibility and an over-inflated role for human agency, are overly modest claims concerning the causal role of poverty and its structural violence. Once again though, expressing this idea in terms of "modesty" is really not powerful enough. The evidence is staring these researchers in the face and practically screaming its obvious conclusions from the rooftops! It should be said straight-out: such "scientists" are incompetent! They should be ashamed of themselves! Social scientists have a *responsibility* to make it clear to both politicians and the public the urgent necessity of a greater commitment of resources to both HIV and TB. In chapter 7, we will examine further the reasons why they are not living up to that responsibility.

One last thing remains to be said concerning AIDS and TB. There is some scientific, political and institutional awareness of what we have covered in this section. There is an international initiative to come to terms with the situation. All United Nations Member States endorsed this goal:

> Developing and implementing a package for HIV prevention, treatment and care with the aim of coming as close as possible to the goal of universal access to treatment by 2010 for all those who need it.[52]

We may judge the likelihood of success of this worthy goal by evaluating an earlier and slightly more modest initiative of the World Health Organization. In December 2003, they announced an initiative aiming to bring antiretroviral treatment (ARV) treatment to three million people living with HIV in developing and transitional countries by the end of 2005. Calling this

---

[52] (2005) *Outcome Document* from the United Nations World Summit on HIV/AIDs, 15 September

[53] http://www.avert.org/aidstarget.htm

initiative "*3 by 5*" (treat *3* million people *by* 2005), the WHO said it hoped to see 700,000 people on ARV therapy by December 2004, 1.6 million people by June 2005 and three million by December 2005. But yet this three million represents only fifty percent of the people expected to be in need of treatment at the end of 2005. Thus, the goal of fifty percent could easily be seen as far too "modest," given the consequences for the other half who will need treatment but will not receive it. However, while too modest in terms of aspiration it may have been, it was nevertheless far *too ambitious* in relation to the resources actually committed so far. The final report on the *3 by 5* initiative was released in March 2006. It revealed that around 1.3 million people in low- and middle-income countries were receiving ARV medication at the end of 2005. This is just forty percent of the intended target. In sub-Saharan Africa, 810,000 were being treated out of an estimated 4.7 million who needed it.[53] The prognosis for the human species does not look good.

Conclusion: Inequality, Charity, Poverty and the Structural Violence of Capitalism

> *But I, being poor, have only my dreams. I have*
> *spread my dreams under your feet; tread softly,*
> *because you tread on my dreams.*
>   William Butler Yeats

> *Do not waste your time on Social Questions.*
> *What is the matter with the poor is Poverty;*
> *what is the matter with the rich is uselessness.*
>   George Bernard Shaw

"Life," said the 17th-century philosopher Thomas Hobbes, "is nasty, brutal and short."[54] The assessment is not at all controversial when applied to life such a long time ago. But with

---

[54] Hobbes, Thomas (1651) *Leviathan.*
http://www.publicliterature.org/books/leviathan/2

the life-extending and life-enhancing technological and medical advances made in the 19th and 20th centuries, the enormous improvements in sanitation and food production, the plethora of consumer goods of all sorts available to middle-class suburban society, the statement seems very far off the mark if applied to today. Or at least it does if applied to the affluent. But for millions of children, life is both shorter and much more brutal than it was in Hobbes's time. The contrast between the desperate lives of these suffering children and "the good life" of the middle classes makes the "nastiness" of life far, far worse than anything that could have been imagined in the 17th century. After all, capitalism was just beginning then.

Once again, we have a kind of contradiction. Apart from the occasional high-school massacre as a result of some bad craziness from a sad alienated soul, and the occasional violent "leakage" from the poor world's desperate struggle for survival, the middle-class suburban world is a gentle, civilized place. If anything, it is a refuge from the violence of the world. Nice Canadian people do not often point guns at children's heads and force them to execute another child. If they employ a 13-year-old to cut their lawn, they see to it that he is well compensated. And though, perhaps, some of them go on sex tourism trips to acquire the services of a child prostitute, such behavior is only engaged in by a minority and is strongly disapproved of by the more moral majority. The vast majority of the suburban civilized world would claim that they do no harm. They tip well and give generously to charity. And yet . . . there is *such a lot of violence* in the world.

There has to be a cause for it. The accusations pointed at "bad" people just don't seem adequate to explain what is happening. True, the brutalized child usually becomes "bad." Callousness and viciousness combined with illiteracy do not make for a "nice" person. But we need to ask: what is the cause of the cycle of child victims becoming victimizers? The dystopia thesis asserts that it is structural. The dystopia thesis asserts that the effects of the structuring of extreme inequality amounts to a violence. The thesis would assert that a treatable disease that goes untreated amounts to a violence. The dystopia thesis asserts that this sort of violence *is actually greater* than the more direct violence, which we find easier to imagine (though not necessarily to understand). The structural violence is more significant than the directly observable violence of the world because most of the latter is itself caused by structural forces, and hence is also a form of structural violence.

Let us look at this argument from a statistical point of view. There are two and a half billion people living on less than two dollars a day. The richest ten percent of the world's population receives fifty-four percent of the total global income.[55] Child prostitution takes place within this context of income distribution. While basic health needs for the world could be provided for thirteen billion dollars, people spend *seventeen billion dollars on pet food* in the United States and Europe.[56] The failure to treat multi-drug-resistant tuberculosis patients takes place within this context of spending priorities.

The wealth of the three most well-to-do individuals now exceeds the combined GDP (Gross Domestic Product) of the forty-eight least developed countries.[57] Bill Gates, for a number of years now asserted by Forbes Magazine to be the world's wealthiest man, has an estimated wealth of *$53 billion*.[58] He and other super-billionaires like Warren Buffet are allegedly giving very generously to charity. In particular, the Gates Foundation

---

[55] Jens Martens, *A Compendium of Inequality,* The Human Development Report 2005 Global Policy Forum (briefing papers), p. 3.

[56] Mary Assunta (1999), "Tobacco and Poverty," *Proceedings INGCAT International NGO Mobilisation Meeting*, Geneva.
http://www.islamset.com/healnews/smoking/INGCAT/Mary_Assunta.html

[57] Figures derived from 1999 World Wealth Distribution – United Nations Development Program.
http://www.cooperativeindividualism.org/wealth_distribution1999.html

[58] Forbes Magazine, *400 Richest Americans List.*
http://www.forbes.com/lists/2006/54/biz_06rich400_The-400-Richest-Americans_land.html

(contributed to by Buffet as well) has given almost *two billion dollars* to the fight against AIDS and TB.[59] This is an exceptionally large charitable donation. However, the shortfalls in the "3 by 5" campaign discussed above, should be seen in the context of Gates' $53 billion. The ongoing AIDS plague in Africa, the failure to eradicate malaria and other medical financing shortfalls should be seen in the light of a global system that allows just three men to have a greater personal fortune than the combined GDP of 48 countries!

Once again, the point must be clarified; this is *not* about "bad men." Indeed, if suburban middle-class Americans are generally "nice" people, Bill Gates is likely a good deal nicer than most. We are talking here about *structural violence*. We are asserting here that *charity connects to this violence*. No, giving to the poor and needy is not a bad thing. But charity is a functional aspect of structured inequality. Charity is a substitute for taxation and governmental expenditure. Of course, it is good to give; but the corollary of that giving is that one only gives what one feels personally comfortable with giving . . . *not what is needed!* And if we were to add up *all that is given to charities,* we can still see that, however great that amount may be, there is a big gap between what is given to solve problems and their continued existence. That is, we can measure the "charity gap" between what the givers feel comfortable giving and what is needed in terms of the pain and deaths of starvation or untreated treatable diseases.

We can further measure the structural violence of the system in the facts concerning the debt burden of the poorest countries of the world. The Jubilee 2000 initiative asked for massive debt forgiveness. The Make Poverty History campaign continues to do so. Limited relief has been given to some of the poorest of the world's poor countries. In 1996, the World Bank and the International Monetary Fund launched the Debt Initiative for Heavily Indebted Poor Countries. Twenty-eight countries are currently receiving debt relief that will amount to fifty-six billion

---

[59] http://www.gatesfoundation.org/default.htm

dollars.[60] But for most poor countries, debt servicing continues to far outstrip the aid that is given. We can see how this structural violence works in terms of the United Nations Millennium Development Goals (MDGs) that we are nowhere near on track for achieving. Or rather, we can measure structural violence in the gaps between the noble rhetoric of the goals and the practical measures actually being asked to be undertaken to achieve them in a kind of half-assed way ("realistic" is the term used by the these bureaucrats) by a target date of 2015. Eight MDGs have been agreed to by all the world's countries:

1) eradicate extreme poverty and hunger;

2) achieve universal primary education;

3) promote gender equality and empower women;

4) reduce child mortality;

5) improve maternal health;

6) combat HIV/Aids malaria and other diseases;

7) ensure environmental sustainability; and,

8) develop a global partnership for development.[61]

However, there is some straining of meaning with respect to phrases such as: "eradicate extreme poverty and hunger." This goal actually only has the agreed practical objective of reducing

---

[60] Yolanda Rivera (2006), *UICIFD Briefing No. 1: Debt Forgiveness,* The University of Iowa Center for International Finance and Development.
http://www.uiowa.edu/ifdebook/briefings/docs/forgiveness.shtml

[61] http://www.un.org/millenniumgoals/

by *half* the number of people living on less than one dollar a day and reducing, again *only by half*, the proportion of people who suffer from hunger. One can see that the descriptive adjective "half-assed," as used above, has a quite literal aspect to it in this context. What about the other half who will still be living on less than a dollar a day? What about the other half of the world's children who will still be seriously hungry?

But never mind that; *these practical goals are not even close to being on target*! If the rich countries do not dramatically begin to act soon, 247 million *more* people in sub-Saharan Africa will be living on less than a dollar day in 2015 than are now. Ninety-seven million more children will be out of school. Fifty-three million people will join the ranks of those lacking proper sanitation facilities.[62] Thus, we can measure structural violence in terms of the gap between the .7 percent of GDP asked of the wealthy countries to contribute to poverty reduction and the United States' (the least generous of the donor countries) .14 percent contribution.[63]

The broader trends in terms of wealth and income distribution are unsurprisingly grim. More than one billion people experienced a drop in earnings from 1980 to 1993! By 1995 in the United States, the middle quintile of income-earners had only enough savings if they lost their jobs to maintain their current standard of living for 1.2 months. That's down from 3.6 months in 1989. In eighteen countries, the current Human Development Index (measuring such things as literacy and health, as well as per capita income) is lower than it was in 1990, when the HDI was

---

[62] Oxfam statistics
http://www.oxfam.org.uk/what_we_do/issues/debt_aid/mdgs_price.htm

[63] Ibid.

[64] Jen Martens, "A Compendium of Inequality," *The Human Development Report 2005*, Global Policy Forum (briefing papers)

first produced.[64] There is every likelihood that these past trends will continue into the future.

Now, it is perhaps difficult to understand the way the world works in terms of horrendous suffering, on the one hand, and in the structural context of a lack of personal control or influence over events, on the other. There is a degree of abstraction to the notion of structural violence, even if the effects of it are all too painfully concrete. The next chapter, examine the world's socio-economic political system more theoretically and analytically.

But we will end this chapter on a simpler note. We will explain one of the reasons why the world's system is so difficult to understand. There are paid professionals whose job it is to make it that difficult. Indeed, whole social scientific disciplines seem to be dedicated to the task of mystification. As John Kenneth Galbraith asserts:

> The explanation and *rationalization* of the resulting inequality has commanded some of the greatest, or in any case some of the most ingenious, talent in the economics profession.[65]
> [my italics]

Economists have long puzzled over the Pareto curve of wealth distribution. It is very unlike a "normal" distribution of talents, abilities or test scores. The bell curve of suchlike distributions has the greatest number of people with average scores and

---

[65] J. K. Galbraith, *History of Economics,* quoted in "Wealth Happens: Wealth Distribution and the Role of Networks," Mark Buchanan (2002), *Harvard Business School Working Knowledge Archive* April 29.
http://hbswk.hbs.edu/archive/2906.html

[66] Mark Buchanan, (2002) "Wealth Happens - Wealth Distribution and the Role of Networks" *Harvard Business School Working Knowledge Archive,* 4/29. http://hbswk.hbs.edu/archive/2906.html

diminishing numbers of both high and low scorers. But a Pareto curve is very different[66].

> Pareto's so-called fat-tailed distribution starts very high at the low end, has no bulge in the middle at all and falls off relatively slowly at the high end, indicating that some number of extremely wealthy people hold the lion's share of a country's riches. In the United States, for example, something like 80% of the wealth is held by only 20% of the people. But this particular 80-20 split is not really the point; in some other country, the precise numbers might be 90-20 or 95-10 or something else. The important point is that the distribution (at the wealthy end, at least) follows a strikingly simple mathematical curve illustrating that a small fraction of people always owns a large fraction of the wealth.

Hence, to use Bill Gates as an example again, we see him at the top of the pyramid possessing more wealth than the bottom 45 percent of American households combined (the bottom of the Pareto curve pyramid). The net worth of the top one percent is now 2.4 times the combined wealth of the poorest eighty percent in America[67].

But what causes this pattern? Mark Buchanan of the Harvard Business School asserts that "Pareto's distribution has, from a mathematical standpoint, stubbornly defied explanation".[68] This sort of assertion/question/false problem is a good example of structural mystification[69]. Why, we might ask, would anyone think the distribution patterns of wealth would be something that would have a *mathematical* explanation?

---

[67] http:www.cooperativeindividualism.org/wealth _distribution1999.html

[68] Buchanan, (2002) "Wealth Happens".

[69] See Chapter 6.

In the next chapter, the complexity of the manner in which the world capitalist system has evolved and its most salient features today for producing dystopia will be analyzed. But to finish, this chapter offers the following very simple explanation for the Pareto curve of wealth distribution. It is not a question of mathematical principles. Rather it is an *elementary principal of capitalism*. This principle is perhaps so basic and so obvious that they do not bother to teach it at the Harvard Business School: "It takes money to make money." The more money you have, the easier it is to make more. As you get more, the easier it becomes to use the wealth to acquire political and economic advantages over your opponents, to dictate, among other things, (unequal) conditions of trade etc.

The dystopia thesis sums up the essence of the principle like this: the rich get richer and the poor . . . suffer and die!

Chapter 5

Oil and Industry: The World Political Economy

> *Advocates of capitalism are very apt to appeal*
> *to the sacred   principles of liberty, which are*
> *embodied in one maxim: The fortunate must not*
> *be restrained in the exercise of tyranny over the*
> *unfortunate.*
>> Bertrand Russell

> *When President Chirac gave [President] Bush a*
> *souvenir statue of the Eiffel Tower... Bush said,*
> *"This is great! A little oil rig!"*
>> Jay Leno

Introduction: The Contradictions of Capitalism in Everyday Living

> *Contradiction is not a sign of falsity, nor the*
> *lack of contradiction a sign of truth.*
>> Blaise Pascal

> *Capitalism inevitably and by virtue of the very*
> *logic of its civilization creates, educates and*
> *subsidizes a vested interest in social unrest.*
>> Joseph A. Schumpeter

Margaret is a member of a group of people that perhaps most defines contemporary capitalism. No, she is very definitely not a yuppie. If young urban professionals ever were very representative of the capitalist system, that time has long past. No, Margaret and others like her are exemplars of contemporary capitalism because they contain so many contradictions within their situation and lifestyle. Margaret is an American and lives in suburbia. But she is no longer middle class. She ceased to be middle class shortly after her husband left her and she was forced to get a job at Wal-Mart. Margaret is both poor and not poor.

Margaret is certainly not rich, but she has equity in her house and only needs to pay a monthly mortgage payment of $485. This was the unilateral settlement her husband visited upon her when he left her and the children. Like much else to do with Margaret's situation, this settlement can be seen as either generous or stingy depending upon your perspective. Margaret's husband definitely thought he was being very generous when he walked away empty-handed from the equity that they (from his perspective, *he*) had built up over the years. But that was that. As far as Margaret knew, he had disappeared off the face of the earth when he left her alone with the full responsibility for their two children. Margaret had been working part-time at Wal-Mart before her husband left her, and now she began to work full-time there in the hope that it would be enough for her and her family to live on. But it wasn't and it isn't.

Margaret and the children live in a quite pretty, relatively new house that is nicely, if sparsely, furnished. Her husband had taken some of the furniture with him, and there were no funds to replace these items. But they own a washer and dryer and dishwasher and three television sets, one for the living room and one in each of the girl's rooms. Twelve-year-old Jenny owns fashionable trainers, an IPod and has her own mobile phone. Four-year-old Alice is beginning to ask for such fashionable items as well but has yet to receive them, an ongoing source of dissatisfaction in her young life . . . and a cause of serious worry for Margaret because she knows that even after the "you're too young justification" has been outgrown, she doesn't think that money for such things will be forthcoming. Jenny's ownership of today's teenage "necessities" derives from the earlier era of middle-class affluence when her father was still part of the household.

Margaret's most serious problem and worry for the future can be easily grasped through simple addition. She exercises enormous discipline with the budget, the food budget in particular. Alice being young, and thus perhaps more adaptable, got used to the bland and repetitive diet, while Margaret simply endured Jenny's complaints, as Jenny endured the food. Jenny is too embarrassed concerning the low-cost diet to ask friends over for dinner . . . which is just as well because they are on such a shoestring that a guest can't really be afforded. The one exception to this austerity plan is the monthly visit to McDonalds. The two Big Macs, a McNugget Happy Meal, two Cokes, and two large orders of French fries come to $13.80. They spend $248 a month on food in total, not including their big night out at McDonalds. Margaret is enrolled in the Wal-Mart employee health insurance scheme, which costs $167 a month, and most months she has to spend another $11 or $12 on medicines out of her own pocket, making a total of $178 on health. The miscellaneous expenses of daily living— including such items as clothing, postage, laundry, paper goods, cleaning supplies, school supplies, and personal care products— is only $113. But Margaret's budget allotted figure does not really cover even all of these things, a source of continual complaint from Jenny. Nor is there room in this strict budget for such things as appliance repair. If the dishwasher goes on the fritz, the dishwasher will be gone for good. Nor is there room even for much in the way of birthday gifts, a source of many tears, not only from Alice but Jenny as well. Because of Margaret's low wages, her daycare costs for Alice are government subsidized and only come to $22 a month. Jenny's telephone habits are a source of confrontation as they always come to way over the "emergency use only" budgeted figure of $5.00. Adding transportation costs, we arrive at Margaret's monthly budget figure of $1,160. And there is the problem. Margaret's full-time after-taxes take-home pay from Wal-Mart is only $1,016.

This small monthly shortfall is not the end of the story, of course. Jenny does not stick to the telephone budget. Margaret's heart is torn apart by her inability to afford presents, and so she buys them anyway. Essentially her budget is unworkable. Like millions and millions of Americans, her credit cards take up the slack. But the interest on them becomes still another budget item. So Margaret takes on another low-paid job. She does some night shifts for 7-11. But this is even worse in terms of diminishing returns, both financial and otherwise. She has to pay for Alice's babysitting or leave her in Jenny's care. Jenny has not done very well at proving herself responsible, and when she babysits, she also thinks she should get the going rate. Eventually, that hard to access house equity money is going to be needed. . . if the equity is still there! Because American housing prices have fallen dramatically.[1]

Margaret's situation is not at all unusual. Many Americans are spending more on living than they are taking in. Many are juggling credit cards and other aspects of their finances to get by day to day with an uncertain future looming. But everything in the future is not uncertain. There is an item in Margaret's austerity budget that is going to upset the entire applecart: *transportation.* l Margaret lives in a suburban housing estate on one side of Salina Kansas. Unfortunately, the Wal-Mart where she works is on the outskirts of the other side of town. Salina has no public transport. Even so the eight-mile round trip Margaret makes to work is actually very modest in comparison to the commute of most Americans. Nevertheless, the monthly $95 budgeted for gasoline, maintenance and insurance on Margaret's 1991 Ford Fiesta is a significant portion of her income . . . and that figure is set to rise dramatically, very dramatically.

The figures given for "Margaret's" budget derive from research and calculations done by Stan Cox, in an article written in 2003.[2] The figures use, where possible, an assumption of purchases made at Wal-Mart, as well as one of their wages at the time. They are extremely conservatively estimated figures, and perhaps the most conservative of such figures are those allotted

---

[1] By 2009, average prices had fallen by around 13% from their 2007 peak, Pressures continue for further decline. Only 4,458,00 new single family houses were sold in 2009, down by 23% from 2008 - a big drop from the average of 11.5 million new single family homes sold annually from 1996 to 2007. Global Property Guide April 8, 2010.
http://www.globalpropertyguide.com/North-America/United-States/Price-History

[2] Stan Cox (2003) "A Wal-Mart Wage Doesn't Go Very Far – Even at Wal-Mart," *AlterNet.*
http://members.cox.net/t.s/walmart.html

for transport. Very likely Margaret would have to do a lot more driving than just to and from work (taking Jenny hither and thither for example). The figure used in the estimate for gasoline is only $12 a month. The price of gas at Wal-Mart on the day of the research was $1.45 a gallon. The eight-mile return commute to work with another 100 miles a month added would be just over $19 if the car managed 21 miles per gallon. But the average price for a gallon of gas had gone up to $2.50 in Margaret's Kansas as of April 9 2007. This is actually very cheap in comparison with Seattle's average of $3.10.[3]

The relatively modest increase in gas prices between 2003 and 2006 shown in the preceding paragraph has nonetheless been a matter for concern, worry and even anger for many Americans. These prices, however, would seem very cheap compared to those of most places in the world. For example, in Holland gasoline is priced at $6.73 a gallon.[4]

However, the dystopia thesis is not predicting modest price increases in gasoline over a long term. It is predicting *astronomical price increases* in a very short time. These price increases will not be due to such short-term factors as the damage to refineries and drilling rigs that occurred shortly after Hurricane Katrina or the setting on fire of the oil fields in Kuwait toward the end of the Gulf War. Such events will, of course, add their compounding effects. Rather, the main driving force for the longer-term price increases will be global economic and geological facts. The price of a barrel of crude oil as of April 19, 2006 topped $72.[5] The dystopia thesis predicts this figure will double within only a very few years and then to triple within only a very few more.

---

[3] http://www.gasbuddy.com/gb_gastemperaturemap.aspx

[4] (2007) *NBC* "Business Questions and Answers."
http://www.msnbc.msn.com/id/12452503/ April 10

[5] Associated Press April 19, 2006.

The above prediction will be explained and justified later on in the section on the *peak oil crisis*. But first it is necessary to reflect upon the *effects* of such enormous increases upon Margaret and people like her, upon Wal-Mart, upon the "American way of life" and upon the world economy.

Some Fun with Arithmetic

> *Money can't buy happiness, but neither can*
> *poverty.*
>   Leo Rosten

Margaret's situation, as can be seen from the budget above, was not really sustainable even in 2003, when this hypothetical budget was calculated. She regularly spent more than she earned; she had no savings; she was amassing credit card debt at high rates of interests; her only asset was the equity in the house. Sooner or later she would be forced to sell up or refinance in order to begin spending that equity . . . providing the house retains its value. For reasons that will be explained later, it is, however, part of the dystopia argument that housing prices will definitely *not* continue to rise and that a staggering price fall is coming. But leaving that aside for the moment, calculations of gas price rises still produce some interesting results.

It was predicted that the price of crude would double in a very few years from now and then later triple that price a few years hence. Gasoline pricing has a great many other complexities to it (importantly including changing refining costs and taxation; e.g., the higher European prices are mainly due to taxation) but nonetheless must bear a fairly close relation to the price changes for a barrel of crude. The gasoline price figures used in the next sets of calculations assume a simple direct relationship; i.e., that they too will first double and then triple that figure, multiplying today's prices by six.

Margaret was very fortunate in only having an eight-mile commute, and the assumption of virtually no other driving done by her was very unrealistic. People must also commute to do just about everything. The label "soccer mom," for example does not come from nowhere. Children simply do not play outside the house anymore; they grow up involved in a range of organized activities . . . to which they must be both delivered to and picked up and taken home. So both for the sake of a simplicity in terms of the calculation and to be more realistic, a 125-mile per week rate will be used. This figure comes to only 6,300 miles per year, only about half of the Kelly Bluebook average figure of 12,000 miles per year. At today's (2006) gas prices,[6] Margaret would be spending $787 a year (using a 20-mile per gallon as approximation). This is a considerable output when your yearly take-home pay is only $12,192. Already, Margaret's earnings shortage in relation to the cost of living has grown dramatically. In the initial scenario, she was only $144 short each month. Now she would be an additional $50 short. Still, we can understand how Margaret could keep her struggling ship afloat . . . barely afloat. But what happens when the gas prices double?

Assuming all other things remain the same, which of course they won't, Margaret will be paying out $1,574 on gas, about the same amount many people are paying now if they drive the Bluebook average mileage. After this price has rocketed up to triple the initially doubled rate, Margaret will have to pay out $4,722 a year on gasoline. This is well more than a third of her total Wal-Mart take home pay. Clearly this does not even come close to being viable. If the 12,000 miles per year that the average American drives is used as the figure, then this lack of viability becomes all the more dramatic. The $9,000 a year that would be spent on gasoline by the average motorist would certainly preclude them relying on a Wal-Mart income, as it would be more than three-quarters of it.

The assumption of "all other things remaining the same'" made in the preceding paragraph's calculations clearly would not be true. Things constantly change. Prices for many products go up, and for a few, they occasionally come down. Perhaps,

---

[6] The figure of $2.50 per gallon is used to keep the arithmetic simple and because it was approximately the Kansas average at the time of writing.

Margaret might even have received a wage rise. But very few of the factors in addition to gas prices that would change would likely benefit Margaret. Indeed, the price of gasoline would be among the forces *pushing up the prices of everything*!

The lack of financial viability for Margaret's Wal-Mart career would itself be a force for significant change in the economic and social arrangements of contemporary America. Wal-Mart has close to a million employees, and while it is true that some of them make more than Margaret, most of them do not. Wal-Mart has a finely graded managerial hierarchy, meaning that it is a system of one person having a gradation of responsibility over another and a *minimally* greater hourly wage. One can climb many grades in the hierarchy before the difference between that pay grade and the bottom entry level amounts to more than peanuts.

Wal-Mart was not an accidentally chosen example. In addition to its owners being among America's wealthiest individuals, Wal-Mart's managerial hierarchy of low wages, big-box suburban sprawl locations and cheap import strategy are all business models widely copied. The entire retail sector is underpaid and usually needs to commute relatively long distances to work. If gas price increases make it unviable for Margaret to continue with her job and suburban living, then that lifestyle will also be unviable for millions. The very impossibility of the millions of low-paid retail sector employees being able to get to and from work will become a factor in the breakdown of the socio-economic arrangements currently in existence. The impossibility of the hundreds of thousands of Margarets being able to keep their suburban homes will exert a strong downward pressure on the real estate market. But the low-wage commuter is only one of the factors involved in the impossibility of the present system.

The dramatic house price fall in the United States and elsewhere was a result of quite different factors attacking the suburban way of life. Factors both act independently and combine to produce effects. The world's political economy is nothing if not complex. Cultural forces push upon everyone to buy their own home in the US. It is a part of the American Dream. But the American Dream is getting increasingly hard to afford. The new (for the last few decades) American Way to acquire the American Dream was, of course, to borrow. Many people borrowed more than they could afford. A whole new financial sector, however, the sub-prime loan market, was built upon loans to such people. When these people finally (and inevitably!) began to default on their mortgages, there was a powerful knock-on effect, becoming a crisis for the entire real estate market and further becoming a factor in the financial crisis of 2008 about which we will say more later.

Shipping Coal to Newcastle

> *If all economists were laid end to end, they would not reach a conclusion.*
> George Bernard Shaw

Those readers not English, and even perhaps most of them who are under a certain age, will perhaps miss the humor in the above section title. *Of course*, coal is shipped to Newcastle. It is still used as a serious or decorative heating source for many old homes with coal-burning fireplaces and augurs. It is still very widely used in the UK to fire electricity-generating plants. But at one time, Newcastle was in the heart of mining country, and the expression "shipping coal to Newcastle" symbolized a kind of absurdity. It has a new resonance of irony now, because after the painful closure of nearly the entirety of the British mining industry, coal is once again touted as perhaps being "economic" after all. Though the enormous costs to restart derelict mines is perhaps prohibitive, and though Britain is soon to face serious energy problems, Margaret Thatcher would probably still think it was all worth it. After all, she still managed to defeat the Miners Union and arguably the entirety of the unionized British working class[7].

---

[7] The miners had gone on strike in the seventies and brought down the Heath government. It was widely believed among both the Right and Left in Britain that the miners were the strongest and most radical of the British unions. To defeat them would drastically reduce the power of

There is another dystopian resonance to the "shipping coal to Newcastle" old saying. The absurdity of sending a lot of something to somewhere that already has a lot of that something (the meaning that was signified in the original saying) is here intended to signify the insanity intrinsic to a world economic system that routinely does just that! Not only is *fresh* lobster on the menu of many restaurants in North American cities thousands of miles inland, but fish are imported to fishing communities. Beef is imported to cattle country. The Niagara apple-growing region of Southern Ontario imports apples not only from the other side of Canada but from Australia as well. No, this is not a particularly Eastern Canadian insanity; the other apple-growing regions of the world all import from them as well. Not only are we provided with apples and pears outside of their normal growing season, we are given considerable latitude of choice with respect to varieties of apples and pears. Does this make life better? The commercials certainly assert that it does. However, there is a longer-term hidden cost to this fantastic trading and rapid shipping of goods everywhere and anywhere. No, that is not quite correct; goods are not shipped everywhere and anywhere. There is a market logic to the distribution of commodities. And there is a deeper logic than that as well.

If one does a casual but contemplative survey of the items in one's house, one begins to see a picture of the world's global economy. In the kitchen is coffee from Columbia, bananas from Costa Rica, maple syrup from Quebec, wine from France and California and South Africa, spices from India and lamb from New Zealand. There are foods from nearly everywhere in the world . . . literally. In the living room, there is perhaps furniture from Sweden made from wood from Malaysia or Brazil. The

---

the entire trade union movement. This Margaret Thatcher set out to do, provoking them into a strike in 1984/85. Though the miners were on strike for a full year, she succeeded in defeating them. For a good historical account of this including the relevant political-historical background see Seumas Milne (2004) *The Enemy within: Thatcher's Secret War Against the Miners*, Verso.

wood the house is made of is Canadian. The knick-knack souvenirs of Vegas and other holidays scattered throughout the house were all made in China. The car in the driveway is Japanese, though its manufacture and assembly was spread out through three other countries. The television in the family room is Korean, and the one in the bedroom is Japanese, as is also the stereo system. Actually, the only thing American-made in this typical American home is the music: a persecuted black woman from the recent past is singing the blues.

We have a world economy that is, and has been, very dependent upon cheap oil. Goods are transported long distances by ship and truck and plane. It is not only the price of gasoline that is going to go up but other forms of fuel as well. Not only middle-class but working-class people (at least from First World countries) fly off to exotic vacations or holiday visits with friends or relations on the other side of the country or the world. Cheap airfares are the backbone of a multi-billion-dollar world tourism industry, which quite a few countries absolutely depend upon for hard currency and employment. But low-priced aviation fuel not only supports tourism, it supports the rapid transport of all kinds of goods and business services. Imagine a six-fold increase in oil prices upon all of this!

However, as I said earlier, the transport of goods is not hither thither or everywhere and anywhere; there is a distinct logic to it. Once again we can use Wal-Mart to illustrate it. Margaret's bottom-of-the-rung employment there may not be very happy, indeed, it is increasingly desperate; but she is not the worst off in Wal-Mart world by any means. Margaret helps to sell, among other things, Kathie Lee handbags. The price of such bags is the bargain Americans made with the devil, as they traded off their communities, values and lifestyles of the small-town age that they are increasingly nostalgic for. Main Street USA can now only be found in Disneyland and films because it could not compete with the Wal-Mart hypermarkets' much cheaper goods. Li Jianguo lives and works on the other side of the Wal-Mart world. She works in the Qin Shi handbag factory in China that makes the Kathie Lee handbags that Margaret, and others in America's thousands of Wal-Marts, sell.

Li Jianguo lives in a dormitory room with 15 other women. She works a 98-hour week with no overtime pay. There is no employment code of conduct, and she has no official contract. In other words, she has no real rights at all to protect her in the crowded unsafe working conditions. She earns the equivalent of four cents American an hour, and she is not the lowest paid in her factory. The lowest only earns three cents an hour.[8] To say she is *exploited* is an understatement.

"Exploitation" is actually a technical term in Marxist discourse, and one that is important to understand in order to appreciate the dynamic logic of the world's political economy. It will also be important to understand that theory's concepts of value and capital and commodity. The importance of economic realities to the present and future dystopia has been a constant theme throughout this book. It is crucial to understand the world political economy. Unfortunately, the social science disciplinary specialism charged with understanding the economy – economics – can be of little help. Mainstream economics has long since lost its way as a discipline, contributing little to any real understanding of the economy and instead performing the role of an ideological legitimator for existing social and economic relations. Although this will be discussed further in the next chapter in the context of the theory of structural mystification, one important point can be made here. Contemporary economics is principally concerned with the mathematical modeling of complex market behavior. One might well ask: just what is wrong with that?

What is wrong is that the enterprise lost any and all material foundation for the numbers. Markets with all their financial complexity are only part of the actuality of our economy. Amounts of capital are not simply numerical abstract markers of money. There are also very concrete material realities involved, which are the flesh and bones, so to speak, of the numerical

---

[8] Figures given in this scenario are for 1999 and come from the National Labor Committee.
http://www.nlcnet.org/campaigns/archive/report00/walmart.shtml

values. Questions concerning the origins and basis of value at one time were questions that economists very much concerned themselves with. They no longer either ask or answer such questions but simply content themselves with the number play of the economy's surface. But to understand the hard realities of dystopia, we must get beneath that sometimes misleading surface. Thus, as a first step toward explaining the present world political economy, a brief return to classic Marxist economics will be undertaken.

Classical Marxism

> *If we could understand reality simply from the*
> *surface of things, we should not need science.*
> Karl Marx

> *All fixed, fast-frozen relations, with their train*
> *of ancient and venerable prejudices and opinions,*
> *are swept away, all new-formed ones become*
> *antiquated before they can ossify. All that is solid*
> *melts into air, all that is holy is profaned, and man*
> *is at last compelled to face with sober senses his*
> *real conditions of life, and his relations with his*
> *kind.*
> Karl Marx

Money was present in ancient societies. There were rich and poor, and wealth was a crucially important feature of life even back then. Quite early on in history, a merchant class made its living from the profits of trade. Because of facts such as these, many people have *quite wrongly concluded* that such social and economic organizations of the past were basically capitalist. But there are particularities to capitalism that actually make it capitalism. These particularities simply were not present in earlier societies. Capitalism as capitalism was not really fully formed until the 17th century and only then in Europe.[9] Marxism identifies distinct "modes of production," the dominant form of economic organization that characterizes societies at different stages of development. Marxism identifies a number of these earlier forms; for example, the "ancient mode of production" is that of classical Greece and Rome. Most importantly though, Marxism analyzed the transition from a "feudal mode of production" to the "capitalist mode of production" that continues to the present day. The details of this transition need not concern us here. It is sufficient to note that capitalism has distinct features that gradually emerged historically.

Capital is actually something more than simply amounts of money. It has a very *material reality* that is frequently forgotten by contemporary economists through their intoxication with numbers and mathematical symbols. Capital is accumulated wealth . . . the tangible assets produced by the past labor of others. Of course, one sort of asset may be exchanged for another; but underlying all amounts of capital will be something real that has already been created. Such material realities as are represented by varying amounts of capital are those products of brain and body as are created through human labor. Labor is the source of all value.

Profit might seem to the individual trader to simply be the result of selling something for more than you paid for it. But profit in a capitalist system is something far more than that on a collective level. It is the key to the dynamic drive of the entire system. It is the manner in which the fruits of labor are fed into the system to create a logic of continual growth. In a non-capitalist world, an individual might work for themselves and consume the majority of the products they have created. This work would most likely be agricultural or very simple craft-based

---

[9] The process actually began much, much earlier, perhaps in the 13th century, by the 14th certainly. The process of emergence was slow, gradual, uneven geographically and fitful in terms of time. It was not really until the 17th century that one could see widespread and fully formed capitalist relations of production dominating all others.

manufacture. But larger-scale manufacture and trade requires a different logic; it requires the logic of the extraction of *surplus value*. The extraction of surplus value is the Marxist technical meaning of the previously referred to term: exploitation.

In a capitalist system, people's capacity to work is bought and sold. They work at any number of diverse and frequently highly specialized activities. But whatever it is they make, or whatever service they perform, it is not usual that they are paid in kind. Rather they receive a wage (in the form of money) from which they purchase the necessities of life and whatever luxuries they can afford. But if one were to add up the monetary value of all that they purchase, one would find it not nearly equal to the value of the goods or services they produce during their work shift. Instead, a surplus is produced for their employer. This surplus is the fundamental basis for all profit in the system. You work and your employer pays you less than the value of the products of that work.

This, of course, is not all pure profit for the employer. No, employers have many other costs. They must pay for the upkeep of whatever tools or machinery are used. They must pay rent (or mortgage payments) for their place of business. They must pay various charges and interest for whatever financing was necessary to begin the business. They must pay for insurance, and of course, they must pay taxes. This last inevitable expense pays for the physical infrastructure – roads, bridges, rail networks, ports and other transport facilities, water, waste removal, and much else – upon which their business and all others depend. Taxes also pay for the health care, education and training of the workforce. All in all, a great deal must be paid for. Profit is what is left over after paying for all these things and after paying their wage bill. The complexity of the situation can obscure its underlying simplicity: the logic of the extraction of a surplus from the toil of the workers. And, of course, by that we mean any sort of paid activity . . . whether "by hand or by brain."[10]

---

[10] The phrase "to secure for the workers the fruits of their labor by hand or by brain" used to be on the back of the membership cards for the British Labour Party. The famous socialist "clause four" of the party's

The logic driving the extraction of surplus pits employer against employee. The relationship between employer and employee may be quite cooperative and amiable or openly antagonistic to various degrees. No matter the level of person-to-person friendliness or its absence, the fact remains that the objective interests of employer and employee are utterly opposed. Ultimately, no matter how much the employer maintains a sense of fairness, no matter how much profit he is able to make while still paying his employees a relatively high wage, it still is a fact that he would make a still greater profit if he could pay them less. The extraction of surplus value from employees is what Marxists call exploitation. The relative amount of surplus value extracted by different businesses is what is called the rate of exploitation. Exploitation, then, is fundamental to the capitalist system. It is why inequality is a fundamental and not an accidental feature of the system.

Ultimately, the logic of profit will dictate the employer's behavior, because the logic of the capitalist dynamic is to maximize profit. The "nice employer," the "kind boss," the "public-spirited corporation," the popular company that stresses it "gives a fair day's wage for a fair day's work" (if any of their claims to do so are actually ever true) may do well for a time, but in the end, if they do not change, they will lose out to the "nastier" ones. Treating their workforce well (relatively) may improve morale and thus performance to some degree. A reputation for fairness can benefit a company. Consumers might well prefer to buy from them. But, ultimately, if there are significant price differences, the consumer will buy the goods or services that (for equivalent quality) are cheaper. And the products that are cheaper will be produced by the company that pays its workforce the least . . . or that pays out the least in terms of benefits . . . or that pushes the limits in terms of safety. In

---

charter from which the phrase comes from has long since been abolished. In this neo-liberal age, virtually almost all such socialist symbolic gestures, even in social democratic parties, have, of course, been dropped.

essence, the very logic of capitalist production pushes for poor working conditions and low wages. Wal-Mart is the perfect model.

Because of its own intrinsic features, capitalism will generate crises. It has, as an absolute demand, a necessity for growth, which among other problems, bumps up against the limiting forces of nature and the realities of finite rather than infinite resources. It has to constantly technologically innovate or otherwise revolutionize the forces of production, but yet capital can only acquire its profit from the extraction of surplus value from the workers; hence Marx's famous law of the tendency for the rate of profit to decline.

The preceding explanation is, of course, merely the very barest of a bare-bones summary of the elements of classical Marxism's analysis of capitalism. Nonetheless, it is necessary to leave it now because there is a further important form of extraction of surplus value occurring in the world not covered in the classic Marxist explanation. Classical Marxism describes well the profit-seeking logic of the system. It describes the necessary exploitative element in the relationship between employer and employee. But it does not properly explain how this relationship is affected by the differing situations and unequal power relations between the different parts of the world. A series of much more recent theoretical developments are necessary to draw from to explain this.

World Systems Theory and the Development of Underdevelopment[11]

The great nations have always acted like gangsters, and the small nations like prostitutes.
        Stanley Kubrick

Classical Marxism and the economists' mainstream development theories share a common mistake. They both subscribe to the principal ideas that will be outlined in the next few paragraphs. Humanity has socially and culturally evolved. An economic evolution has accompanied this process. The wealthier countries such as America and the Western European nations

---

[11] This section is a synopsis of the fundamental points of the theories that have become known as world systems theory. Immanual Wallerstein was the progenitor of world systems theory with his ground-breaking three volumes: *The Modern World-System: Capitalist Agriculture and the Origins of the European World-Economy in the Sixteenth Century* (1976); *The Modern World System II: Mercantilism and the Consolidation of the European World-Economy, 1600-1750,*(1980), *The Modern World System III: The Second Era of Great Expansion of the Capitalist World-Economy, 1730-1840s* (1988), all published by Academic Press: New York. The important essay "The Development of Underdevelopment" in *The Monthly Review* (September, 1969) and the book *Capitalism and Underdevelopment in Latin America* (1969), both by Andre Gunder Frank, were also seminal pieces of work explaining the relationships of exploitation between countries and regions, particularly the Americas. But in addition to these classic works, there has been considerable refinement of these theories. Indeed, there is a contemporary academic journal, *The Journal of World Systems Research*. This journal, along with its publishing institution, the Institute for Research on World-Systems based at the University of California, is devoted to further refinement of the theory and application of it to contemporary issues in development and international political economy. Also see *The Underdevelopment of Development: Essays in Honor of Andre Gunder Frank,* Sing Chew and Robert Denemark (eds.) (1996), Sage: London.

underwent a transition from primarily agricultural societies through a process of industrialization to the evolution of industrialized capitalist economies and political democracies. These simple facts are not contentious.

Some political theorists like to argue that industrialization and the accumulation of wealth facilitated the growth of democracy and vice versa. Others simply concentrate upon the economic process. Regardless, the essential feature of these theories is the assertion that economies like the United States economy went through a series of evolutionary stages to arrive where it is today: a post-industrial society dominated by the service sector of the economy and increasingly becoming a "knowledge economy." This too is also relatively un-contentious.

Other countries are at earlier stages of development. But it is here that the perspective of "world systems theory" begins to strongly disagree. Both classical Marxism and contemporary economic development theories believe that these not-quite-so-developed countries need to pass through *the same stages* as did the Western economies. Particular countries, and indeed whole geographical regions of the world, can be seen to have reached *different levels on the hierarchical pyramid of stages*. We see China now rapidly industrializing. We see what were once called the "tiger economies" of Southeast Asia being very highly developed in this regard. And tragically, we see virtually the whole of sub-Saharan Africa on the bottom rung of the pyramid. Most of these countries have failed to initiate any significant process of industrialization at all. Various explanations have been proffered for this failure to develop, with political corruption and endemic violence being a favorite among Western politicians. As for explanations as to why corruption is so widespread and why violence so virulent, we find assertions concerning "the failure to properly establish the democratic institutions common to Western civil society" frequently given, with such ethnocentric notions sometimes augmented with a dollop of conscious or unconscious racism. Classical Marxism would, of course, reject all these sorts of racist causal elements in these theories; but it unfortunately shares with them the notion of there being differing stages of development that the regions of the world all must pass through.

This "stage of development hypothesis" (though it is often put forward simply as "fact") then, as well as being a measure of economic development, wealth and financial complexity, is also a historical thesis. That is, the "less-developed" nations (sometimes called "developing," "underdeveloped" or "undeveloped," depending upon their place in the hierarchy) are not only less developed but in a certain sense are *back in time* too; they are at an earlier historical stage of development. So, for example, the 1980s development of the auto manufacture industry in the Mexican Maquiladoras took place, in one sense, in the earlier time frame of the 1920s. That is, the Detroit auto industry evolved with the American economy at that time, and the Mexican one will follow a similar, if not exactly identical, path just a few decades later. Mexico needs only to look at American to see its future. From this perspective, the outlook for most countries' economies is extremely hopeful, to say the least. They are fast developing, and the American consumer lifestyle is surely on its way.

Of course, for a few countries, the outlook is not so rosy. They seem stuck at an elementary stage and unable to move out of it. And though the dystopia thesis utterly rejects the concealed and unconcealed racism underpinning most of the explanations that branch off from the dominant development theory (e.g., the failure to implement democratic institutions explanation mentioned above), nonetheless, it shares the bleakness of the dominant thesis's vision for these countries. Indeed, the dystopia thesis has a new term for such countries: "never- to-develop" countries. When the crunch with respect to shortages of the world's energy resources comes (as will be discussed below), a new level of inequality of an already very unequal distribution will occur. The poorest have always got the smallest share, and as the coming crisis emerges, that share will increasingly be nothing at all. The poorest countries simply *will not be allowed to develop*. While, of course, one does need to analyze the social, political and economic institutions of such countries, the dystopia thesis does not put the explanatory emphasis upon the causal force of such institutions. Rather the emphasis is upon the relation these countries have with the rest of the world. Rather the emphasis is upon the *totality of an interconnected world economy*.

Humanity's cultural and political-economic evolution was by no means a simple linear progression from nomadic hunter-gatherers to the more complex agrarian societies of the past. Indeed, great agrarian civilizations grew, flourished and declined in one part of the world or another without the people in many other parts ever knowing they existed. The world was *not* one single inter-related socio-economic entity. Societies traded with one another and engaged in orgies of conquest and destruction. Adventurers sometimes traveled great distances to bring home new treasures and culturally cross-fertilized one society with another. Nonetheless, intercultural influence was most significant between geographically proximate areas, while some parts of the world remained relatively isolated until near present times. Regions developed along the same path, not the entirety of the world. Though minimal trade between far-flung corners of the globe sometimes existed, there never was what one could call a "world economy." That is, there was not... until the advent of capitalism! *Capitalism and a united world economic system evolved simultaneously!*

Capitalism evolved in an inter-related process of European internal economic development and increasing international trade. It also evolved in the business of Empire. The conquest of most of what is often called the "Third World" by the European nations was a political and economic development that did not take place separately from the European (and later American and Japanese) internal evolution of their capitalist economic system. Imperial politics dictated what was produced at home for export and what was produced in the colonies for import. This is where conventional development theory is so very badly mistaken. The Southern colonized Third World countries are *not* on the same multi-stage development process as the Western/Northern developed nations. They are *not* at an earlier stage of development. The conquests took place just as capitalism emerged. The economic relations of trade were dictated by the political relations of Empire. First World and Third, North and South, colonizer and colonized, town and country, all developed together in single system. The development of one part of the system conditioned the development, or lack of development, of the others.

The Third World did not just fail to develop industrially. The Third World was *prevented* from developing in this manner. For example, the textile industry was *not allowed* to develop in India by the British. Rather the mills of Lancashire were kept busy producing cloth, not merely for England but also for export, while India was left to export to its colonial master the spices, tea and other raw materials for items of which they were fond. This was the essence of the colonizer/colonized economic relationship: the colonizer imported raw materials and exported manufactured goods, while the colonies did the reverse. Economic development was thus stymied in the Third World.

Capitalism is not a static system. It organizationally and technologically evolved, and as it did so, economies changed, as did as the relations of world trade. Assembly-line production was invented. This perhaps was the zenith of the possibility for increasingly specialist tasks as a form of the division of labor. We see it perfected in Henry Ford's automobile assembly lines in the early part of the 20th century. Here we see another of capitalism's contradictions: a system of putting together a product of extreme sophistication and complexity by a labor force of individuals each doing a task so simple and repetitive that the stupidity such mind-numbing work inflicted upon them approached retardation. But while the work may have been boring, while the tasks robbed the workers of any creative satisfaction they might have taken in the labor, while their employment conditions left them alienated from their fellow workers, there was nonetheless one crucial advantage for the employees. Mass production brought the price of automobiles down. Mass production and cheap imports brought the relative price of everything down. Soon ordinary people were not only employees and workers but consumers as well. Or at least they were in the First World.

The colonized world threw off its colonial oppressors and gained economic independence. The Americas were the first to do so. The United States and Canada joined the older imperial masters in reaping the major benefits of the increasingly global capitalist economic system. Central and South America, however, became early examples of a new form of colonialism. A formal political independence was conjoined with a continued and even enhanced economic dependency and exploitation. This pattern, begun by them long before the 20th century, was repeated in the other parts of the world, while the European powers lingered over their imperial dream. Formal political independence for most of the Third World did not come until after World War II.

However, though countries gained *formal* political independence, the reality of that independence was *severely* circumscribed. This is what the economists and political scientists fail to understand. Most Third World countries, most of the time, suffer from incredibly poor governance. The liberal academics are distressed by the abundant evidence of corruption and the absurdly harmful policy decisions; they are distressed because their limited understanding of the dynamics of the capitalist world system pushes them in desperation toward the racism they deplore in notions such as the "African mind."

But it is certainly not a result of either genetic or cultural predilections for certain kinds of political-economic policies that produced the repeated African economic disasters. They, like all in the Third World, are locked into a *world system*. The structural logic, the power relations of that system, dictates policy. It dictates for *some* a continuation of the old raw materials for manufactured goods trade relation with the richer nations.

I emphasized the word "some" in the last paragraph because the world system has evolved. While the dynamic of the old raw material/industrial regional trade imbalance remains, there is now a further division. The former industrialized nations have undergone a circumscribed but nonetheless substantial *de-industrialization* process. The heavy industries that were their prime source of wealth in the past have been farmed out, so to speak. Britain, for example, had thriving steel and shipbuilding industries. These are now virtually completely gone. But it is not the case that the world's economy is now primarily a knowledge economy. No, as we shall see in the next section, it is still primarily an oil economy. But the First World has shut down a good deal of its heavy, dirty industry. It has, as it were, exported its polluting industries to the Third World. Steel is as important as ever. Shipbuilding did not cease in the world economy because Britain stopped building them. Not only do these activities still take place, they are done on a larger scale than ever. No, it is just that the First World economies are more service oriented, particularly more financial service oriented. The stock markets, the banks, the insurance companies of the First World largely control the economies of the newly industrialized economies of the Third World.

But there is a crucial difference in the historical situation governing this industrial development of the Third World. In the early 20th century mass production of consumer goods, the workers were able to perform the dual role of producer and consumer. Ford assembly-line workers were able to afford to purchase Ford motor cars. The scale of mass production in America and other First World countries went hand-in-hand with the evolution of a consumer society. The Third World industrialization process has a different dynamic. Southern Third World mass production (in the main) is not intended for Third World mass consumption. The consumers are still located in the North.

Now one might think that these trading relations – in the past purely a raw material/manufactured good exchange, and in the present, a financial service/heavy polluting industry exchange – is an example of extraordinary irrationality in the policy decision-making processes of the losing partners of such unequal exchange. But such is not so. Politics and economics are inseparable; the government is a crucial economic player. The capitalist system has inbuilt contradictions concerning the relations of individual logical decisions and apparently irrational, collective outcomes. The economic policy-making logic of the poorer countries is two-fold and quite simple. First, the ruling elites can dramatically economically benefit from selling their country cheap, so to speak. This may take various legal forms or may involve outright corruption. Either way, the collective good is being sacrificed for the benefits of the few. The collective good of the poor country is being sacrificed for the benefit of their rich Northern "partners." Corruption or apparent ineptitude is not a contingent feature of the system; it is a result of the system's collective logic.

The situation underpinning the second aspect of the two-fold logic of economic policy-making for the poorer countries is equally simple. The financial institutions of the First World, including not only banks and multinational corporations but also international institutions such as the International Monetary Fund (IMF), the World Bank, The General Agreement on Trades and Tariffs (GATT) and the World Trade Organization (WTO), *impose* policy upon the weaker nations. Capitalism requires capital to make things happen. Capital flows from the richer to the poorer nations, the developed to the less developed. It comes in the form of loans and aid grants. It comes with strings attached. It comes with conditions. These conditions, regardless of the rhetoric of altruism in which they are sometimes dressed up, are always to the benefit of the "donor" countries, the lending nations, the investors. The conditions may well benefit the rulers of the exploited country *personally*. But they do *not* benefit the debtor nation. Not in the long run. Not ever!

The creation of the world's present world political economy can now be summarized. Capitalism and a world economy emerged simultaneously. Capitalism possesses a two-fold logic for the extraction of surplus. The first aspect is in the employer/employee relationship. The employees produce a surplus for the employer. They produce products or services worth more than what they produce in wages for working. This surplus is the basis for all profit. Accumulated profit is capital. It has a money form, an electronically numerical symbolic form. But these symbolic counters are attached to real things. They are the things people have built in the past. The system requires the accumulation of capital and the maximization of profit. But the employer/employee relationship is not the only relationship of extraction. There is a regional process as well. The Third World employers extract a surplus from Third World employees; but a portion of that surplus is in turn extracted from them, in a regional transfer of wealth from Third World to First, from South to North, from country to city. The imbalance of power, both economic and political (this latter power can sometimes be quite nakedly military power), ensures that this process is accomplished through unequal relations of trade.

However, the world is more complicated than a simple division of North and South, First World and Third, rich and poor. There is a continuum of wealth and development. This is not simply between nations but within them. The process of industrialization taking place in the Third World is not universal among these nations. Some of that development is taking place in the special economic zones such as are found in the Philippines or the Mexican Maquiladoras.[12] In such places, industrialization does little to enrich the host nations of foreign corporations. Workers, primarily female, feel the personal domestic freedoms being a worker brings. They suffer long repetitive soul-and-body-destroying hours for this sense of freedom and limited entrance into the consumer world. But their working life there is limited. Before they reach 30, they are cast aside to be replaced by their younger more nimble and less demanding sisters. That they face mandatory "retirement" at such a young age is not accidental. They are gotten rid of before the needs of motherhood become too insistent; they are gotten rid of before their knowledge of their world and sense of injustice has time to fully develop; above all they need to leave before they can properly begin to organize. But elsewhere it is different. A middle class emerges as the country develops. Consumer society is born. And these regions and nations exploit those who are less fortunate. Just as in turn they are exploited by the true core of the world system.

The very existence of a Third World middle class serves an ideological function. Simply by existing, they obscure the obviousness of the unequal social division of the world's wealth and power relations. They have the political effect to mute and deflect a resistance to the main power. Those at the bottom aspire to climb to the middle; those in the middle aspire to climb to the top. This is true of both people and nations.

---

[12] See the 1986 film *The Global Assembly Line*, New Day Films.

The semi-peripheral nations exploit the truly peripheral regions of the world.[13] Sometimes this means the exploitation of their own hinterland. The "city" exploits the "country." The political centers of all countries are to be found in cities; this is so regardless of the fact that some of these countries are primarily agricultural economies. Farm laborers, today's contemporary peasantry, may live out in the country. They may own a small amount of land but must supplement their income by working on the land of others. These "others," the wealthy landowners, the local or foreign corporate agricultural enterprises, all have their offices and lives based in the city. Or at least they have the significant power intersections of their economic and political exploitation of the outback there.

We see other Third World divisions corresponding to this economic relationship. The rich and the middle classes aspire to modernity; that is to say, they aspire to the consumer lifestyle. The poorer country folk are more traditional, with their social conservatism and religion-based morality frequently being used against them as a justification of the status quo that leaves them impoverished.

The simplest, and indeed most prevalent model of this, is an agricultural economy. At one time, the vast majority of humanity toiled in the fields. This is changing, but it is only in the last couple of years that we can find a majority of the world's population living in the cities. Farmers in North America and Europe may have problems as they struggle with the rapid changes of the global market and the complicated structures of subsidies and the futures market. These First World farmers, however, are now more properly described as agriculture business managers, as computers and accountancy knowledge become more and more a part of their daily work lives. But the agriculture of the Third World, though equally dependent for success or failure upon vacillating world markets, is not like this. They are at

---

[13] World systems theory uses its own terms — core, periphery and semi-periphery — rather than the more intellectually loaded terms of First World, Third World, North and South etc. They are more accurate and more easily express divisions that are not strictly between nations.

the wrong end of the world's economic direction and force. They face increasing impoverishment. They face increasing failure in a constant struggle for survival. The peasantry of the Third World is less and less a peasantry and more and more a workforce of agricultural laborers.

What is the difference? Well, most significantly, though peasants must need give up some of what they produce as a ground rent to a landowner or work this person's land for a part of the year, still much of what they produce is for their own consumption or to be taken and sold by them in the market. But an increasing portion of every Third World country's arable land is "factory farmed" for the production of a selection of cash crops, usually for export. So, the peasantry works on huge banana (from whence the expression "banana republic" came) or coffee plantations. They produce the consumer luxuries so loved by us in the First World. This increased agricultural specialization has been very beneficial . . . to us in the West. But it has not improved the lives of the "former peasantry."

However, the exploitation of the periphery by the semi-periphery, the exploitation of the country by the city, need not be agricultural. Indeed, the extraction of most of the world economy's "raw materials" depend upon just this same set of relations. In Nigeria, for example, the Niger Delta receives little economic advantage from the rich oil fields found there. They receive little in the way of direct financial benefit. The skilled workers in the main come from elsewhere. Only unskilled labor is hired locally. They certainly receive little in the way of petroleum products . . . except, of course, that which they steal from a leaking pipeline. And who does benefit from these oil riches? Well, the local corporate management, the bribery infested civil service, the rich city dwellers and small middle class of the city, these people of the semi-periphery benefit from the exploitation of the resource rich hinterland. But they do not benefit the most because the semi-periphery is in turn exploited by the core. It is a multinational corporation that reaps the real oil wealth; in the case of Nigeria, it is mainly Shell. The other beneficiaries, of course, are the First World consumers of energy – the SUV drivers of America get to indulge their prolific fuel consumption at prices guaranteed by the power relations of a world system of exploitation.

The Peak Oil Problem

My grandfather rode a camel, my father rode a camel, I drive a Mercedes, my son drives a Land Rover, his son will drive a Land Rover, but his son will ride a camel.
> Sheikh Rashid bin Saeed Al Maktoum
> (Emir of Dubai)

The United States has compensated for its production decline by importing oil. The planet does not have that option.
> Russell A. Brown

SUVs have become a kind of public symbol of irresponsibility recently. They are retaining their currency as a status symbol of affluence, but the currency has become devalued for two related reasons. First, these vehicles now symbolize a wealth that is careless of the environment. Secondly, they now symbolize a curious notion of anti-patriotism. Their excessive gasoline consumption plays into the hands of "dangerous foreigners" who would hold America "hostage" over oil. There is also an interesting mix of horrible political reality, absurdity and underlying economic contradiction involved with SUVs that allow them to symbolize dystopia as well.

The beginning of First World worries about energy came with the formation of OPEC (the Organization of Petroleum Exporting Countries) and its resultant big increases in oil prices in the 1970s. For just a very brief period of history, the American public and American politicians were both concerned about energy supplies. The politicians didn't really do much about it except mouth some platitudes, but the car-buying public began seriously looking for better gas mileage. The global economy brought it to them as a Japanese import. The enormous market success of small imported cars rocked American auto manufacturers. They tried yet seemed unable to compete . . . until the government gave them some help. The success of the SUV was born of tax advantages and contradictory policies. There was legislation mandating emission controls on vehicles (as an anti-pollution measure rather than anything to do with global warming), speed restrictions on the highways to reduce fuel consumption and regulations directly concerning auto manufacture and fuel efficiency. All of this seemed to favor superior Japanese (and other foreigners') engineering. Ford and GM needed help to keep from being wiped out. The enormous gas-guzzling SUVs were classified as "light trucks" rather than cars and thus were exempt from much of the "interfering with the market" legislation. Purchasing a truck could be written off as a business expense. In short, the US government subsidized the purchase of SUVs. It is this that makes SUVs a symbol of dystopia.

Of course, the market is going to be "interfered with." Of course, it is going to be interfered with in a way that derives from economic considerations. And finally, of course, it is going to be interfered with in a way that goes against the long-term interests of humankind.

It should be noted that the expensive hybrid cars, (e.g., the Prius) now being bought by "environmentally conscious" movie stars and the like, are also symbols of dystopia. They encourage dangerous illusions about the relation of politics, economics and the environment. Such cars suggest that the peak oil problem can easily be solved. They suggest we only need some market incentives to apply the engineering skills humanity has in abundance and our looming transport and energy crisis will be easily managed. The dystopia thesis not only asserts that managing this crisis would be anything but easy but argues that it will not even be possible at all without a fundamental system change . . . a change that at present there are not even any preliminary signs of it coming.

The "peak oil crisis" is quite simple. We will soon be running out of cheap oil, and there is literally *nothing to adequately replace it* for performing the role it has played for the last century in the world's political economy. Our contemporary world system that gives some people at least (a very great many people actually), an incredible standard of living based upon technological marvel, is fundamentally oil driven. Or rather it is fundamentally *cheap* oil driven.

There has always only been a finite amount of oil in the world. Oil is a result of geological processes and circumstance. The geological processes move at a speed outside of any possible human time frame of reference. New oil may come into being but not in any time frame whereby we could use it. Some oil was easy to find. Some of the places where it was found were easy to get to and access. Some of the oil in these places was easy to extract. All of *that* oil has already been consumed. The search for oil now largely takes place under the ocean. The extraction of oil takes place in the North Sea and the Arctic. Even in the much more readily accessible deserts of the Middle East, pressurized salt water often needs to be pumped in to maintain the flow that once came so easily and cheaply. The physical limitations of the amount of oil in the earth, the physical limitations upon the possibilities for getting it out of the earth, ensure that there will come a point when, no matter how much demand for oil there is, no more can be extracted to meet that demand. This is the oil production peak. The years subsequent to the peak will produce less oil world-wide *in spite of demand*.

Oil production could fluctuate for a variety of reasons. This makes it difficult to know in advance precisely when the peak will be. It will only be retrospectively that we will know for sure . . . after we go for years producing less and less.

The significance of the oil production peak is not merely that it means that someday we will run out of oil entirely. That is not the real problem. Long, long before that day arrives, we will have been in serious crisis . . . a crisis perhaps from which the human race will never recover. It is not that there are not other ways of powering and organizing our economy. Potential for a positive utopia remains even as dystopia emerges. The problem is the way in which we have our transport and energy systems organized now. The problem is the coming transition away from a system that is unsustainable. The problem is that we will attempt to retain the present system until oil prices are so unstable in short fluctuations and so nearly impossibly high that everything has to change. The change to a new material basis for the world economy, the change to an entirely new energy dynamic, will not be smooth, orderly and rational. It will be wrought with irrationality, extreme violence, injustice and suffering.

The Unique Importance of Oil and Transport

> *Nothing succeeds like reports of success.*
> Sue Sanders (US oil producer)

> *If it weren't for electricity, we'd all be*
> *watching television by candlelight.*
> George Gobel

Electricity has been absolutely key to the development of the modern age. Electricity powers everything from computers to trains to the lights in our bedrooms. It was and is essential to both the industrial and post-industrial age. It is perhaps the single most crucial material element of civilization. Thus, it may seem paradoxical that it is not crucially pivotal in the dystopia thesis concerning energy. Electricity is, of course, centrally related to the main problem; but it is not *the* main problem. The main problem is transport. The main problem is oil.

Oil is widely used in the generation of electricity. This, quite obviously, has to stop. The dystopia thesis is comparatively optimistic concerning this. Other theorists of the coming peak oil crisis see electricity generation as a major problem, and one that is perhaps insoluble[14]. They point out that the immense variety of

---

[14] See, for example, Richard Heinberg (2002), The Party's Over: Oil, War, and the Fate of Industrial Societies and (2004) Powerdown: Options and Actions for a Post-Carbon World; James Howard Kunstler (2005), The Long Emergency; Matthew R. Simmons (2005), Twilight in the Desert: The Coming Saudi Oil Shock and the World Economy. There are a great many others. Indeed there are a number of organizations and websites devoted to the issue. The Association for the Study of Peak Oil & Gas has chapters in a great many countries and a number of websites see http://www.peakoil.net/ for a linkage. The Post

other means of electricity generation – coal, natural gas, nuclear, wind, tide and others – all depend upon an oil-based economy for their construction, maintenance and, above all, any expansion in their current output levels. This is true, but once again it needs to be repeated: the oil problem is not an absolute shortage but a *price problem*. This may seem like less of a potential crisis. It is not. *The price problem will be so severe that it will change everything!* One of the things that will change will be government plans concerning electricity generation. The peak oil crisis will emerge with startling rapidity. But there will be a short period of gradual emergence before the true extremities of situation begin to manifest themselves. The exigencies of even this less extreme period will be severe enough to wake up the politicians and money people. They, of course, will instigate many stupid, short-sighted, self-interested and, generally speaking, unwise actions; but nonetheless they will still inject money and urgency into every other viable form of electricity generation. This will certainly not be easy. But the bottom line is that we will still have the lights on (for a while anyway), and oil will no longer be used in electricity generation. This, at present quite important usage, will simply be placed at the bottom of the list in terms of oil usage priorities.

Taking oil away from electricity generation will, of course, greatly aid the conservation efforts that will be both government mandated and market driven. Different countries presently generate electricity in different percentages for different sources. Many experts believe that nuclear power is really the only practical source of generating capacity expansion to meet the coming crisis. However, France is about the only country where this could be done relatively painlessly. There has not been a new nuclear power station built in the US since the 1970s. Coal is perhaps the next most practical energy generator available for expansion. Different countries, of course, are differently endowed with accessible (read economically feasible) amounts of it.

Carbon   Institute   is   another   of   the   major   organizations.
http://www.postcarbon.org

Britain, for example, will come to greatly regret the shutting down of its enormous pit infrastructure, when it finds itself forced to reopen the pits it shut down as "uneconomic."

Of course, coal has other problems. It is a prime carbon emission generator. The "peak oil crisis" is set to interact with the global warming crisis in an interesting way. At some point, there will be a reduction of carbon emissions because of less usage of carbon fuels. The advent of global warming suggests the wisdom of conservation. Thus, perhaps we will save more oil for future rather than present use. Optimists see the two problems as offsetting one another in a beneficial way. The dystopia thesis, of course, possesses no such optimism. This is no "glass half full, glass half empty" kind of question of perspective. The glass is a lot more than half empty. The two problems will interact but not in any kind of balancing way. Their time scales of cause and effect will be quite different. Long before oil has sufficiently run out to physically impose sufficient restraint in its usage to lower carbon emissions, humanity will be feeling the worst effects of global warming. To conserve upon oil, there will be a resurgence in coal-fired electricity-generating plants, which will exacerbate and speed up the warming effects.

Regardless of these difficulties, electricity will continue to be generated throughout the First World and even in the Third. There will be controlled regular interruptions of service and uncontrolled crises of cold and darkness. In this way, the First World will come to more closely resemble the present state of the Third. There are, in fact, fairly serious problems with the power-generation infrastructure,[15] which are quite unrelated to the fuel sources issue. But politicians will act, things will be done, the market will respond. It is not an electrical blackout that will be the dramatic change of dystopia. The uncharacteristic optimism of the dystopia thesis in this regard is simply that these political and

---

[15] The North American transmission infrastructure is in bad shape for example. The great blackout of 2003 was merely a foretaste of trouble to come. See for example this report:
http://www.researchandmarkets.com/reportinfo.asp?report_id=364040

market forces are not themselves negligible (something that other peak oil crisis analyses sometimes underestimate); the technical problems, though difficult, are manageable without a complete social system changeover. The oil and transport aspects of the economy are another manner entirely.

The "heart of the beast" was a phrase widely used in 1960s radical political circles. It indicated the United States' central position in the world capitalist system. It indicated that it was in the US that one would find the "contradictions of capitalism" at their sharpest. The transport infrastructure of contemporary North America (Canada is as bad or worse!) makes this viewpoint quite apt. Some countries are better placed than others to attempt a non-catastrophic "weaning off" of the oil tit, so to speak. Many countries possess, if not magnificent, at least adequate on some level of utility, public transport systems. This is so for most Western European countries, for example. London has not only its famous "underground" for intra-city travel, but it has recently established an inner-city congestion tax policy, which has successfully reduced car and truck traffic significantly. Unfortunately, among the things that were rundown for political reasons in Maggie Thatcher's 1980s Britain was the inter-city rail network. However, even in its reduced condition, a comparison with the US Amtrak rail service can only provoke the adjective "pitiful" about the latter! Some American cities have subway systems and rudimentary bus systems for that small portion of the population too poverty-stricken to own even a battered old car; but these systems are usually not either very extensive or very good.

Two key points come out of the preceding paragraph. The dystopian effects directly deriving from the end of cheap oil will be geographically and nationally variable. Different places will be hit with varying degrees of, yes, market-driven economic force. Some of the small Caribbean island states, which are more or less wholly economically dependent upon tourism, will be completely ruined once the cheap airfares that support present-day mass tourism are gone. Even here, though, there will be variance. All flights there will not cease, and those that do certainly won't all cease at once. The more up-market resort tourism will fare better.

This variance will be true for the US as well. Business people will continue to fly to destinations within the country and to the rest of the world, albeit much fewer of them. But those Southern US resort towns highly dependent upon the drunken-college-kid phenomenon now known as "spring break" may well be financially crippled, as these are just the sort of trips that will soon become unaffordable.

Much, much more important than the effects noted in the preceding paragraph is the whole economic transport and housing infrastructure of the United States. Suburban living, the commuter worker and soccer mom, at a certain point, just no longer will be feasible. Change will come, but the manner in which it comes will be chaotic and painful. It is interesting that even the US government is able to look into the future a bit with respect to this. It commissioned a report[16] into the economic consequences of large unstable market fluctuations, shortages and large oil price rises and other effects of "peak oil" to the economy. The report concluded unsurprisingly that the severity and longevity of negative effects would be dependent upon preparation. They produced three scenarios.

The first is quite optimistic. With a 20-year head start before reaching the oil production peak, and an emergency program being implemented, the US economy could gradually change and adjust without too much disruption. If that emergency program's lead in is only 10 years, however, significant intense disruption would occur. If the emergency program is not implemented until peak oil is actually reached, the report concludes in its last scenario, then economic disruption would be so severe that recovery might never occur. That is, the US economy of that possible future would be unrecognizable, and the differences would all be negative in the extreme. The reasoning behind this is simple. To fundamentally alter the whole physical transport

---

[16] R.L. Hirsch, R. Bezdek and R. Wendling, (February, 2005) *Peaking of World Oil Production: Impacts, Mitigation & Risk Management,* Science Applications International Corporation (SAIC) Project Report commissioned by the US government.

infrastructure will take time. Cars have a physical and economic lifetime; today's gasoline-gulping SUV does not immediately and magically transform itself into a hydrogen-driven vehicle once the desirability of such become apparent. Capitalism has an inertial force carrying its present into the future. Interestingly, this government-commissioned scientific report upon future possibilities in relation to oil depletion has been officially ignored and the publication's suppression attempted by . . . the government.[17]

When will we reach the oil production peak? Well, as said before, it will be very difficult to tell, until some years after it has actually been reached. Okay, but then what is the range of estimates? Well, by far the most optimistic one is, in all practical terms of human scale, effectively never: 50 years, 100 years or more. Who supports these optimistic perspectives? Well, an interesting array of characters do, actually. First, and most credible on the list, are Saudi oil ministers and oil company CEOs. These people all have extraordinarily obvious vested financial interests in this conclusion . . . or at least its public pronouncement. The real status of Saudi oil reserves are a state secret, and the issue is controversial. However, there are a lot of good reasons to suppose the truth is very, very different from what is being told.[18]

There is a degree of latitude within the range of more independent and respectable estimates. The more conservative end of the spectrum suggests sometime a little before 2020. This, it should be noted, is a lot shorter than the 20- year scenario for emergency transition plans seeing us through. And, of course, if one looks around, one sees no signs of any such emergency

---

[17] Richard Heinberg (2005), "Where Is the Hirsch Report," *Global Media Studies Group* http://globalpublicmedia.com/articles/441. This issue, both in a more general fashion, and with other specific examples will be discussed again at greater length in chapter 6.

[18] See, for example, a report prepared in 2004 by the Institute for the Analysis of Global Security (IAGS) http://www.iags.org/n0331043.htm

transition plans being implemented, or even developed. One sees no plans to speak of whatsoever on any reasonable scale at all. California has gone the furthest in preparing for a future oil crunch. They have opened the "hydrogen highway." British Columbia has followed their lead and now has one too. President Bush and Governor Schwarzenegger have trumpeted hydrogen vehicles as the technological brave-new-age solution to the problems of resource depletion. Unfortunately, however, the two hydrogen "gas stations" (one in San Francisco and one in Sacramento) can only support a "fleet" of two cars and two buses together. While this sorry state of development seems unlikely to do much with respect to California's commuter problem, they are, nonetheless, miles ahead of BC. British Columbia's much-vaunted hydrogen highway is only virtual, with barely enough government financing to support even that.

For the other end of the respectable estimates for when peak oil production will be reached, we need look to the past rather than the future. Sometime in 2005 is an estimate sometimes given. If this figure is correct, then we shall soon see that it is. After four or five years of less oil being produced, whatever the short-term market fluctuation effects may be, it should be obvious that that much oil never will be produced again. The serious disruption effects should be coming soon.

Among the possibilities would be a crash in the housing market. It is an interesting problem with consequences difficult to predict. It is generally agreed that this market is a kind of bubble. The price increase expansion of the bubble has been going on for a very long time. What is meant by this? Well, first of all, it should be noted that, like many other of capitalism's features, it is at once exceedingly complex with regional and national specificity and yet fundamentally very simple. There is not the space in this book to devote to the complexity, so what is presented here is the simple basics of the structure and dynamic.

Housing prices, in the final analysis, must somehow be related to wages, and the wages of society's lowest paid at that. Workers need to live somewhere. The poorer ones cannot afford to own, and so they rent. The rent they pay must, however, be related to the monthly mortgage payments of the owner. Perhaps rent is so high that families cannot afford a house or apartment for themselves. They share with others and cram several families into a single dwelling. Regardless of the distribution, a total rent is paid to the owner. There are physical, not to mention social, limits upon how many people can live in a single dwelling. There are the financial limits to how much rent these people can put together because of the limits set by how much they earn. If the rent paid is significantly less than the mortgage payments for the property, then the owner has, in effect, what is a losing business. What occurs in a real estate bubble is that, year after year, the value of this losing business continues to rise. This has been going on throughout the First World for decades.

Regional and national legal and economic structures profoundly affect this general trend. In Hong Kong, for example, such structures have produced a particularly acute situation. New office and apartment buildings are subject to a highly volatile and speculative market situation long, long before building commences. Small down payments secure huge loans for buildings upon the speculative future value of the individual apartments or office spaces. There can be as many as nine sale and re-sales before building commences and many more before it is finished. The person who actually moves into and lives or works in these spaces is, therefore, at the end of a very long chain of profit-taking that has put the price up many, many times over its original, usually already quite inflated, value. Because of some of the limiting factors noted in the previous paragraph, it is only the high end of the market, so to speak, that can afford such properties. Ergo, Hong Kong has an enormous surplus of office space and luxury homes at the same time as a very severe housing shortage for ordinary people.

Again, as an example of regional and complicating factors, the UK provides us with some interesting variation. The ludicrous speculation of the Hong Kong situation would be forbidden by law there yet speculation exists nonetheless. Indeed, speculation is fundamental to the real estate bubble everywhere. The UK situation is complicated most significantly by government involvement in the market. Two principal entries occurred. First, in the decades subsequent to World War II, the government engaged in an enormous building and subsidized rental program. Council houses and flats, as such subsidized dwellings were called, were variable in quality but, generally speaking, from the point of view of the working classes, a very good deal. The next significant government intervention was done in the 80s by the Thatcher government. They re-privatized the housing stock through subsidizing the buying of council houses and flats by their tenants. This gave both short- and long-term gains to some new council house owners, an immediate injection of some cash to others before they fiddled the system and transferred ownership to a richer class of people, and finally left the worst council housing to deteriorate completely as maintenance was underfunded. The bottom of the UK real estate market now means that poorer citizens cannot afford housing without the underfunded local government subsidizing most of the cost and the rest of the market going up and up and up. But the only things that allow most people to make their mortgage payments is the "profit equity" they have because of the increase in housing prices and relatively low interest rates. First-time buyers are effectively frozen out of the market because of the lack of the former and in spite of the latter.

UK housing prices are on average double that of Canadian prices in relation to average income and cost of living. One would therefore think that the North American situation is less acute than in the UK and certainly far less so than in Hong Kong. This is certainly true for the present and shorter term. The bubble is less of a bubble. But in the longer term, the effects of the oil market upon the real estate bubble will likely be more profound. Oil will affect the whole world. Prices will go up, businesses unable to adjust to the new transport realities will collapse all over the world, but this effect will be more profound in the no public transportation, suburban strip-mall, long-haul trucking business, residential and lifestyle realities of North America.

Any substantial increase in interest rates would force a succession of mortgage foreclosures. Essentially the government cannot allow such to occur, though multiple factors of the peal oil economy will be providing extraordinary pressure for it. Yet at the same time, there is little the government can do to prevent it.

The dystopia thesis does not predict a simple bursting of the housing bubble (though the recent price "adjustments" of the American Market supports such a prediction in part). Whatever else happens, the future economy will retain its complexity. No, what the dystopia thesis predicts is that, under the pressure of the peak oil price rises, capitalism will face its most extreme crises of instability with profoundly unpleasant and intense effects upon ordinary people.

The 2008 financial crisis and its related effects outside the financial system have already caused enormous hardship. People have lost their jobs, their pensions, their life savings and their homes. The worst is not yet over. Though, after the bank bailouts, the capitalists themselves are breathing easier. The fact that there is such extreme poverty amidst such plenty is not really their problem; it is ours. The sad fact is that, though economic crises always generate suffering, they also present opportunities, and thus far, the Left in most parts of the world have significantly failed to take advantage of them. This issue will be addressed in chapter 8.

The Market, Science, Engineering and Other Saviors

I confidently predict the collapse of capitalism and the beginning of history. Something will go wrong in the machinery that converts money into money, the banking system will collapse totally, and we will be left having to barter to stay alive. Those who can dig in their garden will have a better chance than the rest. I'll be all right; I've got a few veg.
        Margaret Drabble

We cannot give over all our corn production to ethanol; I mean, we gotta eat some.
        G.W. Bush

The reasoning behind the so-called law of supply and demand is quite sound. However, the forces of supply and demand do not produce singular and easily predicted effects. Rather, they produce tendencies that will be prevented from fully actualizing themselves by countervailing forces. In the case of oil economics, the laws of supply and demand will be superseded by laws of a different order: the physical laws of the universe. No, the market will surely not save us from this set of coming disasters.

Oil, the peak oil skeptics sometimes concede, may become costlier to extract, perhaps even unsustainably so in present quantities. So it will end up costing more. That is the way the marketplace works. But this very cost increase will bring the price down again eventually. The cost increase will discourage wanton usage, encourage conservation and make presently uneconomic extraction economic. Market-driven greater efficiency in production, in combination with reduced demand, will eventually lower prices again. Wonderful. As the economists like to say about the market: "God couldn't do better." Except the situation is just not quite so perfect as they believe.

It is not simply that individuals buy or don't buy gas dependent upon prices. There are collective de facto decisions that are taken and taken over time. You live where you have to commute long distances or you don't. Perhaps gasoline prices have gone up sufficiently that you want to stop paying them. You want to move. But this price motivation affects everyone. A lot of people want to move. The value of your house goes down accordingly. Now you can't afford to move. You can't afford to move; you can't afford to stay. This is exactly what the dystopia thesis asserts. Your year-old SUV has fallen dramatically in price. You sell it at a big pain-in-your-pocketbook reduced price to a poor person who can now afford it before you buy your Prius. Yes, adjustments are made through the extraordinary complexity of inter-related markets. That is not at all what is at issue between contemporary economists and dystopia theorists. The latter merely assert that the adjustments will be extraordinarily painful and inefficient. You shut down a nationwide coal mining industry because it is uneconomic; you triple the real energy extraction costs you would have had if you had kept the pits open, when you *reopen* them.

The market logic underpinning suburban malls, big-box stores and hundred-mile commutes will change at the same time as the economics of shipping goods around the world in the globalized division of labor changes. Contracts for the purchase of jumbo jets designed to transport millions of tourists will not be fulfilled when the price of travel goes up in relation to the price of aviation fuel; many potential international tourists think they will stay home this year instead of flying to Jamaica or the Canary Islands; in the light of reduced demand for flights, the need for the new jets is removed. There will be a market-generated, complex series of lawsuits and bankruptcies. Underneath this will be pain. There will be pain in tourist industry Jamaica, pain in Boeing worker suburbs in Seattle, pain everywhere. This is because the one area where the laws of physics trump the laws of supply and demand is with respect to supply. All the market pressure in the world cannot increase the amount of oil in the earth. All the market pressure in the world cannot change sufficiently the energy-extraction rations. All the market can do is cause prices to go up regardless of its consequences in a complex interconnected system.

The energy-extraction ratio is the proportional amount of physical energy required to extract (and transport and all the other production energy costs) the fuel, compared to the amount of energy that the fuel can produce. If it takes the same amount of energy to get the fuel out of the ground as that fuel can produce when burned, you have a ratio that is clearly uneconomic . . . in a physical sense. Perhaps, a distorted market might make it financially viable for a time. But eventually, this market logic will be trumped by the physical logic underlying the extraction process.

What is fundamentally wrong with the optimism of the marketplace ideology in this case is that there is a sometimes acknowledged, sometimes not, but regardless, always-false supplemental appendage to it. That is, there is a technological thesis upon which it depends to make everything turn out all right. It is unquestioningly believed that market demand and the increase in prices will generate technological miracles on two fronts: discovery and extraction techniques. "Miracle" is by far too strong a term, but nevertheless, the dystopia thesis would certainly concede improvements will be made because of this incentive. It is merely that the dystopia thesis would posit limits to those improvements; for oil economist optimists, "miracle" is the *precise* term required, because real miracles as phenomena are required, for their ideological dreams, to be realized. Given sufficient stimulus (read market incentive) and humanity can accomplish anything. The widespread collective feeling about the possibilities of technological marvel are, unfortunately in most cases, based upon a deep ignorance of the science that underpins the technology we do have.

The science of oil discovery and the engineering of oil extraction have each undergone qualitative jumps in efficiency since the early days of oil production. However, in spite of such amazing improvements, there are two extremely powerful and depressing facts about discovery and production. Global satellite surveying notwithstanding, the number of new oil field finds have been diminishing for many years. More and more money has been pumped into searching for oil, more and more sophisticated technology has been utilized in the search, yet, contra marketplace logic, less and less oil has been found. The supply is finite. The supply is non-renewable. The average energy expenditure in extraction today is many, many times more than it was 100 years ago or 50 years ago or 20 years ago. Technological improvements do not remotely come close to matching the increasing difficulties of extraction. The easy to find oil, and the easy to get out of the ground oil and the easy to move to where it is needed oil has all been used up long ago. Today's oil, and tomorrow's even more so, is extremely difficult to extract and found most usually in harsh, isolated, inaccessible parts of the Earth.

The other ideological manifestation of ignorant optimism is to do with the possibilities of alternative energy supplies. Virtually all of them, with the exception of the hydrogen fantasies discussed earlier, are to do with electricity generation. Some of these alternatives are practically sound, others are less so, but coming with them all are the dual problems of scale and change. That is, there is the present-day too small a scale to make much difference on the one hand, and there is the extensive investment, planning and physical infrastructural change required to upscale them on the other. There is really only one energy source where these factors are not applicable: natural gas.

Natural gas is cleaner and more efficient than oil, and the physical infrastructure already exists for significant electricity generation, as well as heating system uses. But can it take up the slack in oil usage for electricity generation? No. We have the same problem as with oil, except that US natural gas production has not only already peaked (US oil production also peaked a long time ago), but by the nature of it as a fuel, importation possibilities are physically restricted.[19] Mexico still exports natural gas to the US, but it just recently peaked in production and is now a net importer. Canada still exports to the US, but its production figures are fast being caught up by domestic demand. This is likely to become a short-term dystopian factor for Canadians. We can expect significant pressure (political-economic bullying would perhaps be a better way of putting it) from the Americans to prioritize their needs over our own with respect to this, as well as other natural resources. They will want them, and they will want them cheap. They will also be quite happy to dispense with the "natural laws of supply and demand" regarding what we might think would be the market's price for goods outstripping demand; in such cases everywhere in the world, the government becomes a significant player, even adding military force into the bullying equation. Though such was routinely applied throughout the 20th century, at present it would be considered unthinkable with respect to Canada. The dystopia

---

[19] Natural gas requires pipeline transport. It is possible to be transported in liquid form, but liquid natural gas (LNG) is for practical purposes essentially a different fuel. Warranted public wariness about having LNG terminals sited near them has meant that there are very few such terminals in North America. Scaling up to make any real difference would be prohibitively costly.

thesis argues that, under the extreme exigencies of post peak oil, the unthinkable just may happen.

Coal production can be expanded (though probably with dire effects upon the environment). More nuclear plants can be built. Wind, tide, solar and other alternative energy sources can and likely will increase in efficiency and usage be expanded. Market-enforced conservation measures will occur. The dystopia thesis does not dispute this. Market forces will have an effect. But the time lag involved before they kick in will be crucial. There will likely be fairly frequent and widespread blackouts in the future (aided by a crucial lack of investment in the improvement and maintenance of the electricity grid's physical infrastructure). However, the dystopia thesis is actually fairly optimistic about electricity. The role of oil in contemporary electricity production is significant but not so much that it cannot and will not be replaced. Perhaps a few (perhaps quite a few) dark cold nights will occur, but the dystopia thesis does not predict that economic crises of capitalism will mainly take place with the lights out. No, as said before, it is transportation that is key. It is with respect to transportation, that oil is key. It is with respect to the economy, that cheap oil is key.

This brings up the last of our cheap oil replacement possibilities: ethanol. Again, as was the case with natural gas, the infrastructure is already in place. But could it economically be expanded? Once again, the laws of physics intervene. The ratio of energy produced by corn-extracted ethanol fuel to that expended in its production make it something of a bad bet. It is controversial insofar as its proponents give it a somewhat positive, though still not high, ratio; those against give it a negative one. The latter case means that it actually takes more energy to produce it than it can produce once transformed into fuel. If this is true, the entire ethanol gasoline industry is nothing more than a concealed subsidy to agribusiness for no good reason except to make these corporations richer. If it is the former case, there are still problems. To power the present US fleet of vehicles would actually take up more farmland than the US presently possesses. This is assuming that such land is entirely removed from food production, the obviously ridiculous possibility that gives a certain degree of relevance to George Bush's stupid remark that was quoted at the beginning of this section.

Sugar cane is better than corn for ethanol production, and Brazil actually has a significant amount of its vehicles powered by such. This has, of course, already led to some dire environmental consequences.[20] But leaving such aside, as capitalism is certainly well capable of doing, turning the whole of Brazil into a fuel factory for the US at the expense of feeding its own population is actually one of the dystopian possibilities that might alleviate some of the transport fuel shortages in the US and other wealthy countries.

Conclusion

> *Madness is something rare in individuals – but*
> *in groups, parties, peoples, ages it is the rule.*
> Frederick Nietzsche

> *Until you change the way money works, you*
> *change nothing.*
> Michael Rupert

The world economy is driven by the capitalist prioritization of profits. There are two primary relations of exploitation in the world capitalist system. The first is the extraction of surplus value from their employees by employers. The second is regional whereby wealth is transferred from peripheral regions to the core regions of the world's economy. This is the power dynamic of the

---

[20] There are a great many forces driving the relentless destruction of the world's forests, many of which were discussed in chapter 3, where the serious environmental consequences of such destruction were also discussed. The governmental pressures and market forces of sugar cane ethanol production are another such force. More and more forest is cut down as more and more acreage is given over to cane production. The positive side of ethanol usage reducing carbon emissions is counter-balanced by this destruction of forest.

net transfer of wealth from countryside to city, from Third World to First, poor country to richer one. Social inequality, a sliding scale of social inequality reaching extraordinary extremes of both wealth and poverty, is thus fundamental to capitalism.

The world economy is not just the economy, it is a political economy. The power relations of the world economy inscribe political relations (including, if need be, military threat and attack) into the economy. The unbridled market dream of neo-liberal ideology is a more utopian dream than socialism ever was. Government interference with the market will always occur because the market always interferes with government. Market protection measures, militarily enforced bad terms of trade and local corruption are all fundamental to the system. The structural power relations of the world economy ensure a disjuncture between the objective interests (principally the interests in maintaining and expanding their own power) of the ruling groups and the collective interests of society. The balance of power ensures that, in the long term, the collective interest always loses out.

These existing relations of inequality and exploitation will continue as the world engages with the twin environmental (global climate change, resource depletion and degeneration) economic (the end of cheap oil and energy) problems of the late carbon economy. The problems will largely be ignored until they cannot be ignored any longer. However, when they do become seriously engaged with, the existing unequal relations of political economic power and its structural dynamic logic will determine that engagement. Would it be possible, for example, to have a reduced consumption, conservationist world capitalism? And the answer to that question sadly is no. Capitalism is driven by a relentless logic of growth. It would certainly be possible to have a happier population with less economic activity, as so much of our present economy is given over to the production of useless and humanly harmful things . . . in a different political economy entirely. But not in this one.

Regardless of the collective insanity of pursuing certain courses of action, they will, nonetheless, be pursued. Oil industry power will continue to oppose sensible change on every level, using all its might in political pressuring and public relations. Efforts at conservation beyond individual altruism will be feeble. The development of alternative energy resources will proceed slowly. Instead, there will be a world-scale political economic and military competition for the reduced supplies of oil. Every effort will be made to maintain both current consumption levels and existing inequalities in standards of living.

What does this mean exactly? It means, first of all, as many commentators have noted, a competition between the US and China as the two biggest consumers of petroleum. But it goes much further than that. As the physical supply side of the world's energy economy contracts while demand grows everywhere, all existing alliances will become strained under the pressures of latent competition. Thus, Europe, Russia, India and the whole rest of the world will be struggling to acquire more than their fair share. A great many of the poorer countries will be struggling even more desperately with their own populations, as their elites try to ensure that their country's rightful share of resources go to their European or Chinese or American "allies."

For oil-producing countries, this struggle will be particularly intense. Who is going to get to use Nigeria's oil supplies? Well, one thing seems clear at least: it is almost certainly not going to be Nigerians. Who will get to use Venezuela's oil? In the present US political climate, connected to the occupation quagmire in Iraq, an invasion of Venezuela may seem very unlikely. It didn't happen earlier in spite of the enormous hostility the Bush administration felt for Chavez. In the future though, the exigencies of expensive oil and economic crisis will change all that. The American people will not allow *their oil* to be consumed by Venezuelan communists, let alone Cubans and the other poverty-stricken Latin Americans Chavez wants to give it away to.

And then, of course, there is the Middle East. The level of existing violence is incredible; but this is no escape valve; the pressure building is immense. It will increase everywhere there is oil and bad government. The future holds a very great deal more terror and war. That is capitalism's only possible response to resource depletion. This last aspect of dystopia will be dealt with and detailed in the penultimate chapter.

The next chapter concerns the role of knowledge and ignorance in the continuance and emergence of dystopia. A crucial point made in this chapter was the interconnection between the economy and governance. The dystopia thesis asserts that our present political-economy has fundamental aspects to it that render it unable to respond to humanity's longer-term interests and keep it firmly on the road to destruction. Ergo, fundamental system change is required. But at present, there is very little evidence of any widespread deep political will for such change. This is because such political will would require a deep understanding of the way our political-economy works and of our collective problems. That such understanding is profoundly lacking is not accidental. The structural relations of knowledge and power prevent it occurring on a widespread level. The next chapter explains these relations in our present and future political economy.

Chapter 6

Structural Mystification and the Failures of Crucial Understanding

> *They keep you doped with religion, sex and T.V.*
> *And you think you're so clever and classless and free*
> *But you're still fucking peasants as far as I can see.*
> John Lennon

> *It is difficult to produce a television documentary*
> *that is both incisive and probing when every twelve*
> *minutes one is interrupted by twelve dancing rabbits*
> *singing about toilet paper.*
> Rod Serling

Introduction: Structural Mystification and Dystopia

> *The supreme art of war is to subdue the enemy*
> *without fighting.*
> Sun Tzu

You are not only multi-tasking, you are also *thinking* about many other things. You are stirring the spaghetti sauce, responding to your eight-year-old daughter's arithmetic homework query, telling your nine-year-old son to stop bothering her, wondering why your husband is late again, thinking about the office politics at work and half-watching and half-listening to the news on TV. The story is about climate change and the criticisms the opposition is making of the Canadian government for its negotiating stance on carbon emissions in Copenhagen. You catch a glimpse of a picture of a drowning polar bear. Apparently, the bears are having a very hard time because of the Arctic meltdown. That part of your mind that was paying attention to the story briefly wanders from its main line to think about bears and fur and snow. It comes back to it to hear a perspective you've heard many times: the experts are not all agreed about global warming. There is a Dr. So-and-So from some university saying it yet again: "It is not absolutely proven that human activity is an important cause of global warming and that it might be part of a natural cycle." You don't believe this "expert" even though you yourself are no expert. The other experts you have heard have quite definitely said global warming really is occurring, that human activity is significantly responsible, and that, if anything, what was wrong with the Kyoto accord was that it did not demand nearly strong enough measures to address a very serious problem and this is even more true now with respect to Copenhagen. You are more inclined to believe this group than the other, but nonetheless you find the fact that even among the experts the subject is still in dispute, curiously reassuring. You are actually more worried about your job, your children's homework, your husband's tardiness and the heating being applied to your gourmet spaghetti sauce, which is beginning to stick to the bottom of the pan. This last is the "warming" problem you are most immediately concerned with.

Dystopia's various future nightmares will come about because the things that could have been done to prevent them will not have been done. These things are not being done because they are difficult. They are not being done because there are powerful forces making sure that they are not being done. What would be required with respect to any of them would be a powerful sense of not only commitment but *urgency*. What would be required to produce the commitment and urgency that translates into the sort of collective will that becomes a political force is deep, confident understanding. The steps necessary to deal effectively with global warming, for example, will not be taken because of millions of people feeling that "yeah, maybe its happening, maybe it's a problem, maybe someone should do something about it." Commitment to action requires deep understanding. It requires clarity with respect to the various levels of complexity as are part of all our serious problems.

The power relations of society are deeply imbricated with its production and dissemination of knowledge, particularly so with respect to questions to do with the power relations themselves and even more particularly so with respect to humanity's most serious problems. Truth and falsity are not most significantly questions of absolutes. We may often find absolute falsity but seldom absolute truth. Truth is rather more a question of degree. Scientific knowledge, for example, is very significantly produced through a refinement of error. Finer and finer refinements of error produce deeper and deeper knowledges. But truth, too, can produce misunderstandings of quite serious consequence. In the scenario sketched above, for example, it is quite true that the "experts" are not *all* agreed upon global warming. The skeptical spokesperson casting doubt upon it could well be both an expert in a relevant field and quite sincere in his pronouncements. Nonetheless, the story as it was presented is not quite right. The consequence of it not being "quite right" repeated millions of times in the mental reception of similarly mystifying media episodes is dystopia.

Knowledge production and dissemination frequently involve conflict. For example, reporters, editors and media conglomerate owners have all been involved in discussions and power plays concerning how to present the global warming issue. The question of "expert" consensus, or the lack thereof, on any given issue is not simply a question of fact. "Do they or don't they all agree?" is a bit too simple a question. How many disagree? How do we actually define "they" in the particular context? Are there any valid reasons as to why we might or might not discount the minority viewpoints of some so-called experts? These, of course, are questions that though they are not necessarily cut and dried with respect to their answers, nonetheless, most often can be answered. Much more significantly with respect to the media dissemination of knowledge is the *power determined decisions* of how to present the issue. The reporter for the story in the scenario above, for example, might have known very well that most respected scientific bodies have little respect for the climate change skeptic's point of view. The reporter may have known very well that the skeptical scientist interviewed has his research consistently funded by an oil or auto manufacturing company, that he is flown all around the country at their expense to discredit "alarmist" stories about carbon emissions. The reporter, though aware that, in an absolute sense, it is true that there is not total scientific consensus about human activity and climate change, nonetheless is aware that most significantly there is. She might personally have felt very strongly that the time has long since passed for including such scientific dissident views in media presentations of the issue. Indeed, the reporter might have regarded the prominent inclusion of the skeptical point of view as ruining the story. But perhaps she was overruled by the editor or even by guidelines put out by the executives high up in the media chain the station belonged to.

The skeptical scientist might well be engaged in conflict as well. This sort of conflict could take many forms. It could involve rhetorical strategies to convince colleagues of his credibility. It could involve secrecy with respect to funding for research. It could take the form of an individual's internal debates as to the morality or not of accepting certain forms of funding. It could involve university pressure to acquire private funding for research, career potential and tenure decisions. Science is certainly not pure. Its institutional battles can involve everything from "office politics," to questions of vanity, ego, conscience, big money and ethics.

The television viewer, radio listener, newspaper and magazine reader, as suggested by the scenario above, come to the stories in a complex fashion as well. The casual readers or listeners are not only impaired from clear critical reception of the media presentation of issues. They are handicapped by previous misconceptions and lack of knowledge. They do not merely intellectually evaluate stories or passively accept them; they do so in an emotionally grounded fashion. That is, the degree of relevance, or again lack thereof, of the various issues to the readers or listeners derives as well from their sense of identity. The harassed mother/wife/cook of the scenario above might well be an SUV owner and somehow feel personally attacked by presentations of global warming issues with implicit criticisms of her lifestyle and consumer choices. Few are aware that this market-choice individuation of collective political issues is itself an important aspect of the mystification of the issues.

The imbrication of emotion with gender, class and ethnic identity, as well as people's lived experiences, profoundly affects the manner in which knowledge is received as well as produced and disseminated. The larger picture is one in which questions of truth, crucially important questions of truth, are intimately bound up with the relations of power in society at large and in the institutions most specifically designed to produce and disseminate knowledge. The way in which we fail to come to deep understandings of our most serious problems is a complicated issue.

The production and dissemination of knowledge most significantly takes place within social institutions. A conflict of interests with respect to relations of power (not always explicit or immediately perceivable) is structurally embedded within these institutions so fundamentally, that one can fairly say that the production and dissemination of knowledge intimately involves a contradictory process of mystification. Structural mystification is this trans-historical dialectical process obfuscating knowledge production and its dissemination. The scientific and social scientific research institutes of government and industry not only produce knowledge, they occasionally outright prevent its production and even more often interfere with its dissemination. The media and educational systems do not simply disseminate knowledge; they frequently restrict the dissemination of such and often work to publicly discredit soundly proven conclusions. In short, all the institutions upon which the public must rely to realize an understanding of our most serious global and local issues frequently generate harmful misunderstandings rather than insight. Structural mystification is thus a powerful force in the realization of dystopia.

Structural mystification is a powerful force in the realization of dystopia but it is a complicated multi-dimensional process that is not easy to fully grasp. We will demonstrate its working in the key institutions designed for the production and dissemination of knowledge in society: the education system and the media. We shall also look at the functioning of the public relations industry. However, before beginning this analysis, we shall endeavor to clarify the theory of structural mystification by putting forward the essential points concerning the relationships of power and knowledge in a more abstract general form.

Structural Mystification and Knowledge

> *It is impossible to make people understand*
> *their ignorance; for it requires knowledge to*
> *perceive it and therefore he that can perceive it*
> *hath it not.*
>   Jeremy Taylor

1) Knowledge is reasonably justifiable true belief.

2) True beliefs are those that correspond *to some degree* with the real characteristics of an independently existing reality.

> i) Truth and falsity are thus most generally relative rather than absolute terms expressing degrees of correspondence.

3) Knowledge is a social product.

> i) It is most usually expressed in language, though sometimes it is embodied in non-linguistic *practices*.

> ii) In either case it is culturally determined.

> iii) New knowledges are always historically dependent to some degree on those which preceded them.

4) The social nature of knowledge production is always directly or indirectly manifest in power relations.

> i) The possession of knowledge is always (at least potentially) an instrument of power.

> ii) Knowledges are institutionally (though not always formally) certified. That is, institutions give their authority to some knowledge claims and deny it to others. They assert what are or are not valid claims; ergo they "certify" what is and is not knowledge.

iii) The process of certification is a contestable one both within and between social institutions. For example, bodies such as the American Medical Association will certify some medical claims as valid that similar institutional bodies in other countries may not and vice versa.

iv) The possibility always exists (and is frequently actualized) that false beliefs (or less-true ones relatively) will be institutionally certified as knowledge and the converse that "truer" beliefs will fail to receive a certification of their status as knowledge.

5) The trans-historical continuity of structured societal inequalities of power continues to ensure a structural contradiction with respect to knowledge production such that the process involves its dialectical opposite: *structural mystification.*

i) The dialectical (as opposed to the logical) nature of this contradiction is that it is manifest in reality *as conflict.* This can be merely latent or actually manifest. It occurs between and within institutions, and between and within individuals. This last point gives a psychological and cognitive dimension to a predominantly sociological and historical phenomenon.

ii) The contradiction is manifest in another form of conflict as well: between belief and reality. As action and practices are undertaken (or conversely not undertaken) the discrepancy between belief and reality will manifest itself as unintended effect (or the lack of intended effect).

iv) Though the phenomenon of structural mystification is trans-historical, in the sense of being constantly present throughout human history to the present, its manifestation has been in historically changing and culturally specific forms. Thus, structural mystification works in a specific fashion in contemporary capitalism. Mass education interacts with an all-pervasive public relations industry and a culturally all-pervasive worldwide mass-media system to ensure the production of ignorance with respect to humanity's most serious problems in a complex sophisticated fashion hitherto unprecedented in human history. Ignorance used to be a much simpler matter. In our contemporary human condition, even the ignorance born of illiteracy is no simple matter of illiteracy.

Before proceeding to specific examples of workings of the relationship between power and knowledge, the theory of structural mystification can be further clarified by a comparison with a simpler kind of theory that does the same explanatory work. This theory, which has been called "the dominant ideology thesis,"[1] contains important elements of truth about the relations of power with disinformation. Yet it is still crucially flawed.

Structural Mystification and the Dominant Ideology Thesis

> *In a time of universal deceit, telling the truth is*
> *a revolutionary act.*
> George Orwell

> *To do evil a human being must first of all*
> *believe that what he's doing is good . . .*
> *Ideology - that is what gives evildoing its long-*
> *sought justification and gives the evildoer the*
> *necessary steadfastness and determination.*
> *That is the social theory which helps to make*
> *his acts seem good instead of bad in his own*
> *and others' eyes, so that he won't hear*
> *reproaches and curses but will receive praise*
> *and honors.*
> Alexander Solzhenitsyn

---

[1] N. Abercrombie, S. Hill and B. S. Turner (1984) *The Dominant Ideology Thesis*. George Allen & Unwin.

The theory of structural mystification conceptually performs the task attempted unsuccessfully in the past by various formulations of what has often been called the "dominant ideology thesis." This sort of thesis gives a causal explanation of the effects of belief and identity formation in the process of domination. Dominant ideology theses explain the legitimation of inequality, for example. Such theories initially seem vary plausible. People accept an enormous lot of horrible things in life because they are tricked into believing that such are inevitable or that such are not horrible at all but actually are good things. People on the bottom of the societal hierarchy accept their position there. People suffering accept their suffering. So, of course, there is considerable truth in this perspective. People are frequently lied to. People are frequently tricked. Nonetheless, there are weaknesses in the dominant ideology thesis arguments.

Structural mystification theory can be distinguished from the various formulations of dominant ideology thesis"(and thus from their shared weakness) by the fact that it is framed *negatively with respect to knowledge acquisition* rather than *positively with respect to belief.* It is the absence of knowledge rather than the adherence to any particular set of ideological beliefs that explains the "collusion" (in this context, now no longer the best choice of words) of the dominated in their own domination. The principal problem with dominant ideology theses is that they translate an enormously complex process into a simple exercise of successful propagandizing. But people believe a lot of very different things, some of them quite plausible though wrong, others absolutely ridiculous. A great many Americans, for example, believe in there having been a government cover-up of visits by extraterrestrials; some of them actually assert that they have been beamed aboard their spaceships and medically experimented upon. It is difficult from within the perspective of the "dominant ideology thesis" to explain the relation of such beliefs to people's collusion in their own domination. However, from the structural mystification perspective, one can actually make such a connection.

Various notions of ideology were employed by Marxists to explain why the Western world's working classes not only failed to *actively* support a class-based socialist revolutionary program but seemed to positively be against such a development. A Marxist formulation of the dominant ideology thesis explains why:

> To consolidate the domination of one class over another for any length of time, it is . . . absolutely essential that the producers, the members of the exploited class are brought to accept the appropriation of the social surplus by a minority as inevitable, permanent and just.[2]

But do the members of the working class (or a significantly large number of them) actually believe that "the appropriation of the social surplus by the minority is inevitable, permanent and just"? To assert that they do, and prove this assertion, would require an empirical study. But a number of questions are immediately raised by the suggestion of such a study. What percentage of the working class is required to positively hold such a belief for it to be considered "significant" enough to prove the thesis? Could the answer to this question be determined simply through a questionnaire? Would the simplest approach to constructing such a questionnaire (i.e., directly putting the question Do you believe the appropriation of the social surplus by a minority is inevitable, permanent and just?) actually get at what we would want to learn? If not, then what alternative questions, or alternative methods to a questionnaire, could be utilized so as to give a confident expectation of discovering the sort of facts which would verify the thesis?

These would appear to be purely methodological questions. But when considered more carefully, they can be seen to have profound theoretical implications. Other questions immediately follow on. For example, how many of the working class understand "profit" in terms of a social surplus? Without engaging in any empirical study, it nonetheless seems probable

---

[2] Earnest Mandel, (1982) quoted in N. Abercrombie, S. Hill and B. S. Turner (1984) *The Dominant Ideology Thesis*. George Allen & Unwin p. 29.

that a large number of people understand profit purely in terms of daily life situations, and thus in purely micro-economic terms. For example, Jo sells a friend a car for $100 more than she paid for it; she also realizes that the corner grocer has a markup on what he sells cat food for. Profit is something she is very familiar with and accepts as a necessary part of daily living. But if this is the case, does that in itself prove that such individuals, by the very fact of their seeing profits in such terms, mean that they have incorporated a ruling-class ideology? Does it make any difference to the initial question that the most usual personal experiences of working-class individuals with those who live on profits rather than wages are with petit-bourgeois small traders, rather wealthy capitalists? On that level, business profits can look very much like a wage. Are many, or most, of the working class, aware that all of what could be considered a "social surplus," is appropriated by a minority? To be aware of income differentials, to know that there are very rich people, is not at all the same as being aware of the distribution of wealth and power.

Income distribution is, in fact, rather misleading with respect to power. This is so, first, because the inequalities of distribution are much more pronounced with respect to wealth. Secondly, a high income does not necessarily securely maintain one's position in the social hierarchy. Illness or redundancy can change a person's life situation very quickly and dramatically. More importantly than these two observations, however, is the fact that it is ownership and control over the means of production that are crucial from a Marxist understanding of class and power. The extraordinary high incomes of corporate CEOs, CFOs and other executives are almost always associated with both personal wealth and stock holdings, as well as decision-making power with respect to corporate resources.[3]

Another question arises from the Marxist version of the dominant ideology thesis quoted above: Why is it necessary to

---

[3] For analysis and statistical detail corroborating these points, see Lundberg, 1968, or any recent issue of *Fortune* magazine for that matter.

conjoin inevitability, permanence and justice? If the present system is just with regard to power relations and distribution of resources, one need not regard it as inevitable or permanent to actively support it, let alone not wish to change it. Similarly, if it is believed to be inevitable, what point could there be to attempt to change it even if it does seem unjust? Logically, it would seem that only one belief or the other is required; yet there is evidence of substantial effort directed at propagandizing variations of both. Mandel's formulation of a dominant ideology thesis is, in part at least, superfluous with respect to what it is supposed to achieve.

For example, the argument is often put that because of human nature capitalism is inevitable. The view is also promulgated that we live in a meritocracy; thus advantage and privilege are deserved. These two commonly propounded arguments are not logically incompatible with one another; but either, in addition to the other, would seem to be superfluous, from the point of view of legitimating the present system. This indicates not coherence but, rather, *incoherence* with regard to the principal points that a dominant ideology would be expected to be achieving in relation to its power maintenance function.

The concept of structural mystification provides an explanation for this lack of coherence by its negative framing. Let us look again at Mandel's dominant ideology proposition, but this time formulated in terms of structural mystification.

> To consolidate the dominance of one class over another for any of time it is absolutely essential that the producers, the members of the exploited class, *be prevented from realizing*: that a minority (ruling class) appropriates the social surplus; that this is unjust and against their interests as a group; that it is certainly not inevitable and need not be permanent . . . if they unite and actively resist this exploitation[4].

This explains what might appear to be the "overkill" of the promulgation of "superfluous" arguments. That is, if the

---

[4] This is in every respect a repetition of Mandel's statement quoted earlier except to make it a negative rather than positive statement.

arguments regarding inevitability and justice are conflated and confused, it is so much the better from the point of view of the working class failing to make an accurate assessment of their position. In fact, all arguments, propositions, half-truths, disinformation, misinformation, lack of information, contradictory beliefs, outdated knowledges or incomplete knowledge, which could be (however indirectly) related to our reworking of Mandel's proposition, serve the same sort of function that a dominant ideology is purported to.

The point is that, rather than a specific set of beliefs that serve ruling-class interests and that are "more powerful, dense and coherent than those of the subordinate classes," it is precisely the weakness, superficiality and lack of coherence of the belief "system" of the dominated class that explains their lack of motivation to organize either a revolution or even much in the way of a reform of existing inequalities. The notion of structural mystification stresses that this lack of coherence in belief, this lack of important knowledge relevant to their exploitation, is neither accidental nor a conspiracy by the ruling class. It is structurally built into the institutions through which knowledge is acquired and disseminated.

Thus far, structural mystification has been explained only in terms of the power relations of class domination, but it is far more than that. The mystification process not only affects the possibility of people coming to understand the realities of class and power, but it is at work with respect to any and all of the power relations in a hierarchically structured society. That is, it is at work mystifying race relations in the United States, gender relations in Saudi Arabia, ethnicity in Bosnia and relations between religious groups in Beirut. It is at work obstructing the understanding of the commodification of natural resources and how such impedes any sensible long-term management of the environment. Basically, the process of structural mystification is always present where it is in the interests of power to obscure the truth. Thus, structural mystification obscures not only awareness of the suffering correspondent with the extremes of inequality in the world but crucially how that inequality interacts with other long-term factors to work against all our common human interests. The contradictory aspect of knowledge production and dissemination ensures that considerable knowledge (both in breadth and depth) of our long-term human predicament is produced and given a limited dissemination throughout the world. But it also ensures, at the same time, that the process of producing that knowledge is misdirected, obstructed and generally mystified and that its distribution is not only severely restricted but presented in a context of considerable disinformation and noise.

Structural Mystification and the Education System

> *The aim of public education is not to spread*
> *enlightenment at all: it is simply to reduce as*
> *many individuals as possible to the same safe*
> *level, to breed a standard citizenry, to put down*
> *dissent and originality.*
> L. Mencken

> *I have never let my schooling interfere with my*
> *education.*
> Mark Twain

Each particular education system has its own unique history and peculiarities, both of its internal organization and its relationship to the wider society. Nor are education systems homogenous. Each country's educational system not only has its own distinct features but also has an extended linkage to other educational systems. Consideration of any particular country's education system has to take into account the fact that, in some respects, the country's education system extends outside the parameters of nationality. This is manifested primarily at the tertiary level and beyond, where there are publications, international conferences, jointly shared research projects, a measure of international acceptance of academic credentials and criteria of judgments, etc. Thus, educational systems are both national and international institutions. As such, they are structurally related to other national and international institutions. These institutions and society's socio-economic political structure more generally exert causal force upon the education system. Nonetheless, the educational system is also, in a sense, self-determining.

The term "relative autonomy" can, at first glance, appear to be an oxymoron. However, the qualifier "relative" when appended to "autonomy," merely qualifies what without such a qualification would denote *absolute independence and self determination*. To say the education system is relatively autonomous, therefore, is to say that it possesses actual autonomy in some spheres of operation. It is to say that its self-governing, self-regulating and controlling aspects are real. It is to say that the institution possesses its own history, the analysis of which explains a very great deal. However, it is also to say that analyses focusing upon this could never be, even potentially, exhaustive as explanations. The institution must be placed in its structural context of cause and effect with respect to other institutions and the power relations of society more generally.

The "events" of an education system's history (as, for example, the organization of a new MA course on feminism and literature, or the recruitment of a large set of students from a particular class background to one university department but not to another) are certainly causally affected by factors outside the institution. But the effects of the wider society upon these "events," as well as upon the internal structuring of the institution, are often mediated by time. This creates a series of "causal displacements" and "time lags," whereby the continuity required by the system's apparent necessity to reproduce itself manifests itself as a defining force to shape that history from "within." This "autonomy," though, is always subject to potential minor or major interference at any time. And further, though perhaps temporally mediated and difficult to perceive in terms of easily identifiable effects, the institution is constantly being affected in a non-disturbing sort of way; this is the cumulative pressure of the totality of its relations with wider social reality. This is only the other side of the same coin: *relative autonomy*. The educational system is always being *co-determined* by its own autonomous history, conventions and principles of organization, *and* the force felt simply by being situated in the wider context of social reality and the specific functional and ideological demands made upon it as an institution from that wider social reality. Thus, the social structure that is any country's educational system is in no way a monolithic static block but rather a dynamic, constantly changing, site of struggle. Knowledge is produced within it. Knowledge is disseminated within it. But attempts to produce knowledge within it are, through bureaucratic and other means, impeded and sometimes completely squashed.

Perhaps most importantly, knowledge dissemination is restricted. Very crucially, the education system operates selection procedures. These procedures are very definitely linked to the hierarchical structure of the political economy. The selection procedures determine who gets to learn what and to what degree of depth. The procedures provide (or refuse) legitimating credentials for the different places students will later come to occupy in the socio-economic hierarchy of their later lives. Most crucially of all, the system does so through procedures that are consistently misrecognized by the participants and that are all the more ideologically effective for that fact. Pierre Bourdieu explains it in his groundbreaking analysis *Reproduction: In Education, Society, and Culture*:

> The agents entrusted with the operations of classification can fulfill their function of social classification only because this is performed *in the guise* of an operation of academic classification, that is, through a specifically academic taxonomy. They successfully perform what they (objectively) have to do only because they *believe* that they are doing something different from what they are actually doing; because they are actually doing something different from what they believe they are doing; and because they *believe* in what they *believe* they are doing. As mystified mystifiers, they are the *first victims* of the operations which they perform.[5] [original emphasis]

---

[5] Pierre Bourdieu (1988), *Reproduction: In Education, Society, Society and Culture*, Sage, p. 207.

The wider power relations of society ensure that the education systems have significant other roles besides the production and transmission of knowledge. The education is directly connected to social stratification and the legitimation of existing social inequality. It goes well beyond merely giving intellectual justifications for a belief in society's essentially just meritocracy, for example. It specifically legitimates the fate of each individual within the alleged meritocracy. Again, Bourdieu provides a succinct explanation of the process:

> The agents themselves have a psychological stake in becoming party to the mystification of which they are the victims - according to a very common mechanism which persuades people (no doubt all the more so the less privileged they are) to work at *being satisfied* with what they have and what they are, to love their fate, however mediocre it may be.[6] [original emphasis]

If the point here perhaps seems somewhat abstract and, for that reason, difficult to comprehend, it can be brought down to Earth through the experiences of a remarkable group of school children, all failures of the Italian school system. These children might well have been victims of the selection procedures of that system but instead came under the tutelage of a remarkable teacher, a priest who helped them gain sociological insight in his one-room schoolhouse. These children learned to think critically, to use statistics through an analysis of the system that had pronounced them failures. The school children of the Barbianna School collectively wrote a remarkable book, *Letter to a Teacher*. They express a very similar analysis to Bourdieu. The fact that they were personally condemned by the system rather than professors perhaps explains their more bitter polemical prose. They sum up their conclusions concerning academic selection and social stratification in a section entitled "Selection Has Reached Its Goal":

---

[6] Ibid. p. 167.

Daddy's boys constitute 86.5 per cent of the university student body; labourers' sons, 13.5 per cent. Of those who get a degree, 91.9 percent are young gentlemen, and 8.1 percent are from working-class families.

If the poor would band together at the university, they could make a significant mark. But, no. Instead, they are received like brothers by the rich and soon are rewarded with all their defects.

The final outcome: 100 percent daddy's boys.[7]

They explain the dynamics of the ongoing process equally colorfully and equally bitterly:

The poorest among the parents don't do a thing. They don't even suspect what is going on. Instead, they feel quite moved. In their time, up in the country, they left school at nine.

If things are not going so well, it must be that their child is not cut out for studying. "Even the teacher said so. A real gentleman. He asked me to sit down. He showed me the record book. And a test all covered with red marks. I suppose we just weren't blessed with an intelligent boy. He will go to work in the fields, like us.[8]

This was Italy of an earlier era. Have things changed significantly? Are countries like the United States any better? Not at all. The inequality reproduction process works, albeit differently organized, in every country, and continues to do so to the present day. For example, Lawrence H. Summers, President of Harvard University, asserted in a 2004 speech that:

In the United States today, a student from the top income quartile is more than six times as likely as

---

[7] The School Children of Barbianna (1970), *Letter to a Teacher,* p. 65.

[8] Ibid. p.34

a student from the bottom quartile to graduate with a BA within five years of leaving high school. And in the most selective colleges and universities, only three percent of students come from the bottom income quartile and only 10 percent come from the bottom half of the income scale.[9]

The education system is simultaneously an agent of power and an agent of truth. Our hierarchically stratified system reproduces itself. The education system plays a key role in that reproduction of inequality and, at the same time, through it procedures and through people's experiences of those procedures, legitimates that reproduction of inequality. It, thus, importantly impedes the realization by people of the manner in which the political economy functions . . . precisely the understanding required to avert dystopia. Yet, at the same time, it also actually produces knowledge . . . including knowledge of how power relations work and how we are moving forward toward dystopia. That is, in its very essence, it is contradictory. The fact of the contradiction makes it all the more efficient in its role as a legitimating mechanism for the social structures that oppress us. We acquire many of our most crucially misleading beliefs not through some system of overt "brainwashing" but rather experientially. That is, amid the falsity, there is always also truth and sometimes the truth of experience.

Imagine simply being told the following: "We live in a meritocratic society. People receive the relative amounts of economic reward according to how hard they work, how talented they and what qualifications they have worked for and possess." Repeated often enough, perhaps the fact of this simply being said might carry some force. But compare that simplistic legitimation process with the one we actually have, as is demonstrated by the following hypothetical scenario.

John and Mary, both of working-class background, take the (British) GCSE English examination. John fails but Mary passes.

---

[9] Lawrence H. Summers, Higher Education and the American Dream, speech given to the American Council on Education 86th Annual Meeting, February 29, 2004.

What are the most obvious explanations each can give to themselves and to each other as to the reasons for their different results? The simplest explanation is that either Mary is smarter (or has greater language proficiency) or worked harder at it than John. John ends up as a casual laborer on and off the dole. Mary ends up an English professor. For each of them, merit is the most obvious explanation for their different financial and status rewards. The fact that Mary and others of the working class *can and do* pass through the educational system makes it difficult to deny the meritocracy of the educational system.

Vertical mobility makes it difficult to deny the meritocracy of the economic system. Thus, the force of arguments about unfairness and inequality in society is severely weakened by the highly publicized experience of those individuals, who like Norman Tebbit are *Upwardly Mobile* (the title of his autobiography[10]). The lived "successes" of the thousands of Marys, as observed by the millions of Johns, is an even stronger support for meritocratic ideology.

Another superficially plausible explanation for the different levels of educational achievement according to class background is a variation of the "culture of poverty" thesis.[11] That is, it is the different *attitudes* towards education held by the different social classes that can explain their differentiation in results. The middle classes value education more highly, are taught to be more ambitious, to work harder, etc. Mary and John, though neither come from a middle-class background, nonetheless probably have personal experiences supportive of this view. They both perhaps believed that Mary did better in the GCSEs because she worked harder than he did. But he didn't try so hard at school because he

---

[10] Norman Tebbit (1988) *Upwardly Mobile*, Weidenfeld & Nicolson.

[11] The culture of poverty theory asserts that not only is there a culture of the poor but that this culture is either an extremely important causal factor in the maintenance of the poor in poverty; or less charitably interpreted, that the "culture of poverty" is *the* explanation for poverty. Oscar Lewis (1959) first developed the theory and coined the phrase.

couldn't see the relevance of the syllabus to his probable future; i.e., he thought he was most likely going to work as a laborer or some other working-class job immediately after leaving school. He believed (correctly, in statistical terms) that there was not a very high probability of him becoming an English professor whether he passed the GCSEs or not. Mary, on the other hand, understandably wishing to appreciate her achievements in terms of her own merit (including her and her family's atypical values) and knowing how much harder she studied than most of her classmates, now, as an intellectual, subscribes to the view that attitudinal change amongst the working class would produce greater educational achievement and hence greater social mobility. Both her experience of "atypical" attitudes towards education, deferred gratification and planning, etc., and her experience of success confirm the meritocracy of the system and a "culture of poverty" sort of theory to explain the inequalities within it.

But what of John's expectations of success within the system? He thought his chances of passing through to its higher levels unlikely and his "career" prospects outside of a traditional working-class job to be minimal. And *objectively, this is correct.* For *his class*, and thus for him as a member of it, the statistical probabilities of his successfully passing through all of the educational system's hoops to reach the position of university professor are small. These probabilities vary from time to time between one country and the next but generally bear out the general assertion. These *objective probabilities* obviously affect *the class's attitude* towards educational attainment. Thus, on the one hand, the objectively accurate intuitions about probabilities of success within the system conditions attitudes towards it; and on the other hand, those exceptions who reach the higher levels of attainment demonstrate that the system is not barred to the working class. Similar objective probabilities (with greater complicating factors) and similar ideological dynamics work with respect to other markers of social inequality (gender, ethnicity and even sexual orientation).

The attitudes and values of the working class toward higher education are grounded in an objective reality that is founded in experience. What to "culture of poverty" theorists is the answer to their search for a neat linear causal connection is, in fact, a vicious circle . . . and worse, it is one from which those who escape from it personally do not usually contribute to a class realization of it, but rather draw the strangling circle even tighter. That is, the working-class background of a professor certainly does not keep him or her from operating the same selective mechanisms of the system as all the rest . . . the same selective mechanisms that over-select his class and serve to reproduce and justify existing inequalities.

Thus, the "class-conscious" working-class (and we could substitute race or gender examples for class here, if we wished) student's comment upon his academic success is misguided: "I try hard because it's important. Not just for me, but for my class. Here at the university I am representing them."[12] Statistically, the mere fact of his or her being at the university at all precisely shows he is not "representative." Implicit in the above quotation is the idea that if he can do well, it will set an example, that others of the class (or ethnic background) will see that educational attainment is possible. That this is *possible* for some individuals is certainly true . . . and there is no shortage of "examples" to point to. But is it possible for all? For many? In fact, is it possible for any more than there actually are?

It has been a constant theme of this book that social inequality and the hierarchical structure of society is a crucial contributing factor to dystopia, and thus, misunderstanding how it is reproduced is a key aspect of the manner in which structural mystification is working against avoiding it. But structural mystification does not only obscure our understanding of inequality. The inequality itself is a part of structural mystification. It works to obscure large numbers of people's understandings of *anything*. Once again, the Barbianna School children express it perfectly:

---

[12] Student at Essex University, UK (1989), name withheld by request.

> You wanted him to repeat the geography of Italy
> for another year. He could have left school without
> ever having heard of the rest of the world. You would
> have done him great harm. Even if he only wants to
> read the newspaper.[13]

The education systems of many countries, both First and Third World, contain elements of excellence. *Some* people really do receive a very good education. But the numbers that do so are severely restricted. The entryway to quality education is frequently directly linked to the economy and a family's position in the socio-economic hierarchy. That is, it is possible to simply buy one's way in. But the system of private schools and Ivy League colleges that exists in the United States, for example, has in addition to the ideological nakedness of simply buying ones way in, of the children of the rich getting the best educations, a supplementary more meritocratic element. Many enter the Ivy League based solely upon the merit of past performance. Some even arrive from the poorer (both in the sense of money and quality of education) public schools. It is the elements of *real* meritocracy that makes the education system so effective as the economic system's legitimating device. Structural mystification and *real* education are actually but flip sides of the same coin. Perhaps the greatest amount of important human knowledge is produced in exactly those institutions that do the most to ideologically mystify and confuse.

The First World has now in its entirety embraced the concept of mass education, indeed even mass *tertiary education*. One might think that, with such well-educated populaces, it would be very hard indeed to pull the ideological wool over their eyes, so to speak. And yet America, with one of the largest inclusion rates in "higher" education, has one of the worst-educated populations . . . at least if you take their "democratic" political choices as any measure of their education level. Americans seem passively content with their four-year choice between Tweedledum and

---

[13] The School Children of Barbianna (1970). *Letter to a Teacher*, p. 23.

Tweedledee for their president, and more often than not choose the "dumb" one of the two. What is the explanation for this? Is mass education a failure? The answer is contradictory. It depends upon what the objective of it was. If the objective was truly to obtain a well-educated general public, then, of course, it is certainly a failed project. Education is so obviously underfunded (this sweeping statement would apply to almost any country one might care to speak of) that it is hard to believe that that was ever the serious intention. If, on the other hand, however, the intention was to continue to provide good education and training to some and to simply adjust an economic hierarchy reproduction mechanism (and ideologically justify it at the same time!), then the mass education experiment carried out throughout the First World has been a resounding success.

Structural mystification works through a process of experiential (mis)understanding to arrive at various mistaken views of how the world works. This is best demonstrated by the education system. But structural mystification also works in a somewhat less subtle fashion. It works *directly* through a production of alleged "facts," "knowledges" and "reasoned opinion." This process, of course, is made all the easier by the fact that the reception of misinformation, disinformation, half-truths, misleading truths and downright lies is received by a poorly educated public. Various sorts of overt propaganda are constantly dished up for an audience that has been *trained* to accept what they have been told uncritically, at the same time as they have been trained to have the attention span of a goldfish. The next section that deals with the public relations industry thus must be read with the understanding that its more overt means of deception and mystification interacts with the structural mystification side of the educational process.

Capitalism and Knowledge of Capitalism: Utopia Now?

*Knowledge is the only instrument of production
that is not subject to diminishing returns.*
John Maurice Clarke

*Education . . . has produced a vast population
able to read but unable to distinguish what is
worth reading.*
G.M. Trevelyan

Imagine a future utopia where informed and critical consumers make ethical choices concerning their purchase of commodities. Imagine a world where myriad individuals concerned about social justice, safety, poverty, sweatshops and vile dictatorships make thoughtful, morally guided investment choices. Perhaps many readers feel they do not need to imagine such a world; they believe that just as dystopia already exists in the present, so too does what is being called here a "utopia." "Socially responsible investing" is already a huge business and growing faster than all others. There are many and various "socially responsible" mutual investment funds. There exists an American organization founded 1992 by 54 politically and morally "progressive" corporations: Business for Social Responsibility. So, have we achieved at least a small step toward combating some of the ills of the dystopia of the present and future?

It is, of course, a sign of something good in humankind that people would prefer not to invest in child exploitation, torture implements, toxic pollution and suchlike evils. But the dystopia thesis is not that people are bad, morally indifferent, uncaring folk. Even those who perhaps might appear to be the most cynical with respect to such matters usually have that cynicism taught them as a good strategy for survival in a competitive world. No, the hope for corporate responsibility and the intention to invest ethically may well be genuinely laudable features of people's personalities and values . . . it is merely that the belief that such actually exists is dangerously naïve. It is the widespread belief in such that is a part of dystopia and a cause of suffering in the present and probable greater pain in the future.

The previous chapter explained the logic of the world's political economy. There is a disjuncture between individual intention and collective consequences. Corporations, legal entities with even more "rights" than people do not possess values. Or rather, they possess no values but one: the *maximization of profit*. Corporations may *profess* values; indeed they frequently do, but that is something altogether different. The fact that these things about capitalism are not widely understood is not at all surprising though. In addition to the creation of a gullible populace, that is, a population significantly *trained not to think critically*, there is an entire industry whose sole purpose is to confuse, mystify, misinform and emotionally seduce them into a mistaken understanding of the system in which they live. Socially responsible investing and corporate social responsibility are entirely products of the advertising and public relations industry.

The Natural Capital Institute founded by Paul Hawken produced a "social audit" of "socially responsible investing (SRI) mutual fund firms." The conclusions reached suggest that "socially responsible" is no more than a public relations label. The findings are instructive.[14] The cumulative investment holdings of the SRI funds examined in the audit are virtually identical to those held by conventional mutual investment funds. Particular fund names and literature are often deceptive. The screening methodologies and exceptions employed by most of these firms allow practically any publicly held firm to be included in a "socially responsible investment fund." And they are. Ninety percent of Fortune 500 companies are included in these ethically responsible investment firms' portfolios. The environmental screens used by portfolio managers are loose and do little to protect the environment. This is not surprising, as the language

---

[14] Paul Hawken and the Natural Capital Institute (2004,) *Socially Responsible Investing: How the SRI Industry Has Failed to Respond to People Who Want to Invest with Conscience and What Can Be Done to Change It.* NCI: Sausalito.

used to describe these funds, including the term "SRI" itself, is vague and indiscriminate and leads to misperception and distortion of investor goals. In other words, socially responsible investment funds are merely material artifacts of structural mystification. They are mystification commodified, a mistaken view of capitalism sold as an investment strategy.

> We believe that striving to obtain the highest rate of financial return is a direct cause of social injustice and environmental degradation, as it consistently leads to an externalization of costs of the environment, the future, workers, or other peoples. Colonization, imperialism, slavery, and most wars are directly attributable to oligarchies trying to achieve the highest return on investment. How the SRI industry came to believe that it could use the same standard to reverse those ills may have more to do with marketing than philosophy.[15]

Indeed, the dystopia thesis would assert it is precisely to do with marketing. SRI is *entirely* a product of the public relations industry. This is further than either Paul Hawken or the Natural Capital Institute would wish to go. It is a measure of the power of structural mystification that even those who thoroughly research a topic seem unwilling to accept the real conclusion of that research and balk at the final hurdle, so to speak, and end up with a hopeful idealistic endorsement of some future good behavior of those who they have just critically cut to ribbons. For example, Hawken writes:

> If every company on the planet were to adopt the best environmental practices of the leading companies – say, for example, Ben & Jerry's, Patagonia or 3M – the world would still be moving toward sure degradation and collapse.[16]

---

[15] Ibid.

[16] Paul Hawken (1993), *The Ecology of Commerce: A Declaration of Sustainability*, Harper-Business.

And then he contradicts this harsh conclusion with statements like the following:

> We believe that with education and connectivity, the current downward spiral of environmental and social conditions, can be arrested and that a just and restorative economy is possible.[17]

This last statement obviously is in *direct contradiction* to the dystopia thesis. Perhaps it may simply be regarded, or indeed the whole positive philosophy of the Natural Capital Institute may be regarded, as an admirable "optimism of the will," which is actually not a contradiction of the dystopia thesis. The dystopia argument is entirely an analytical assessment of the odds against humanity, rather than a call to defeat without a struggle. No, where the analysis and perspective of the Natural Capital Institute seem to be dubious is where they take perfidious behavior to be *accidental* rather than an *intrinsic* part of the system. The dynamic logic of "striving to obtain the highest rate of financial return" is not the hallmark of "nasty capitalist enterprise" or "evil capitalist enterprise" or "particularly ruthless capitalist enterprise." It is *the* logic of capitalism. Striving for anything less is simply the logic of a failed, or a soon to fail, capitalist enterprise . . . or a PR stunt . . . or a pitch for a liberal conscience niche market.

Cruelty Without Beauty

> *Capitalism is the astounding belief that the most wickedest of men will do the most wickedest of things for the greatest good of everyone.*
> John Maynard Keynes

---

[17] Vision statement, Natural Capital Institute Website: http://www.naturalcapital.org/

Perhaps more than any other company that exists, if not in the world, in the UK at least, The Body Shop and its founder Anita Broddick embody the notion of a politically progressive business. That is, it is not just a business that happens to be politically progressive but rather a company whose politically "right-on" attitudes and (alleged) practices are intrinsic to its undoubted financial success. The Body Shop evolved from a single-store, shop-front small business to an international conglomerate of franchises. Its success was fueled from the very beginning by the perception of social responsibility . . . in the first case, with respect to animal testing – the inspiration for the famous advertising slogan "Beauty Without Cruelty" – but later extending to Third World labor practices, and other environmental and social justice issues. If it only it were true!

The Body Shop's success was built upon the public perception of its social responsibility. Producing such perception is not necessarily easy. It requires careful planning and strategy. It requires creativity. It requires an advertising and public relations campaign. This is not necessarily easier than actually being socially responsible, but it is more effective. Actually being socially responsible would mean decisions being consistently determined according to a criterion that was *not* the maximization of profit . . . which, from the dystopia perspective upon capitalism at least, is the sure road to bankruptcy. PR entails no such (financial) negative outcome; PR is very good for business.

The following propositions about The Body Shop are all widely believed as a result of the PR work that was done:

1) The Body Shop treats its employees fairly both in the First and Third World.

2) The Body Shop acts in accordance with a strong sense of social justice.

3) The Body Shop is *honest* in its financial dealings with respect to both its own franchisees and the wider world of business.

4) The Body Shop respects the environment and is non-polluting.

5) The Body Shop uses natural ingredients in its products.

6) The Body Shop does not engage in animal testing.

The above assertions are not *all* false. They do not engage in animal testing, for example. However, while animals are certainly still used for testing of a great many things, the cosmetic industry *as a whole* has long since abandoned it . . . before The Body Shop won so much public approval for refusing to engage in it. They *do* use natural ingredients in their products; however, they do so in combination with various chemical agents. They are merely getting enormous positive PR because of an incorrect assumption by the public; i.e., that they use *100 percent* natural ingredients. This is not ever directly stated; it is merely implied. That they do use "non-natural" ingredients is not necessarily a bad thing, as some chemicals are much safer for use upon human skin. But The Body Shop does not merely refuse to engage in animal testing; it fails to engage in sufficient health and safety testing to properly ensure the safety of its products. It exploits Third World labor and abuses its own franchise owners. It regularly simply dumps its plastic and other waste products in landfills. In short, image and reality are very different.

The Body Shop is as ruthless as any other corporation, perhaps even more so. The flip side of producing an enchanted positive image is aggressively attacking any who would critique it. The above counterclaims and criticisms of The Body Shop all come from an article by Jon Entine,[18] and though he was able to support his claims with evidence – most of it from disgruntled Body Shop employees and franchise owners – and also won an award from

---

[18] Jon Entine (1994),"Shattered Image: Is the Body Shop Too Good to Be True?" *Business Ethics,* and also see the website: http://www.jonentine.com/body_shop.htm

the National Press Club, he was legally prosecuted and generally harassed and had articles suppressed from publication.[19]

The Public Understanding of Science

> *Formerly, when religion was strong and science weak, men mistook magic for medicine; now, when science is strong and religion weak men mistake medicine for magic.*
> Thomas Szasz

> *Science can be introduced to children well or poorly. If poorly, children can be turned away from science; they can develop a lifelong antipathy; they will be in a far worse condition than if they had never been introduced to science at all.*
> Isaac Asimov

The flip side to the power-determined manipulation of perception through falsity is the intrinsic power of truth itself. It has its own force. And yet, in addition to the imbalance in resources, even some of the intrinsic power of truth is removed from it because of the complex interaction of the different institutions involved with knowledge dissemination, e.g., the education system and the public relations industry. Not only the public at large, but many scientists and scholars as well, are rather naïve in their understandings of science and just what should count as knowledge. This naivety is the source of a great deal of misunderstanding in itself and further gives a huge opening to the manipulation of public opinion by the public relations industry.

Truth, as said before, possesses its own intrinsic power. Science derives its enormous prestige and authority because of its connection to that intrinsic power of truth. One must have a correct understanding of physics and a number of other sciences and correctly apply that understanding to the building of a bridge

---

[19]http://dir.salon.com/story/books/review/2004/07/26/killed/index.html?pn=3

or a skyscraper or an airplane . . . otherwise they fall down or crash. Ergo, science's great authority as a producer of knowledge is largely deserved. One can set science up in opposition to ideology with respect to truth, and yet one is beginning to tread upon dangerous and potentially misleading ground here. The relationship between science, truth and ideology is tricky. Science is not a guarantee of truth. Science not only sometimes errs, it errs ideologically. That is, it is manipulated by money and power. This is made all the easier by the general public's over-simplified view of "truth," "facts," "probabilities," "theories" and so on.

Truth is not usually a matter of absolute certainty, and that is also frequently the case with scientific knowledges. That something is "only a theory" should not be grounds for dismissing its significance. There are good theories and bad theories. There are theories that are brilliant in their simplicity and logic and well supported by masses of evidence. Probabilities are sometimes facts about which we can be absolutely certain, and sometimes merely wild guesses. All of this means that most of the most interesting scientific questions are subject to ongoing debate and refinement. The existence of this debate, perhaps the most intellectually healthy component of scientific discourse, is frequently exploited by those who wish to mislead the public. We find within the perfectly healthy struggle for truth an ideological component to science itself.

Thus it is that the institutional workings of structural mystification are not uni-causal and limited to the relatively autonomous workings of single institution but rather causally interact to obscure understanding of important issues. The uneducated, poorly educated and "educated" (yes the quotation marks are there to signal irony) public's understanding of science derives from the educational institutions they have been through. But these confused notions of scientific practices, criteria of judgment and epistemology interact with a sometimes prostituted and debased scientific practice, which is itself ideological. This, already murky grip upon key issues is then engaged with by a cynical, clever and well-financed public relations industry, which works to further confuse them, most often intentionally.

In chapter 3, for example, the debates about global warming were considered. The global scientific consensus (by any reasonable measure of such) now asserts its existence as a fact, and further, attributes a significant element of human causality to the phenomenon. But the consensus is far from unanimous. There are a number of possible reasons for that, and it is actually likely that all of them are, in fact, part of the debate's past and present state of play. First, it may simply be the case that some scientists, purely for reasons of evidence and argument, are quite reasonably skeptical and reject the conclusions of most of their fellows. Truth is not necessarily a matter of consensus. However, much of the evidence upon which these scientists base their conclusions very likely would not exist were it not for the fact that the research that produced this evidence was guided by relations of power and money. Science costs money; very often it costs a very great deal of money. The outlay of this money frequently derives from elements with a vested interest in certain conclusions. The search for the "truth" about global warming is not a disinterested search for truth. Indeed, we can see this search for truth as, in some sense, a kind of contest between the largest amount of evidence and a strong money-driven desire to find things to contradict it. Thus, the evidence convincing the skeptics was produced only because it was searched for so much, directed by the power of money . . . and yet, one could say, precious little was found in spite of that. Nonetheless, all of the skepticism concerning global warming and its human causation is not *totally* without foundation.

There are two further elements underpinning the skeptical perspective upon global warming. Scientific commentators, scientific journalists, pronounce upon the subject publicly. The skeptics among this group are well-funded, again by vested interests. They are not lying when they assert that there is less than a unanimous conclusion in the scientific community upon the issue. They are not lying when they say there is some evidence supporting the skeptical point of view. They are not lying when they say that they themselves are skeptical and that they are scientists concerned with the issue. Nonetheless, in spite of all this "truth" with respect to the issue, the public is being misled. One can be a scientist and pronounce upon debates outside of one's specialty of expertise. One can over-exaggerate the lack of consensus. It doesn't take much to confuse a public that assumes science deals in black and white and absolute truth. The human causes of global warming become "just theories," not "facts."

Finally, we have the least interesting, and usually the least effective as well, way in which skepticism is generated: outright lies and simple propaganda. It is usually the least effective because it is the most easily combated by simple truth and the revelation of its falsehoods. In the case of science, as in the media and education system, structural mystification works most effectively through partial truths rather than complete falsity.

The Global Climate Coalition is an industry funded scientific public relations group. In their self-description they assert:

> Science must serve as the foundation for overall global climate policy decisions, and enhanced scientific research must be the first priority. A bedrock principle addressing global climate change issues is that science – not emotional or political reactions – must serve as the foundation for global climate policy decisions.[20]

But actually, they simply provide public platforms for the handful of scientists who are skeptical of the consensus that there is a human influence on the global climate. As SourceWatch claims:

> These scientists generally do not participate in the accepted process of publishing research in refereed journals in order to test hypotheses and conclusions. They also generally do not have expertise in the topic. Moreover, the GCC went even further than just providing public relations services for these skeptic scientists.

---

[20] *AccuWeather's Science for Hire,* SourceWatch.
http://www.sourcewatch.org/index.php?title=Accu-
Weather%27s_science_for_hire

They also attacked credible and preeminent scientists who are experts in the field.[21]

Structural mystification works on yet another level as a causal factor for dystopia. To avert the dystopia, to even mitigate significantly the suffering of the present, requires strong political action. Considerable confidence in people's understanding would be required to generate the requisite political will. The majority of people in the United States now believe that global warming is: a) real, b) a very serious problem and c) significantly caused by human activity. There is as yet, however, no serious political outrage over the US's refusal of the Kyoto accord. The activity of GCC and other suchlike institutions, even if they fail to persuade people of their skeptical perspective, nonetheless undermines the confidence of the public in the other side. The public, too, has a vested interest in disbelieving many things. Whether to do with global warming or many of the other dystopian phenomena and trends, the First World affluent public has an inbuilt inertia. To recognize it fully would be to grasp a sense of enormous urgency for change, and to change in such a fashion as to forgo a good deal of their comfortable illusion fueled lifestyle.

Climate change and carbon emissions are not, of course, the only arenas of public life in which science is ideologically manipulated through power and money. The American Council on Science and Health is a good example of the institutional workings of structural mystification in the field of health in relation to the food-processing and chemicals industries. The very name of the corporate-funded organization contributes to mystification because it attaches to itself the authority of science. It claims to be independent and has non-profit status. It has any number of scientists whose names are attached to it. But it works just like the Global Climate Coalition. That is, they attack credible scientists and their reports, but yet seldom subject themselves to the rigor of the peer review publishing process that is the judgmental touchstone of more respectable scientists.

---

[21] Ibid.

In fact, the examples of organizations seemingly dedicated to the sole pursuit of structural mystification are too numerous to mention. It is necessary to take a step back to analytically describe the workings of the process as a whole in its relation to dystopia.

For Love or Money: Structural Mystification and Political Struggle

> *Today's PR industry is related to democracy in the same way that prostitution is related to sex.*
> From *Toxic Sludge Is Good for You*
> John Stauber and Sheldon Rampton

> *The fact that corporations and governments feel compelled to spend billions of dollars every year manipulating the public is a perverse tribute to human nature and our own moral values.*
> Also from *Toxic Sludge is Good for You*

Image most often can trump reality . . . at least for a time. We can measure their relative power – or at least we can get some sense of it – through a comparison of expenditure. A small group of under-resourced investigative journalists like Jon Entine (mentioned earlier in relation to The Body Shop) go up against a huge *industry* in the struggle of truth against misleading image. The revenues for the US public relations industry exceeded $2.9 billion in 2002,[22] for example. This is actually a very conservative estimate; others reach as high as $10 billion a year on average in recent times[23].

---

[22] Council of PR Firms (2002) press release, 22-4, quoted in: http://www.corporatewatch.org.uk/?lid=1570

[23] John Stauber and Sheldom Rampton (1995), *Toxic Sludge Is Good for You: Lies, Damn Lies and the Public Relations Industry*, Common Courage Press, p. 13.

This enormous expenditure is not so alarming . . . until things are put in their proper perspective in relation to dystopia, until we understand what the public relation industry *really* is. Yet the few billions of dollars of annual public relations expenditure should actually be seen as more alarming than the many billions of dollars spent on the war research and weaponry, which will be considered in the next chapter. This is because of the simple reason that, were it not for the workings of structural mystification, such misguided direction of human intelligence and energy would not be possible.

Structural mystification, as this chapter has shown, as the analysis of the education system has shown, can be extremely subtle and complex in its forms and activity. However, it can also be very simple. There are two sides to the public relations industry. One side essentially is nothing more or less than the production of structural mystification in its simplest form: that of direct lies, disinformation and deliberately sown seeds of confusion and doubt.

Public relations has its relatively benign and innocent side. Public relations firms work to get positive publicity for their clients. They draw to the public's attention all sorts of information concerning good aspects of products, companies and policies. They try to downplay media exposure to undeserved critical attacks and occasional bursts of ignorant public hysteria about issues relevant to their clients. A description, somewhat along these lines, is often how individual public relations firms and the industry as a whole describes themselves and their activity. They would assert they are providing a service . . . directly to their clients, of course, but also, indirectly to the public at large. The service is disseminating information. The service is one of the production and dissemination of knowledge. And there is *some* truth in this. However, it is also true that it is a very small portion of truth attached to very small amount of their activities. The rest is given over to mystification.

The public relations firm of Mongoven, Biscoe and Duchin, though occupying a specialist niche in the public relations field, nonetheless exemplifies the relationship between the industry as a whole and dystopia. They describe their own activities in the following fashion:

> [MBD] assists corporations in resolving public policy issues being driven by activist organizations and other members of the public interest community. We help clients anticipate and respond to movements for change   in public policy which would affect their interests adversely . . . Forces for change often include activist and public interest groups, churches, unions and/or academia . . . MBD is committed to the concept that it is critical to know who the current and potential participants   are   in   the   public   policy   process,   to understand their goals and modus operandi, and to understand their relative importance. To this end, MBD maintains extensive files on organizations and their leadership. [24]

According to MBD documents,[25] the issues they engage with include:

> . . . acid rain, clean air, clean water, hazardous and toxic wastes, nuclear energy, recycling, South Africa, the United Nations, developments in Eastern Europe, dioxin, organic farming, pesticides, biotechnology, vegetarianism, consumer groups, product safety, oil spills.

This may seem to some as a pretty eclectic list of issues of interest. Well, it is certainly by no means a comprehensive list of dystopian problems; but just to put it in perspective, and to give an indication of whose side they are on and to what use the information they compile is put, the South Africa they were researching was *apartheid* South Africa and the client was Shell.

The dystopia thesis is a reasoning chain accompanied by a mass of diverse yet awful facts leading to a painfully dire

---

[24] "The Truth About Breast Cancer: Part 2," *Rachel Environment and Health Weekly* #572, November 13, 1997.
http://www.corporations.org/cancer/r572.doc

[25] Quoted in J. Stauber and S. Rampton ,*Toxic Sludge Is Good for You,* p. 54.

conclusion. Structural mystification is a key point in the reasoning chain. The urgent and necessary changes required to ameliorate the suffering deriving from poverty and disease and various forms of sometimes violent enslavement, the drastic measures required to solve a host of environmental problems, the policies required to achieve peace and security etc., etc., etc., all the problems facing us, require a large-scale intelligent dramatic change of direction. A host of committed individuals have banded together to form organizations to attempt to broaden and deepen understanding of these various issues and to attempt to generate the political will for the requisite changes. MBD's self-described mission is to spy on such people and organizations . . . and (though unstated, but nonetheless implicit) to discredit them and their activities, thus *preventing change.*

Preventing change that would do what? The dystopia thesis gives a dual connected answer: 1) preventing change that would adversely affect the profits of their clients in the short or long term, and 2) preventing change that would save the world from its horrendous dystopian future.

Could they accomplish this on their own? No, the imbrication of knowledge and power that produces their little niche of political war on those who would save the world from any of its horrendous problems is not carried on in a vacuum. Yes, it takes billions of dollars to deceive and disarm the public; ignorance and apathy are not conditions of the baseline of human awareness upon which knowledge and motivation might be planted; rather, ignorance and apathy are conditions that are *produced.* They are produced in and by the media. They are produced by the educational system. They are produced by the public relations industry. The various present and future horrors of dystopia would be ameliorated or prevented were it not for structural mystification. There certainly is evil in the world. But the evil of the world is not the most significant generator of evil in the world; that causal pride of place must be allotted to ignorance; though, of course, when that ignorance is structurally generated and the effects so painful and catastrophic, one perhaps might well be justified in naming the structures themselves as evil.

In the next chapter, some of the most "evil" aspects of the human condition will be considered: torture, and terror and war. Such terrible instances of such as are occurring now will interact with the other trends that have been examined in this book. They will mutually exacerbate one another in ways that are both complex and frightening. Albert Einstein, when once asked about the weaponry of the wars of the future, famously asserted that if there was to be a nuclear third world war, we could be certain that any fourth world war would be fought with sticks and stones. The dystopia thesis does not predict a total nuclear holocaust, though such is a real possibility. The dystopia thesis does not predict a third world war. Rather it predicts wars . . . wars all over the world. It asserts the third world wars have already begun. It considers the possibilities of any number of them going nuclear. It suggests a future depopulated planet where nascent low-level conflict with crude weaponry could well be remaining dregs of humanity's fate.

Chapter 7

War of the Worlds: Insecurity, Terror and Torture

*You can't say that civilization don't advance,
however, for in every war they kill you in a
new way.*
>Will Rogers

*Ah, this is obviously some strange usage of
word "safe" that I wasn't previously aware of.*
>Douglas Adams

Introduction: The Quality of Barbarity

*Every gun that is made, every warship launched,
every rocket fired signifies, in the final sense, a
theft from those who hunger and are not fed, those
who are cold and not clothed. This world in arms
is not spending money alone. It is spending the
sweat of its laborers, the genius of its scientists,
the hopes of its children.*
>Dwight D. Eisenhower

You are a policeman, and you are filled with righteous anger. The terrorist is responsible for the killing of dozens of innocent women and children. You are ready to tear him apart. "Just give five minutes in a room alone with him Sarge," you say.

You've been watching too much TV. Unfortunately, Donald Rumsfeld had also been watching too much TV. Unfortunately, the American public has watched too much TV. Many people actually think in clichés.

So, five minutes in a room with the evil terrorist; what're you going to do? You're going to mash his face pretty good. You're going shout a lot and call him names while you do so. If only the nasty liberals would stop protecting the criminals, we would all sleep safer in our beds. But this is where the television fantasy departs from reality. It is not that the cliché of the "gimme five minutes with him" is untrue. No, that mentality is alive and well and very widespread. No, it is that the power of the liberals to restrain such people and protect civil liberties is very much exaggerated. No, the liberal is not actually even there to "baby" the terrorists. The rules of decency and civilization and law are not there to protect the terrorists. The rules of decency and civilization and law are no longer there even to protect the innocent. Five minutes, some name-calling and vicious kicking and punching? Five minutes!! No, if you are a torturer, you've been given weeks, months, years even, to do *whatever* you like. You have a budget for tools, access to scientific knowledge and were trained as well as encouraged to be imaginative with respect to the infliction of pain. "Getting him to talk" might serve more of an intelligence purpose perhaps, if you spoke their language, but you don't. "Intelligence" might once have even been the justification. But now it seems more just like revenge . . . or perhaps not even that. Torture becomes an end in itself. You were given a choice between civilization and barbarism. You chose barbarism.

It is worth recalling, at this point, some of the lessons from the past from chapter 3. The example of Uruguay's decent into barbarity shows how fragile and easily discarded are the democratic institutions that protect our human rights; it also showed how dehumanized and dehumanizing torturers are produced. Barbarism is a social product. But in the My Lai case study, there was courage and humanity, as well as barbarism. Some people committed the war crimes; others tried to stop them. It is worth stating again that the dystopia thesis is not about good and bad individuals. The world has plenty of both. The former perhaps provide us with a sense of human redemption. But the dystopia thesis is about *structural forces*. We can recall that those responsible for the My Lai massacre received little in the way of consequences. We can recall that those who refused orders, and those who actively intervened to protect the weak and innocent, were severely punished. That is the structural reality underlying atrocity. It is the reality sometimes recognized in the past (the assembly-line element to the Holocaust) or in various depictions of more current enemies (Saddam Hussein being the most recent with regard to the *systematic* gassing of the Kurds) but never with respect to our own present day barbarities . . . these are always portrayed as aberrations.

This chapter deals with the intensification of conflict that the future is going to bring. It deals with the expansion of the surveillance society, with torture and the erosion of civil liberties, which derive from the War on Terror. The chapter also explores the motivation for terror and propounds an unpopular argument concerning the base causes of it, as well as for war itself. Once again, social inequality and the internal logic of capitalism provide the key to understanding a very great deal of what is horrendous now and for the greater horrors which are to come. Many people can fully condemn cruelty yet be willing to acquiesce to the use of torture by the authorities in the name of expediency in the face of the greater evil of terrorism. Such people shudder when they consider the possibility of such being inflicted upon the innocent; but again can be persuaded to accept it as a necessary evil.

But we can, or at least we should be able to, empathize with the pain inflicted upon people whether innocent or guilty. We should be able to rationally reflect upon the facts that torture does not have a proven track record of effectiveness in subduing rebellions. We should be able to reflect upon the fact that in the torture chamber it is not only the tortured who lose their humanity but the torturer as well.

Torture and Terror: A Moral Evaluation

> *The healthy man does not torture others —*
> *generally it is the tortured who turn into*
> *torturers.*
> Carl Jung

This is likely to be the most controversial section of a book that is full of controversial stances. The argument is that torture is seldom, if ever, morally justifiable; while frequently terrorism is.

Let us imagine an evil terrorist has planted three nuclear bombs in three large cities. If you can just twist his testicles with enough savagery, he will tell you where the bombs are, so that they can be defused and millions of lives saved. This is essentially the plot of the recent Hollywood film *Unthinkable*.[1] It is, of course, ideologically loaded. We are supposed to carry this moral justification through to Abu Graib and Guantanamo Bay. But these American political prisons (torture chambers?) are, for one thing, located in other people's countries. Surely the how and the why of that fact must play some moral bearing upon the situation. Are these prison guards (torturers?) saving millions of lives with their twists of the testicles. Well, the ideological implication is that that is always exactly what it is about. Invasion, occupation, subjugation, policing, torture . . . they are always ostensibly about protection, about security.

Maybe one could morally justify torture to save millions of lives, but that is *never* what it is *really* about. No, it is more closely something like this question: Is torture morally justifiable for slightly cheaper gasoline prices in California. Torture is a form of warfare, particularly barbaric warfare, but warfare is itself barbaric. If we are working out moral justifications, we need to work out the various motivations between the sides involved in the war. . . and the War on Terror is no exception.

Torture and terror go together. The militarily stronger side uses torture; the militarily weaker side uses terror. That should tell us something in itself. Iraqis use IEDs. They are terrorists. Americans torture Iraqis. But who is in whose country and why?

Those who are conquered and occupied, those who are colonized, sometimes use terror. It is called "terror" for ideological reasons on the one hand, and a practical recognition of military weakness on the other. "Terrorists" plant bombs in stores and parked cars and cafes and beside the roadside because they lack an air force. They attack isolated police stations or small army patrols because they lack a large well-equipped modern army; or as in the cases of Iraq or Afghanistan, for example, the

---

[1] *Unthinkable* (2010) ChubbCo Film.

army has already been defeated. In the film *Battle of Algiers,*[2] which dealt with the Algerian war of independence, a captured rebel leader is asked, in the press conference that followed his arrest, how he can possibly justify having women carry baskets with bombs to explode in cafes full of innocent civilians. His answer is that he would gladly trade his basket-bomb-carrying women for the French air force (which, of course, had a much higher death toll in its bomb usage).

But the ideological framing of terror is never presented as a political-military struggle between disparately matched forces. No, the terrorist act is considered politically (and thus morally) illegitimate. In fact, frequently the political dimensions of the act are ideologically suppressed in their presentation. The Irish Republican Army's (IRA) struggle and usage of violence is a perfect example of this. The IRA and Sinn Fein (the political party for which the IRA was the military wing) understood Ireland as a colony of Britain (Ireland was Britain's *oldest* colony in fact); they were struggling for national liberation. The official British governmental stance was that all the acts of political violence carried out by the IRA were not really political at all but were merely reprehensible *criminal* acts. The prison hunger strikes led by Bobby Sands were over the issue of the classification of rebel prisoners. Sands, Sinn Fein and the IRA insisted they were *political* prisoners of a liberation war. The British government insisted they were simply common criminals breaking the law.

One can view the arguments over the moral justification of terrorism to some extent in relation to this debate. The IRA used violence, ergo they were criminals; their nationalistic aspirations were irrelevant; the conquest and colonial history of Ireland were irrelevant. But Bobby Sands, while in prison, was elected to the British parliament. Though, of course, he never took his seat. Instead he fasted unto death. The practical winner of this debate was the British government of course. Sands' election, Sands' fast

---

[2] *Battle of Algiers* (1966) directed by Gillo Pontecorvo is considered a classic.

were irrelevant. They had the power; they had the physical force; they had the edge in capacity for violence. But it also seems equally clear as to who won the moral debate; Sands' actions and those of his comrades were clearly and obviously political.

The Cause of Torture and Terror, the Cause of War

> *Of all the preposterous assumptions of humanity*
> *over humanity, nothing exceeds most of the*
> *criticisms made on the habits of the poor by*
> *the well-housed, well-warmed, and well-fed.*
> Herman Melville

This section will offer an explanation of the cause of torture and terror and war. It will outrage many intellectuals for its "simplistic economic determinism." But though it argues that the structural forces of capitalism are the ultimate cause of these phenomena, the explanation is anything but simple. Race, ethnicity, gender, sexuality, religion, language, culture and nation are all factors that overlay, and sometimes underlay, economics as a factor in the generation of violent conflict. The interconnecting causal forces have complex manifestations. But still it is possible to understand the workings of our political economy as an *ultimate* causal force.

Race, ethnicity and language frequently form the basis of cultural identities upon which economic and political forces act to guide inequitable distributions of resources. Religious fanaticism, so often believed today to be the principal cause of acts of terrorism, is fed into this indirectly through the past and present political and economic injustices directed against the religious group. Politicians on all sides always call upon patriotic fervor to stoke the nationalistic forces of war; but the real reasons for the conflict usually have their roots in conflicts of economic self-interest.

As has been constantly reiterated throughout this book, political and economic inequality are crucial factors with respect to all of humanity's problems. What this means with respect to inter-group conflicts is that the powerful emotional forces that shape people's identities as Arab or Jew, Catholic or Protestant, Serbian or Croatian, Hutu or Tutsi ultimately derive from these political and economic inequalities. Would they be meaningless without them? No, that is not what is being argued. But the grounds for identity-based conflict would be greatly diminished. Injustice and inequity are *the* principal grounds for conflict.

This directly contradicts media portrayals of terrorism, whereby it is seen as more or less directly synonymous with Muslim fundamentalism. They are the principal enemy in the War on Terror. Obviously, this is not completely true. American and European liberals will point to the terrorist acts of other non-Muslim groups. For the English, the recent past of the IRA quickly comes to mind. The more liberal liberals will go beyond saying that "not all Muslims are terrorists" and include even *most* fundamentalist Muslims in their gestures of tolerance and notions of a pluralist society. However, displays of cultural relativism are beside the point with respect to the real issues of causality. The average American apparently finds it very comforting to believe in the "seventy-six virgins in Paradise" motivation for suicide bombers. An American comedian once quipped that "Americans can't understand suicide attacks . . . I mean, how do they get paid?" Yes, well, the Muslim fundamentalists may get the after-death virgins, but what does the secular atheist Palestinian suicide bomber get paid?

What is wrong with even the tolerance of most of the American liberals is that it is based on little understanding of the real causes of conflicts. They read the cold calculations of their leaders as misguided error; they usually read atrocities as the result of accident, stupidity or ignorance. Sometimes it is that, of course. But there is a *logic* running through the nasty actions of all sides. It is comforting to think of your enemy's motivation as being stupid, shallow and self-interested. To see the motivation of suicide bombers in terms of an after-death "pay-off" makes them at once understandable and at the same time dehumanized. "What reasonable human being could believe such nonsense. It would be laughable if it weren't so evil." No, it seems the difficulty in understanding comes from an emotional rejection of the possibility that the terrorists are motivated by a concern for social justice.

The difficulty seems to be in understanding that the sense of injustice done to their group is based upon a *reality* of injustice done to their group. If Muslim fundamentalists see Western culture as immoral and decadent, it is, in part, because that perception is based upon a truth: the truth of extravagant and conspicuous consumption while others starve. The ideologically sexually repressed observe the sexual exploitation practiced by the West. If one gets past the surface of things, the apparently contradictory evidence to the causal emphasis the dystopia thesis places upon economic inequality disappears. Just because a portion of the leadership of Al Qaeda was wealthy does not mean economic inequality disappears as the most plausible fundamental cause of conflict with the West. Just because the understanding of injustice is somewhat twisted in its articulation through fundamentalist Islam does not mean that the realities the religious dogmas misunderstand do not play a powerful role in the motivations of the conflict.

The correction of group disadvantage – whether the disadvantage is rooted in gender, sexuality, race, ethnicity, nation, language, culture or religion – is not only in the interests of justice, but it is also in the long-term objective self-interest of the human species. The sooner we begin to start remedying the extreme inequalities between races and cultures and nations, the sooner we will leave barbarity. The sooner we cease to fight wars to maintain privilege, the sooner we will achieve a civilized world.

The essential argument here is that, barbaric though they are, both torture and terror are best understood as aspects of war. And war simply *is* barbaric. An end to barbarism would necessitate the end of war. An end of barbarism is the end of injustice. Injustice is the ultimate cause of war.

The dystopia thesis recognizes the causal complexities of any particular war; yet it also finds an ultimate common cause for them: our world socio-economic political system. The way identity (national, ethnic, racial) politics graft on to economic inequalities in the lead-up to conflict will be examined in the next section. But the ultimate cause of war is inequality – because inequality is injustice. Ideological differences will not diminish in the near future, but they will play out on top of struggles for control over resources. But still, war will be less the competition of rival empires and more the struggle between two worlds.

The War of the Worlds

> *If we don't end war, war will end us.*
> H.G. Wells

Global military expenditure stands at over $1.5 trillion. This represents a 49 percent increase since 2000. Even after the 2008 economic crisis – which after the various economic stimulus packages (read bailouts to the banks and big corporations), all the G8 leaders are now trying to cut back on spending in the crucial areas of health and education – the US is still substantially *increasing* military expenditure, as are 16 other G20 countries. That said, with respect to this colossal misdirection of resources, the US is still the major culprit accounting for nearly half (46.5 percent) of the total military expenditure. By contrast, its old cold war enemy Russia only accounts for 3.5 percent and perhaps its most significant future rival China 6.6 percent.[3]

But the gross misdirection of resources is not restricted to military expenditure alone. No, the War on Terror and the "surveillance society" are very much a part of it. The widely quoted (on both TV and in the newspapers) infamous figure of *one billion dollars* budgeted for "security" in the Toronto 2010 hosting of the G20 summit can be contrasted with the *total* higher education budget for Ontario in the same year of only $6.2 billion.[4] An interesting fact is that when you Google "torture

---

[3] All these figures come from Anun Shah (2010) "World Military Spending," *Global Issues*.
http://www.globalissues.org/article/75/world-military-spending

[4] *Reaching Higher: The McGuinty Plan for Post-Secondary Education.*

devices" the first thing that comes up are two paid ads by companies specializing in the sale of "crowd control devices."

The war of the worlds is substantially about the allocation of resources; there are other components to it, but still the allocation of resources is crucial. There is the world of the wealthy, the world of the privileged and there is the rest. But the conflict will not be nearly so simple as one side against the other. Among the vast population of humanity who are not yet privileged, who are not yet wealthy, are those who are chasing the dream of it, are those who would and will sacrifice anything, including their fundamental humanity, to try and get there. Many, most even, of these will never make it to the ideologically promised land. They will struggle for but never achieve wealth and power, no matter how ruthless their ambition.

Most of the human viciousness that occurs is a struggle for just a little bit more, a little bit of relative privilege, in a condition of powerlessness and scarcity. This desperate struggle conditions the emergence of leaders in the less developed world. These struggles for survival bring to the fore leaders who betray their own people. The elites in poor countries maintain their elite status in large part owing to their willingness to sell cheap the assets and resources of their people.

So in the poorer countries, we have the wealthy who, as it were, side with the wealthy world, in the struggle for control over resources. And in the struggle for social justice, we often also have the poor who choose to be the servants of the elites, who become the corrupt police force of the "planet of slums,"[5] who become the bouncers at the door of "Club Privilege."

It is a key element of the dystopia thesis that in a world of poverty and suffering the very existence of excessive affluence is key indicator of barbarity. The inequality is barbarous. However, poverty is barbarous in and of itself. We may have a world of

---

[5] Mike Davis's book *Planet of Slums* (2006), Verso, provides an excellent, though harrowing, portrait of the urban living conditions for much of the world's poor, as well as an insightful Marxist analysis of the situation.

mal-distribution through the mechanisms of capitalism rather than any simple condition of scarcity, but outside of "Affluent World," in the world of the poor, in the "planet of slums," there is a barbarism in and of itself. The brutality, the violence, the sheer viciousness of the desperate struggle for survival is overwhelming. There are (for example, Darfur[6]) and will be many more future occurrences of the insanity that was the Rwandan conflict (see chapter 1) where the genocide was carried out with machetes rather than guns.

In the "war of the worlds," then, we have traitors on both sides. We have the millions of poor who in essence side with the rich against their own collective self-interest (and frequently personal self-interest as well, because they are often tricked and do not always get their "thirty pieces of silver"). But in the privileged countries, too, there are "traitors." There are those who are on the side of the poor; there are those who are on the side of justice . . . and ultimately of humanity. We too have an important role to play in the future of the world (see chapter 8).

Wars, as has been argued here, will be fought over resources. In the past, there has been war, between Britain and Iceland for example, over fishing rights. Various other resources will be and have been fought over. For example, the world economy of diamonds conditioned the fighting in countries like Liberia, Sierra Leone, the Democratic Republic of the Congo and Côte d'Ivoire. Such disputes may or may not become serious issues in the future. But there are two principal resources that certainly will be the *most* fought over in the near future. These conflicts will most significantly shape humanity's future. We will discuss them

---

[6] The civil war conflict in the Darfur region of Sudan began in 2003. The Sudanese government give figures of only about 20,000 killed in the fighting while various international NGOs estimate as many as 400,000. Many more have died through disease and starvation. Millions of refugees have been displaced! In 2005 the conflict spread into neighboring Chad and the Central African Republic. See the BBC's background news report on the Darfur conflict for further information. http://news.bbc.co.uk/2/hi/africa/3496731.stm

together, because they are most profoundly intertwined where the drivers of the conflicts are the sharpest.

Water and Oil: The Causality Mix

We will never again permit any foreign nation to have Uncle Sam over a barrel of oil.
          Gerald Ford (former President
          of the United States)

Let me tell you something that we Israelis have against Moses. He took us forty years through the desert in order to bring us to the one spot in the Middle East that has no oil!
          Golda Meir (former Prime Minister
          of Israel)

The grass is not, in fact, always greener on the other side of the fence. Fences have nothing to do with it. The grass is greenest where it is watered.
          Robert Fulghum

The oil slick in the Gulf is estimated to cover 2,500 square miles.[7] It is an environmental catastrophe of proportions not yet wholly clear at this moment, except to say that they will be unprecedented in their extremity. Oil and water do not mix well.

Water is, of course, the very stuff of life. Our dependency upon it is literally a matter of survival. But as chapter 3 made clear, the clean water necessary for so many aspects of life is increasingly in peril. So there are fundamental grounds for conflict. But will there actually be water wars?

---

[7] Matthew Bigg, "Progress Toward Gulf Oil Well Cap," Reuters (2010-05-03), retrieved 2010-05-13.
http://www.reuters.com/article/idUSTRE6424KO20100503

Well, first we need to define what we mean by water wars. Vandana Shiva, in her book *Water Wars*, speaks of them with a number of different meanings. She speaks of "paradigm wars," essentially wars of understanding. This is the question as to whether water is to be understood and treated as a humanly shared resource, sacred because it is essential to life; or if instead, it is to be understood and treated as a commodity. The dystopia thesis asserts that it is very clear which paradigm we are operating with at the moment (see the earlier discussion of this in chapter 3). But the differences in understanding, the different priorities of local communities (with some help from the wider world) are producing real struggles and conflict.[8] This will be taken up again in the final chapter which explores what should be done about dystopia. Here, however, we are still diagnosing it. Thus, the water wars we will be concerned with in this chapter will be of a more conventional nature.

This restriction of analytical focus may seem as if it reduces the issues to relative simplicity: who is going to attack who and precisely why. But it is not so simple. The first and perhaps most crucial observation to make concerning water conflict is that the conflicts will be conditioned by the context provided by the *ongoing conflicts over oil*. Water wars in the main will be truly wars of desperation and driven by an economic context of extreme poverty on the one hand and attempts at development on the other.

Forty-percent of the world's population lives in the 250 river basins that are shared by more than one country. Water wars directly caused by conflicting desires for usage would seem, then, to be definitely on the horizon as the water resource commons shrinks in supply, just as the demand increases. But Mark de Villiers (making reference to arguments by Thomas Homer-Dixon) asserts:

---

[8] See Vandana Shiva, *Water Wars: Privatization, Pollution and Profit* (2002), Southend Press: Cambridge, MA, for a description of these.

Wars over water between upstream and down-stream neighbours are likely only in a narrow set of circumstances. The downstream country must be highly dependent on the water for its national well-being; the upstream country must be able to restrict the river's flow; there must be a history of antagonism between the two countries; and most important, the downstream country must be militarily much stronger than the upstream country.[9]

He goes on to say that Homer-Dixon only found one country that fit this criteria: Egypt, with respect to the Nile. I don't wish to dispute this here; if in any particular aspect, things aren't quite as bad as they first appear, we can only be pleased. But regardless of the truth or not of this narrow perspective upon water war causality, a wider perspective is much grimmer.

Water shortages very seriously affect agriculture. They may produce famines and displace hundreds of thousands of people. The refugees provide further potentially war-causing political-economic stress. Water shortages can make development impossible . . . the Nile case makes this clear. Egypt is simply *not going to allow* significant upstream damming. They will go to war over this issue, and they possess overwhelming military superiority over their upstream neighbours.

Essentially, what is being argued here is that inequitable and ecologically unwise water policies will indirectly, if not directly, feed into conflict and war. The complex imbrication of oil politics and water politics make Egypt a crucial case in point. Egypt does not have a water dispute with Israel. Israel does not have any oil. Yet Egypt is lined up both for and against Israel in the long list of nations involved in the trickiest and most complex politics of oil and water on the planet.

We will make just one brief preliminary excursion into the politics of oil before directly tackling Middle Eastern politics and its probable future wars. China will become the biggest future rival for control of the oil resource. China is developing fast.

---

[9] Marq de Villiers, *Water* (2003), McClelland & Stewart: Toronto, p. 417.

Simply extrapolating from past GDP growth figures, the Chinese economy should catch up to the US in purchasing power somewhere between 2012 and 2015; by 2025, it should be the world's largest economic power.[10] That development is, of course, dependent upon a future increase of oil consumption. We have already considered peak oil in terms of shortage-driven price increases. But it is unlikely that any approximation of a free market in oil will continue long. The resource is just too crucial. The US will try very hard to control its supply; the customer with the biggest guns will get likely served first. And the US certainly has the biggest guns.

But the situation is complicated by global finance and China's relationship to US debt. China is the largest shareholder of Treasury bonds (887.5 billion dollars[11]). This gives them a certain amount of economic-based political clout with respect to US policy. But if there is another major financial crisis in the world, and as we analyzed in chapter 6, there almost certainly will be one soon, then who knows what a rash US government might do.

This is only part of the "external" contextual political-economic framing necessary to deal with the full complexity of Middle Eastern politics. To fully do so would be beyond the potential of this chapter and this book. The scare quotes around the word "external" derive from the fact that the politics of the Middle East are, in many respects, fully global; and though it might seem that the electoral politics of the US are as external to the Middle East as China's internal politics, the analysis put forward here puts them right at the center of it.

Not all American Jews are Zionists, not by a long shot. The American Jewish community is diverse in culture and politics.

---

[10] Carsten A. Holtz, "China's Economic Growth 1978-2025: What We Know Today about China's Economic Growth Tomorrow," *Hong Kong University of Science and Technology* (2005). http://129.3.20.41/eps/dev/papers/0512/0512002.pdf

[11] U.S. Treasury Department (2008), *Major Foreign Holders of U.S. Treasury Securities*.

However, it is *politically* dominated by a Zionist perspective and unquestioning support for the State of Israel. This group of people are very well-organized with respect to political connections and lobbying and fundraising. They exert a disproportionate degree of control over US Middle Eastern policy. Quite likely without them, the US policy would have always been one of purely naked political-economic pragmaticism . . . (about which we will speak about in a moment) because that actually is also a huge driving force in their decision-making. Nonetheless, it is not economic pragmaticism entirely. While there *are* politically and economically *pragmatic* reasons to support Israel, that is not the entirety of the US motivation. The ideological commitment to Israel and Zionism is also a powerful force. There is an economic dimension to that too of course. It is the lobbying and funding dimension of US electoral politics.

The purely economic pragmatic component of US policy, however, while complex, can nonetheless be summed up simply: the largest proportion of the world's oil is contained within Middle Eastern States, the largest being in Saudi Arabia and Iraq. The political motives of the Iraq invasion are thus not very difficult to figure out. The ongoing support for the Saudi monarchy is no less difficult. The US effectively maintains an indirect but nonetheless quite powerful hold on these oil supplies.

The situation is, of course, more complicated than that. However, we should not let any confusion arise as to the real drivers of US foreign policy because of their self-stated motivations. That is to say that the American public's widely accepted ideological notions of the US being a "good guy," of them only intervening in the affairs of other nations to serve the causes of freedom or human rights, are entirely fictitious. Their more particular justifications such as "weapons of mass destruction," barbarity toward the Kurds in the case of Iraq or the alleged concern over the Taliban's suppression of women's rights in Afghanistan are equally untrue. Such concerns form no part of US policy and never have. In general, one could safely assert regarding any issues with respect to freedom or democracy or justice in the world that, since World War II, the US has *always been on the wrong side*. They have always supported vicious dictators (including, of course, the latterly demonized Saddam Hussein) in their suppression of any indigenous democratic movement. No, the ideology propagated for home consumption is just that, pure ideology, and plays no role in actual policy-making (except insofar as credibility issues with the American public sometimes emerge).

But as said earlier, the US role cannot wholly be reduced to their political-economic pragmatic interests because of its domestic political relationship with Zionism. The conflict between Israel and the Arab nations complicates thing where the US is closely allied with the Arab nation. On the other side, we have the misdirected opposition to imperialism directed through fundamentalist Islam. Not that the opposition to imperialism is misguided; no, just the way resistance is guided through ignorance and prejudice.

As a further complicating factor, in addition to oil, there is the powerful economic force of the arms industry. The US has made Israel a military power in the region, and then Israel made itself one of the world's major arms merchants. The US is as well, of course, significantly being *the* major supplier of armament for most of the Arab nations (Egypt, for example). There are further complexities stretching both within and outside of the Mid-East. There is the fundamentalist opposition (an extension of the official fundamentalism!) within Saudi Arabia that found its way to Afghanistan with US support, the complexities of Pakistan's border politics and the big business of heroin that was reinstated after the Taliban was deposed. The US appears to be fighting on *all sides* of the War on Terror and the War on Drugs, as well as on both sides of the Israeli-Arab conflict.

Well, even with all those complicated inter-linkages, the picture painted is an oversimplification. We haven't, for example, even mentioned Lebanon. The US supports some Arab regimes but not others. The monarchy of Saudi Arabia, fundamentalist Islamic though it is, is supported. Syria and Libya are enemies (the degree to which they are shifts over time and circumstance, but that is the basic orientation. The attitude towards Egypt and Iraq has done 180-degree shifts over relatively short periods of time, culminating in Iraq's case in the present occupation. But the support of Israel is a constant. And this is where the politics of oil meet the politics of water.

Water, since Israel's beginnings as a modern state, has always been a matter of national security. The conflict with Syria over the Golan Heights, for example, was and is significantly about control of water. Most of Israel's water comes from the Jordan River. Perhaps the primary fact of the Israeli-Arab tension comes from this reality. As Marq de Villiers put it: "No one in Israel forgets that two-thirds of the water Israel uses originates in territory it now controls through military conquest, in the Golan Heights and the West Bank."[12] So in order to understand the complexities of the volatile region, it is important to know that the US's principal ally has resource issues fuelling conflict with its neighbors that go beyond ideology and oil.

The US, as stated earlier, has its own domestic political reasons for supporting Israel and also oil control pragmatism. But though Israel and the US are bound to one another, not only their policies, but the very long-term interest basis for those policies is different. Water provides an ongoing source of tension in the Mid-East that is escalating. This tension *has to escalate*, as the demands on a very limited resource become more intense. The annual water deficit for Israel (360 million cubic meters), Jordan (200 million cubic meters and the West Bank (140 million cubic meters)[13] is increasing.

Most people and media commentators can easily see that the political mix of the region is bad. But they are less aware of the bad economics driving the politics. There are two constant features of capitalist political water economy to understand as causal forces. A large portion of the water Israel uses goes toward irrigation of the Negev, land formerly desert. Short-term economic gain is a constant in the world's utilization of water, as many governments continue to facilitate a diversion of water to deserts. But this policy, whether carried out in the American

---

[12] De Villiers, *Water.*

[13] Ibid.

southwest or Israel, is working to create crises for the future. There are political issues and disputes (legal rather than military) over water diversion in America; it is just that the Middle Eastern situation is so, so much more intense.

The second principal feature of the political economy of the Jordan River and other water sources of the region is extreme inequality. Vandana Shiva uses the term "water apartheid" to describe its distribution between Jews and Palestinians in Israel.[14] Palestinian villages consume only two percent of Israel's water.[15] There will not be enough water in the future to continue to irrigate Israel's farmlands and golf courses, and the Palestinian farmers will face starvation or die of thirst . . . or fight. Inequality, whatever its complications of history, culture, ethnic identities or ideology, is a constant in capitalism. Inequality is the primary driver of dystopia.

Panopticon World

> *Prison continues, on those who are entrusted*
> *to it, a work begun elsewhere, which the whole*
> *of society pursues on each individual through*
> *innumerable mechanisms of discipline.*
>   Michel Foucault

> *Once a government is committed to the*
> *principle   of silencing the voice of opposition,*
> *it has only one way to go, and that is down the*
> *path of increasingly repressive measures, until*
> *it becomes a source of terror to all its citizens*
> *and creates a country where everyone lives in*
> *fear.*
>   Harry S. Truman

---

[14] Shiva, *Water Wars*, p. 73.

[15] Helena Lindholm, "Water and the Arab Israeli Conflict," quoted in Shiva, p. 73.

The panopticon is an invention of the philosopher Jeremy Bentham, most famous for his exposition of utilitarian moral philosophy. In more recent years, he developed a subsidiary posthumous fame through Michel Foucault's usage of the panopticon as a concept in a broader analytical framework: to diagnose knowledge, discipline and power in the modern surveillance society. The panopticon is a form of prison design whereby there is a central control area looking out with a 360-degree view of a circle of cells, all facing outward and open to the guard's view. The prisoners are not *always* being watched, of course, but they are always aware that they *could* be. This conditions their behavior. The panopticon design is thus an efficient way of maintaining control over the inmates.

Today prisons have technological surveillance devices (cameras and recorders) that achieve the same effect regardless of the physical layout of the buildings. Today, not only prison, but society generally, is subject to the usage of the same technology to keep a watch on all of us. This is Foucault's concept of the panopticon. We are all under surveillance some of the time. We are caught on the security cameras inside a store or a nightclub or while using an ATM. Many cities now have cameras set up to cover their downtown streets. We know that sometimes we are being watched and other times don't know but believe we might be. Just like the prison inmates, we live our lives in the consciousness that we may be having our activities observed and monitored. Just like the prisoners, we modify our actions accordingly.

Our phone may be tapped; our emails may be read; our Internet usage may be tracked. Though this much is a simply a fact about contemporary life, most of us simply make our calls and send our emails without thinking much about the fact that they may be monitored . . . until we begin to do something that someone (anyone!) might think is subversive or illegal. It doesn't actually have to be subversive; it doesn't have to actually be illegal; we just need to think that someone (exactly who can be very vague but always connects to some concept of the "authorities") could conceivably think so. Do we moderate our behavior then? Maybe, maybe not. But we live with the consideration that maybe we should. We all live today with the paradox of paranoia. It might be paranoid to believe that someone is following you, that someone is spying on you . . . but crazy or not, they might be.

The War on Terror does not only make terrorists fearful of arrest and retribution, of Guantanamo Bay and torture. We all know that completely innocent people have been taken by mistake; we know that normal legal rights get suspended. This affects *everybody*. You feel everyone looking at you, wondering if you are a criminal or a terrorist, when you are singled out at the airport and your bag is searched. You realize that you actually *have committed an offence* when your nail scissors are discovered in your carry-on luggage or the mouth wash that you failed to put inside a plastic bag is ceased. Or though perhaps you live in the UK and have good friends in New York but because you have an Arab name you think perhaps the risk of the trip is no longer worth it.

The very notion of rights is a complicated one. There are the legal rights afforded to all citizens. These vary from country to country, with some having many more than others. But in all countries, these legal rights are always subject to "emergency" suspension at particular times and circumstances. There is always an ongoing struggle between authorities pushing for further extension of the panopticon and people attempting to maintain the sanctity of hard won legal rights.

There is also the broader notion of human rights. This is maintained variously in the minds of men and women as a conception of freedom and justice and a vision of how the world *ought* to be. Many aspects of these conceptions are enshrined in various collective documents. The United Nations Declaration of Human Rights was signed by all the members of the UN General Assembly in 1948. This was an important step toward civilization. But the signing of the document by no means ensured the reality of compliance with its spirit. No, as a reality, the rights are by no means universal; what is universal is their violation.

Rights, therefore, should not be understood as an existing reality but rather as a pious hope. They are a *privilege* afforded us by various governments. That is, they are a privilege until they are fought for and won as being *inviolate* . . . without exception . . . without being subject to suspension because of "exceptional circumstance." The War on Terror is thus in essence the very antithesis of human rights and civilization. It is in its very *essence* barbaric.

In the London protest against the G20 meeting, an apparently innocent bystander (that is, innocent in the sense that he was not a protester) was killed by the police.[16] In the G20 protests in Toronto of 2010, over 1,000 people were arrested.[17] Though there has thus far not even been any allegations by the police that any of these people could in any sense remotely be considered terrorists, there is nonetheless a connection. Much of the protest was directed at the diverse set of issues relating to the economic inequalities of the world, the destruction of the environment and the military political imposition of injustice. The protest as whole could be seen as part of the struggle against dystopia, as part of the struggle to build a better world and civilization. Whereas on the other side, the meetings of the world political leaders were essentially about how to manage and maintain barbarity, how to cooperate in the delivery of privilege and dystopia. The exceptional suspensions of "rights" ultimately derived from the same justifications of the War on Terror. The two worlds were fighting.

---

[16] The man was pushed to ground by the police and immediately had a heart attack. This was caught on video, which can be seen on the website of the British newspaper *The Guardian*.
http://www.guardian.co.uk/uk/2009/apr/07/ian-tomlinson-g20-death-video

[17] http://www.cbc.ca/canada/toronto/story/2010/07/01/toronto-g20-protest.html

The Dystopian Future: 2020 Vision

> *The function of science fiction is not always to*
> *predict the future but sometimes to prevent it.*
> Frank Herbert

> *I do not know how the Third World War will*
> *be fought, but I can tell you what they will use*
> *in the Fourth — rocks!*
> Albert Einstein

Mortality rates had begun to rise sharply over the last few years, but the number of people who died in the year 2020 was beyond anything anyone could have imagined in earlier years. So many disasters had struck nearly simultaneously. So many diverse factors seemed to come together at once to produce mutually reinforcing catastrophes. There had been so much fighting. It seemed that, all over the world, the weather had conspired to torment humanity. But all the horror that seemed accidental was not. All of it had its seeds in actions taken by people long ago.

A new flu pandemic swept over the world. Unlike the last one that had its origins in pigs, this one came from birds. It appeared first in Cambodia in chickens. By the time the authorities became fully aware of the problem and began to cull them, it had spread to a third of the country. The peasant farmers had known of the presence of the virus long before this but had been very reluctant to have their birds destroyed because the government provided no compensation for this. At this time, there was a brief flurry of condemnation. But the attention of both media and governments soon shifted. The chickens were very contagious (initially only to other birds, of course, though that later changed), and wild birds soon became infected . . . wild birds that made their way to North America . . . wild birds that infected the domestic fowl.

The Canadian and American domestic fowl lived in the perfect conditions for an outbreak of colossal proportions. In 2019, the World Health Organization insisted on the decision to eradicate *all* the factory-farmed chickens and turkeys in North America. This was a huge financial disaster and one that affected the diets

of nearly everyone on the continent. But, of course, this .
widespread slaughter did not get *all* the birds, and the flu
continued to spread among the bird populations of the world.
Though there was substantial bird-to-human transmission of the
virus, by the end of 2020, there still had not occurred that
horrible, frightening mutation: human-to-human contagion. The
world's scientists and medical establishments lived in fear of this
possibility but disagreed among themselves as to what to do about
it. The public was disturbed, but they had other worries on their
minds as well.

There were an unprecedented number of tsunamis and
hurricanes in 2020. The killer waves were bigger than had ever
been seen before. They pounded the coasts of Japan, Thailand,
Indonesia, Malaysia and Bangladesh on one side of the Pacific
then engulfed the parts of Southern California that had only just
recovered from disastrous mud slides and, even before that, from
out-of-control brush fires above the LA suburbs. Bangladesh was
the hardest hit of all. The floods which killed millions were
followed by uncontrolled disease epidemics and starvation.
Unlike in the previous flood disasters that had befallen this poor
country, this time there was no international relief effort. Other
places had problems of their own.

The tiny Pacific Island nations were similarly swamped. A
hurricane had hit New Orleans . . . *again*. It finished the job
begun so many years ago by Katrina. It finished New Orleans.
But hurricanes hit many other US cities as well: Charleston,
Galveston, Biloxi (again!) and Miami. Most of the Caribbean
Islands were also devastated by the savage storms. The island
deaths were mainly locals. Few tourists were hurt because few
tourists were there. The price of aviation fuel had seen to that. But
the storms killed many people nonetheless. A tornado hit the
glass-and-steel center of Chicago. The steel held. The glass killed.

Hurricanes and tidal waves were by no means all the ways
nature mounted its assault on humanity that year. The Atlantic
conveyer did not actually come to a stop, but it slowed down
considerably. The effect of this upon the weather was profound.
The Arctic ice cover had reached what scientists had called the
"tipping point" unexpectedly earlier than had been predicted. The

permanent ice of the pole had all melted. There was still a deep snow and ice cover over Greenland, but the melt there had been phenomenal, releasing megatons of fresh water into the ocean. The conveyer slowed down, and the winter of 2020 was a winter that no one in Europe had ever experienced before. The terrible ice storms that had become an almost yearly feature of the Eastern US and Canadian winters now had come to Europe. They were unprepared. Their power transmission infrastructure came crashing down under the weight of the ice that clung to the lines and to the trees that fell into them. People huddled around coal fires. People spent weeks in emergency shelters as the frozen pipes in the tower blocks of London and Paris burst beyond easy repair. People died on a massive scale.

The climate change of the North had its counterpart in the South: drought. And with the drought came a plague of locusts. In a region already fraught with civil war, crop failure and starvation, this proved to be its own "tipping point." The region simply collapsed in terms of being able to support human life. The region was huge. The region covered a third of sub-Saharan Africa.

But what nature did to humanity that year was nothing compared to what human beings did to themselves. The world was undergoing what the economists called a "painful readjustment process" of the globalized economy. The oil production peak had been reached some years ago. Less and less oil had been produced every year since, and prices had risen in dramatic fashion accordingly. The burning of the Iraqi oil fields and the complete collapse of their production capacity added to the price spikes. The world, Japan, Europe and particularly the US had had such hopes for Iraqi oil. But the previously only simmering civil war began raging immediately following the ignominious US troop pullout a few years earlier. It had not been done in either the most sensible or honorable fashion. Indeed, older people said the media pictures of Baghdad were reminiscent of the US evacuation from Saigon at the end of the Vietnam War.

But now they are contemplating going back. There is no talk this time about any "democratization" of the Middle East. There is no talk about justice. The talk is only of oil. Much of the public thinks that if the US has to directly rule the country in an old-fashioned colonial kind of way then so be it. Most Americans now support a new invasion. The exigencies of the "re-localization process" of the new economic order have been painful, and Americans want their automobile lifestyle back. They are willing to fight for it.

Americans are also angry at the deaths of the thousands of people from the terrorist "dirty bomb" attacks on major US cities in the last two years. People had feared and still fear that terrorists will get hold of nuclear bombs or fly a hijacked plane into a nuclear power installation. Either or both of these possibilities could still occur, but as of 2020, they had still not happened. No, the greatest loss of life through an explosion was not nuclear. It was the accidental detonation of a liquid natural gas (LNG) port facility. The facility did what the company officials who had bullied the local population into accepting the facility had said was impossible: it exploded into a huge fireball. Most of the "NIMBY alarmists" who had so adamantly opposed the siting of the facility in "their backyard" were not around to say "I told you so." Most of them, like everyone else within a mile radius, were dead.

The explosion had killed more people than any of the terrorists' dirty bombs. These, of course, were nowhere near as lethal as even small nuclear bombs would have been . . . at least in the short term. The longer-term casualties of the radiation dispersal have not yet even been calculated, and the economic costs are in the billions and billions. The nuclear terrorist attacks perhaps never materialized because the terrorists found out that acquiring the materials and making the dirty bombs was so much easier. "Dirty bombs" are simply dynamite, or indeed any explosive at all, encased with radioactive material. The radioactive waste products of nuclear power plants and many other industrial processes made such materials very easy to come by. And so the centers of three US cities are uninhabitable, and many, many people are dead.

The terrorists seemed to understand the American psyche quite well through their choice of attack upon Hollywood and Beverly

Hills. The American public seemed more upset by the deaths of the scores of famous than the thousands of ordinary people.

And so they are angry. They are ready for war, even to the point of nuclear attack. They are ready for this even though they have seen the effects of a full-scale nuclear Armageddon. In 2020, Pakistan and India went to war. India and Pakistan had gone to war with each other three times previously since the partition of the Indian subcontinent and their post-colonial formation as independent countries. The wars, of course, had their roots in the manner in which the British had used religion to divide the populace and cement their own rule. The new countries were formed on the basis of Hindu and Islamic rivalry. There were border disputes. There were problems to do with water rights. There was the persecution of minorities. So they fought. But nothing compared to the war of 2020. There had never been a war like that in the whole of human history.

Pakistan covertly supported insurgencies in Kashmir and the Punjab. India warned it of serious consequences, even all-out war if they continued. They meant by this conventional war, of course. But conventional war presented nuclear dangers. There was a military imbalance between the two sides. This was one of the reasons for the Pakistani clandestine support of rebellions against the Indian government. They saw it as a way of weakening their militarily superior rival and so did not desist. But when the tide turned against the Indian government and the Pakistani support became more overt, India did what it had long threatened. It attacked.

The Indian air strikes significantly damaged the entire Pakistani military infrastructure, not to mention the severe economic destruction. The Indian army advanced quickly in Pakistan, capturing Lahore and marching on Rawalpindi and Islamabad. Pakistan, with its territory now invaded and seeing the emergence of ever-increasing air superiority by the Indians, became increasingly aware of the possibility of total defeat at the hands of their old enemy. They issued an ultimatum: cease all offensive operations; completely withdraw from Pakistan's territory; or, face utter destruction!

The Indians knew well what they meant by this. It was not the first time either side had threatened the other with nuclear annihilation. As long ago as December 30, 2002, President Musharraf of Pakistan said that he had warned India that it "should not expect a conventional war" if Indian troops moved across the "Line of Control" that divides the disputed province Kashmir. And India's defense minister, George Fernandes, replied that in any nuclear exchange, India would easily absorb a nuclear hit, whereas Pakistan would "cease to exist." India could "take a bomb or two or more. . . but when we respond there will be no Pakistan," the Press Trust of India quoted him as saying.[18] And now India had moved deep into Pakistan itself.

As it turned out, neither side was bluffing. India attempted to take out Pakistan's nuclear capacity with a pre-emptive series of conventional air strikes. When it seemed for a moment that they might succeed, Pakistan unleashed its Hatf 3/M-11 ballistic missiles. They carried 20 kiloton bombs, just a little bigger than those the Americans had dropped upon Hiroshima and Nagasaki three-quarters of a century earlier. India used its Jaguar, Mirage-2000, MiG-27 jets to respond rather than missiles. They were equally effective. Ten cities, five of each country were hit before they stopped.

In Bangalore, 314, 978 people were killed. In Mumbai, 477,713 were seriously injured and 357,202 dead. The death toll of Madras and New Delhi brought the Indian total to 1,690,702 lives lost. Another 892,459 people were very seriously injured. In Pakistan, the city of Faisalabad suffered the greatest number of fatalities with 336,239 deaths. India withdrew its military occupation of Lahore, then dropped a nuclear bomb upon it. Together with the bombs dropped upon Islamabad, Karachi and

---

[18] *CNN*, Wednesday, January 8, 2003.
http://www.cnn.com/2003/world/asiapcf/south/01/08/pakistan.india/index.html

Rawalpindi, this brought the total Pakistani dead to 1,171,879.[19]
A further 614,400 were horrifically injured.

These figures were, of course, only the blast fatality and injury
figures. The further deaths and illnesses from radioactive fallout
remain to be seen. This further suffering will not be as bad as it
could have been. With a bizarre measure of sanity in their
collective exercise of madness, both sides used air-burst
detonation rather than ground. Had they used the latter, much
more radioactive fallout would have been produced. Though it
may have been accidental, the Faisalabad detonation, however,
was apparently a ground one and the radioactive cloud is drifting
over other parts of Asia and may be responsible not only for more
deaths and illness but significant "political fallout" as well. The
war may widen. Though the majority of the world's population
had simply watched in horror as these events unfolded, some
countries seem to have been made more belligerent. The logic of
the connection seems very unclear, but it was only within days of
the India-Pakistan nuclear exchange that a "dirty bomb" was
exploded in Tel Aviv.

As of 2020, the "war to end all wars" had not yet occurred.
The passing of the oil production peak had necessitated serious
conservation measures and considerably upped the ante in the
dangerous poker game being played over oil supplies. The major
players were principally China and the US, but their strategies
were complicated by European plotting and the now open
domestic unrest in Saudi Arabia. The politics of oil were no
simple matter of price increases due to shortages. No, military
force, or rather thus far at any rate, the threat of military force,
was playing a crucial role in the exclusive trading agreements
being made (and covertly broken!) by oil producers with
countries like the US. They (and everyone else!) wanted to get

---

[19] All of the figures used in this speculative piece derive from figures
used in a nuclear exchange scenario produced by the Natural Resources
Defense Council in a piece titled *The Consequences of Nuclear Conflict
between India and Pakistan.*
 http://www.nrdc.org/nuclear/southasia.asp

more than their fair share of a dwindling supply. China had already given a shot (in the balls, as one political commentator put it) by putting an enormous number of the US treasury bonds that they owned on the market. Wall Street was thrown into panic; shares plunged wildly over economic uncertainty. The US first asked politely, then asked with an implied threat, for China to withdraw these bonds from sale. The Chinese quite graciously obliged, using the language of diplomacy and good neighbors. However, even the general public knew that that such cooperation was and is crucially related to both military threat and the necessities of growth and survival and oil in the People's Republic.

The oil peak precipitated one of the most shameful genocides in human history. It was accompanied by the worst example of media distortion and American public ignorance their history. The scale of evil rivaled the holocaust. America had gone into Somalia before. In December 1992, they involved themselves in an alleged humanitarian mission ("Operation Hope") into the famine-ravished, war-torn dysfunctional country. It ended badly. The American public never forgot (or if they had, the media repeatedly reminded them) the images of a dead American soldier being ignominiously dragged through the streets of Mogadishu. In 2019, the American military forces entered Somalia again.

Global warming had affected all of Africa in terms of desertification, disease and famine. Disputes over land rights and water shortages once again led to a complex civil war that dragged on for years. In the equally strife-torn cities, particularly Mogadishu, the largest city and one-time capital, things reached a total breakdown of order. There was no longer anything that could be called the Somali state; there was little that could be called government at all on even the smallest local scale; instead there were warlords and gangs.

But the world oil-supply pressure meant that, somehow, systematic oil exploration was nonetheless undertaken. This was a complex undertaking with apparently warring chaos all around. Many foreign soldiers, many Somali fighters, many engineers and geologists lost their lives. But this was nothing compared to the slaughter that ensued when the presence of significant oil reserves was actually found. The US went in full force. This time there was not even an ideological pretext of humanitarian motives. And there was no central power in the country to negotiate a surrender.

Rather than negotiate the terms of US proxy rule neighborhood by neighborhood, valley by valley of rural enclaves, with hundreds of gangster or paramilitary leaders, they simply took over by direct force. Altogether it is estimated that half a million people were either killed directly or died from indirect causes deriving from the military occupation . . . out of a population estimated to be only about 15 million (though this is a guesstimate, as the last reliable census taken back in 2009 showed a population a only a little over 9 million).

As of 2020, only a very small percentage of the American public are at all aware of the shameful slaughter perpetuated by their troops. The major news networks all colluded in keeping the public ignorant of even the worst excesses of brutality. More worrying in this regard, however, was the government's unprecedented success in censoring the Internet.

Science Fact, Science Fiction: Left, Right or Wrong?

> *It is change, continuing change, inevitable change,*
> *that is the dominant factor in society today. No*
> *sensible decision can be made any longer without*
> *taking into account not only the world as it is, but*
> *the world as it will be. This, in turn, means that our*
> *statesmen, our businessmen, our every man must*
> *take on a science fictional way of thinking.*
> Isaac Asimov

Was the preceding scenario unrealistic? In the next chapter, we will be discussing the limits of prediction, the incorrect logics of inevitability and so on. But we can say here that the preceding scenarios of the future all had some kind of factual basis located in the present. Nuclear warfare casualty rates, for example, all had some kind of expert basis in controlled speculations relying on existing military capacity and real political tensions. All the horrific things that occurred in the scenarios are not only possible but have some degree of probability.

For example, the explosion of a liquid natural gas (LNG) installation has some probability because: a) it is a very, very volatile substance, b) the means of avoiding costly safety protocols are available, and c) the economic motivations to do so are strong. With respect to points b and c, we can look to aviation disasters of the past. Common sense tells us that there is a certain danger in flying, and the public's desire is for every safety measure possible to be taken. In the US, the Federal Aviation Authority (FAA) has extensive and detailed mandatory safety measures and also punishments for non-compliance. Nonetheless, a considerable number of crashes are the result of intentional avoidance and deception with respect to these regulations[20] . . . precisely because of economic motivations. That similar violations of safety protocol would take place with respect to the building and operation of an LNG terminal thus has, by virtue of the analogous circumstance, a certain degree of probability.

What about a terrorist usage of dirty bombs? Well, the relatively easy to acquire technological knowledge and capacity to build them exists now. And we certainly have a past of terrorist attacks showing little regard for human life. Such attacks as described in the scenario would only be an increase in scale. Again, of course, it is not certain such attacks will occur; but there is a degree of probability grounded in reality that they will.

Perhaps one could say that the nuclear warfare between India and Pakistan scenario or the invasion of Somalia have too much of their alleged basis dependent upon some controversial political assumptions. Well, in one sense, this is true; the assumptions *are* controversial. But I believe they are nonetheless well-founded.

---

[20] See the National Geographic series *Seconds from Disaster* and *Mayday*. These first dramatize plane crashes through recreations, then also recreate the official crash investigations and search for causes. Many of these show failures to complete proper maintenance in accordance with regulations, over-working employees, keeping the planes in the air too much and a variety of other factors that can be traced back to motivations that place profit over safety.

The dystopia thesis prognostications about the future stand upon an analysis of the past, of the present and, to some extent, extensions of already existing trends. It draws from many sources, but it does, of course, have a "left-wing" orientation. So what about the Right? What are *they* thinking is on the horizon for the future in terms of conflict? Matt Carr sums up the thinking of the US and UK military establishments for us:

> This new military futurism sees threats to the Western way of life emanating not only from rogue states, weapons of mass destruction and terrorism, but also from resurgent nationalism, conflicts over dwindling resources, migration, disease, organized crime, abrupt climate change and the emergence of "failed cities" where social disorder is rife.[21]

This is pretty much the picture I painted in the previous section. I left out organized crime, however, which is a pretty serious omission. It is, of course, responsible for an enormous amount of violence and human suffering. Earlier in the chapter, I did mention the fact that the heroin trade had been re-established in Afghanistan and made a brief reference to the "blood diamond" trade that has featured as a prominent factor in a number of African civil wars. But the effects of organized crime are much more significant than this. Organized crime accounts for something like fifteen to twenty percent of the global economy.[22]

From the perspective of the dystopia thesis, however, we can assert two things. First, that the distinction between legitimate and illegitimate business, as is operational in every country in the world, possesses many legal and practical implications; in terms of morality, the distinction is so blurred as to be virtually meaningless. Secondly, this leads to difficulties in believing that the military foresees organized crime per se as a threat to Western

---

[21] Matt Carr, "Slouching Towards Dystopia: The New Military Futurism," *Race & Class,* Volume 51 (3) (2010), Sage.

[22] Glenny Misha, *McMafia* (2009), House of Anansi Press: Toronto.

life. The dystopia thesis would assert that organized crime actually is very much *a part of Western life*. That perspective, does not, of course, rule out military actions being undertaken against a variety of organized crime bastions.

The "left-wing" perspective of the previously quoted author is interesting. This segment comes from the abstract of his article that concludes with the following:

> This article provides a survey of the genre, showing how the grim predictions of the military futurists provide a justification for an endless global war *against enemies that may never exist.*[23] [my italics]

If this is in any way representative of a left-wing political perspective, I find it very worrying. It would appear that, in this case at least, it is the Right which is investigating reality and using it as a basis for their imagination of the future. Does Carr seriously think that there will *not* be conflicts over dwindling resources? Or that there will *not* be resurgent nationalism? Or believe that failed cities will *not* emerge? He should read Mike Davis's *Planet of Slums*; they are already here. But I suspect he is already aware of this; I suspect he knows that these predicted future threats are real enough. What he doesn't want to accede to is the increases of military budgets that the threats will be given as justification for. What he doesn't want is the newer weaponry and training for armed intervention against civilian populations.

Well, that is fair enough; I don't want that either. I may well agree with much of the prognosis for future conflict produced by military think tanks . . . but I am certainly not "on their side." Indeed, I am sure that, at sometime in the future, I will be identified as an enemy of the state precisely because I am on the side of the poor, and because I believe that it is necessary to be so for the future of all humanity. However, I do agree with the military think tanks on a surprising proportion of their understanding of the probabilities as to how the future will

---

[23] Matt Carr (2010) "Slouching Towards Dystopia".

unfold.[24] What I don't agree with, of course, is what is to be done. What I think should be done is the subject matter for the next and final chapter of this book.

---

[24] Project for the New American Century, *Rebuilding America's Defenses: Strategy, Forces and Resources for a New Century*. http//www.newamericancentury.org/RethinkingAmericasDefenses.pdf

Chapter 8

What Is to Be Done?

*Things alter for the worse spontaneously, if they be
not altered for the better designedly.*
Francis Bacon

*Without a revolutionary theory there cannot be a
revolutionary movement.*
V.I. Lenin

Introduction: The Speed of Change

*We live in a moment of history where change is
so speeded up that we begin to see the present
only when it is already disappearing.*
R.D. Laing

From the standpoint of prediction, the future is simply a question of assessing probabilities. And the probability is that things will truck along more or less the way they have been doing for a number of years to come. The experience of our recent past, along with this probability, produce a sense that the feared (or even hoped for) change will never come. It will always be on the distant horizon but never be imminent. And then one day, very suddenly, it happens. You live your normal day-to-day life, and then everything goes black; the entire North American Eastern seaboard is without electricity. Everything is different. But then the lights come back on, and we carry on as before. Or perhaps you lived your normal day-to-day life in East Germany, and then one day the Berlin Wall was brought down; and hence forth *everything* is different. Things are never the same again.

This is how dystopia is likely to be experienced in the affluent countries. We will witness catastrophe . . . elsewhere . . . just as we have been doing . . . because dystopia is already here for some of the world. We ourselves will experience incremental change for the worst but scarcely noticeable from the perspective of everyday living. We will also experience sudden shocks, like the puncture of the real estate market bubble, for example, or the related financial crisis of 2008 . . . but then things will slowly right themselves again. The world will never be *quite* the same again, but it still will be *recognizably* the same world. That is because these incremental changes are only preliminary shocks building towards something; that is because these shocks are not the earthquake, they are only tremors. But when a number of the various dystopian tipping points have been passed, then things will happen fast. We will suddenly be accelerated into an unrecognizable world of horror.

I say "we" but that is actually inaccurate; because again, some predictions may be hazarded with respect to time frame and which people will be affected. I expect to live out my life in a world that is recognizably like the one of today; I will continue to live a kind of lifestyle that is similar at least to that which I live today. I will live in "this world" until I die of natural and non-dystopian causes. I may be wrong about this; the major "all-life-as-we-know-it" altering change may come next year. A year before the Berlin Wall came down, there were few, if any, East Germans predicting it. So, we don't know for sure just how soon a painful dystopia will come.

We don't know, that is, on the near end. I will probably live out my life in "this world" because I am 60 years old. But we can say with a fair degree of probability that that *will not* be the case for people in their twenties. We can say with *near total certainty* that it will not be the case for people born today. Dystopia possibly may come quicker, but it is pretty likely to arrive before 20 years are up, and almost certainly will come before 30. This likelihood has some implications for the core question of this chapter: What is to be done?

At my age, it makes sense for me to be thinking about my pension, to be working out how I will live my final years. If I, and others my age and older, were to be totally selfish in our plans and perspective with regard to dystopia, we could say to ourselves that it probably won't be our problem. We should enjoy the good life in our remaining time and bugger those who are suffering now; and also say to hell with our children and grandchildren.

Dystopia: What is to be done?

Dystopia, survival of the species, the big problems, will be theirs to experience and theirs to solve. However, if that is your perspective, then there is little to be said to you . . . except perhaps some pointless insult about how selfish you are.

Most people care about their children's and/or their grandchildren's future. Most people, if they stopped to think about it, would realize that they feel somehow emotionally bound to the human race as a whole, and that the idea of extinction, even after their own life is over, is a disturbing prospect.

Planning for a Future That Will Never Come

If anything is certain, it is that change is certain. The world we are planning for today will not exist in this form tomorrow.
Philip Crosby

It is disconcerting, therefore, to realize that, with respect to dystopia, most are not even contemplating the question of what is to be done, let alone seriously trying to answer it. People, of course, are thinking about *the* future; people are planning for the future. But most people's thoughts and plans are all based upon the wrong supposition. They are based upon the supposition that life will carry on in a recognizably similar fashion to today.

Educational savings plans are a perfect example of this. In Canada and in the US and many other wealthy countries, they are a part of the culture of parenting. To ensure that their children have a chance for a good life, responsible parents open a savings plan to later pay for their children's university education. Though such plans are usually facilitated through governmental institutions and tax breaks, parents are still putting out a significant ongoing financial commitment. To *not* make such a commitment to one's children would be considered irresponsible.

The education system, the skills and job market and many other things about our contemporary situation are tacitly presumed to remain more or less constant, so that today's life-chances market necessities will be tomorrow's. But this presumption is almost certainly false! What will be the future with respect to skills and jobs and qualifications? I have no idea. If we were being *utopian*, we might think that people will have collectively smartened up sufficiently to have demanded a well-funded, free public tertiary education system and that by the time children born today will have grown up such will have actually been implemented. Perhaps, agitating and campaigning for that and similar sensible strategies, might well be more important than the individualist solution (paradoxically, engaged in by everybody!) of saving money for *your* kids' education. Such a collective-oriented action would go along with others that would be addressing the problems the child born today will be facing as a 20-year-old. Such, it seems to me, would be a very wise thing to have done.

The thing is that, though we do not know for sure the timescale of dystopia, we *do* know that probably twenty years from now it will be striking hard. Educational savings plans will not be much of a preparation for the exigencies of peak oil, water wars, dirty bombs and global warming. Instead of just making a financial commitment to their children's future, parents *urgently* need to make a political commitment to it.

Charity: The Wrong Side of Collective Altruistic Action

> *Charity is no substitute for justice withheld.*
> St. Augustine

> *When I gave food to the poor they called me*
> *a Saint, when I asked why the poor have no*
> *food they called me a Communist.*
> Doia Helder Camara

Some people are doing things that seem so obviously good that it is hard to criticize them. They are donating food to homeless shelters; they are financially adopting Third World children; they are running marathons to raise money for cancer research. They are making a considerable commitment of time and/or money to directly address important problems and issues. But nonetheless, in spite of the worthiness of the intentions, in spite of the, in some cases enormous, amount of time given to altruistic pursuit, in spite of the, again in some cases enormous, amounts of money raised, we still can say that such action is simply a variant "of planning for a future that will never come." That is, charity will not on any appreciable scale reduce the suffering of dystopia nor prevent its onslaught.

Worse still, I am sorry to say, amidst all the good done in terms of the amelioration of immediate suffering, charity still on balance does harm. Yes, the answer given in this section to the question of what is to be done is: don't do any more charitable work; refocus your efforts politically.

Slavoj Zizek argues that:

> when we see a scene of starving children in Africa, with a call to do something and help them, the true message visible through the (ideological) glasses would have been something like: "Don't think, don't politicize, forget about the true causes of their poverty, just act, contribute money, so that you will not have to think!"[1].

We live in a world where so many harmful activities are extremely well-rewarded. And the corollary to this is that we live in a world where so many important collectively needed activities are left to charities to provide. Though, of course, charity has been with the human species historically much longer than has capitalism, the form it takes now is different; its function is different. In terms of tending wounds, it is a mere band-aid; in terms of ideological function, it is essential. It is the phony human face of capitalist indifference and cruelty.

Let's consider the relationship between cancer, capitalism and the funding of research in the wealthy countries (the shorter life expectancy and other killers in the poorer countries of the world make it less of a priority problem for them). First, we can observe

---

[1]   Slavoj   Zizek   (2009),   *Denial: the   Liberal   Utopia*, http://www.lacan.com/essays/?page_id=397

that, though a lot of research is being done overall, it is inadequate to the scale of the problem. We all know someone with cancer. Would there be a public outcry if the balance between taxation and governmental spending on research were to be shifted? I think most people would recognize the need. Charity runs make people feel good; but they help to obscure the ill-chosen spending priorities of governments. Privately funded research is directed not simply by the priorities of treatment and cure but even more significantly by the priorities of the commodification of medicine and the probabilities of patents paying off.

And what of poverty? Jean Paul Sartre exhorted us in the wealthy world to look at the world differently if we truly wished to understand it. He told us we should try and "see the world through the eyes of the most oppressed." If we genuinely do this do this then, we will see that they do not want our pity; they do not want out charity; they want our hands of their pockets and our feet off their necks!

The issue of charity here directs us now to the larger issue of capitalism and reform.

Capitalism with a Human Face: Plus ca change, plus c'est la même chose

> *Same old, same old.*
> Anonymous

Slavoj Zizek quotes John Caputo to make a point about utopian thinking concerning the possibilities of reforming the capitalist system:

> I would be perfectly happy if the far left politicians in the United States by providing universal health care, effectively redistributing wealth more equitably with a revised IRS code, effectively restricting campaign financing, enfranchising all voters, treating migrant workers humanely, and effecting multilateral foreign policy that would integrate American power within the international community etc., i.e.,

intervene upon capitalism by means of serious and far-reaching
reforms . . . If after doing all that Badiou and Zizek complained
that some monster called Capital still stalks us, I would be
inclined to greet that Monster with a yawn.[2]

Zizek does not dispute whether such reform would make for a
better world, or even if we might be better able to remain within
the system if such fare reaching reforms were possible. Instead he
argues that:

The problem lies with the "utopian" premise
that it is possible to achieve all that within the coordinates of
global capitalism. What if the particular malfunctionings of
capitalism enumerated by Caputo are not merely accidental
disturbances but are rather structurally necessary?[3]

Just to be completely clear, I will answer Zizek's rhetorical
question. The "malfunctionings" are not such at all; the ill
treatment of migrant workers, for example, is certainly a moral
shame, but it is not because of an accidental flaw in the system.
No, it and the rest enumerated by Caputo, are *structurally
necessary to the system*.

On the other hand, of course, it may be the case that there also
is a certain, necessarily utopian element, to the dream of
overthrowing of Capital, and we will speak of this later. But here
we can certainly say that most reformist programs are based upon
illusion and a misunderstanding of the central dynamics of the
capitalist system.

It is not that capitalism is not susceptible to reforms. Indeed,
its very flexibility is one of the things that makes its overthrow so
difficult. The state management of capitalism ranges from neo-

---

[2] John Caputo and Gianni Vattimo, *After the Death of God*, pp. 124-
125, quoted in Slavoj Zizek (2009), *First as Tragedy, Then as Farce*,
Verso: London. pp. 78-79.

[3] Slavoj Zizek (2009), *First as Tragedy, Then as Farce*, Verso, London,
p. 79.

liberalist regulation of unregulated market forces to Keynesian state intervention in the market, to the so-called socialist interventions of social democratic governments. The "socialist" measures taken are always only the *minimal* demands of a an increasingly rebellious public with expectations of justice and a better world. Keynesian intervention takes the edge off economic crises. Both kinds of measures "save" capitalism, as it were, from people's rising expectations and from itself.

Capitalist reforms have brought socialized medicine and pensions, the welfare state in its various forms, as well as state-funded public education and an enhanced physical infrastructure construction for transportation and other crucial structures. Reform has also redistributed wealth . . . though not nearly as much as is generally thought. For example, post-war Britain engaged in a massive public housing building project ("council housing," it is called there) and established the National Health Service. Many, many industries were nationalized, coal and steel and power being the most important among them. There was a relatively massive transfer of wealth . . . about five percent from the wealthy elite to the common people, from the ruling class to the working class. The distribution of wealth remained fairly stable after this, in spite of the back and forth between successive Labour and Tory governments . . . until, that is, the election of Margaret Thatcher. Her time as prime minister and neo-liberal agenda saw the *transfer back* of that five percent. The opening years of the 20th and 21st centuries saw about the same wealth distribution in United Kingdom.[4]

The point here is that capitalist reform is always going to be limited by the fundamental features of the system. Unemployment is not an accidental feature of capitalism, something that might be fixed by a more robust economy and better governmental initiatives. Unemployment rates will fluctuate, but they will *always* be significant. Unemployment is a fundamental functional part of any capitalist economy. As Marx put it, the unemployed

---

[4] Michael Haralambos and Martin Holborn (2004), *Sociology Themes and Perspectives*, Collins Educational.

are the reserve army of labour; they fulfill the function of putting checks upon rising wages and other worker demands.

Inequality of wealth and income, extreme inequality of wealth and income, both within and between nations, is a fundamental feature of the global political economy. The commonly heard adage "the rich get richer and the poor get poorer" is expressive of the structural dynamic of the system. So what about the possibility of various environmental reforms? These push up against the limits of parliamentary democracy. Election campaigns are financed by corporations that have the logic of profit as their bottom-line agenda; environmentally protective legislation will thus be diluted. True environmental protection is replaced by governmental and corporate public relations proclaiming such measures and concealing a much uglier reality. If capitalism has a human face, it is a very ugly face when stripped of the cosmetic doctoring of the public relations industry.

We can turn to Britain again to see the ultimate logic of the urgency of "realistic" immediate reforms. The post-war Labour government produced change. It was seemingly enormous change! But in reality, it was minimal . . . that is, it was minimal with respect to what was not only hoped for at the time, but expected, *demanded*. The Labour government that produced these changes got elected on an enormous wave of popular demand for change. But the Labour party was itself changing. It began a process of change shortly after its very inception. It was born of a genuine workers' mobilisation and self-organization. But as the founding moment was predominantly social-democratic rather than genuinely socialist, it proceeded with a continual logic of compromise. The argument remained the same. In government, Labour had to move to the right in order to stay in power; in opposition, Labour had to move to the right in order to stand a chance to get elected again. These arguments were propounded throughout the entire history of the party and actually, of *every* social-democratic party.

Supporters of the NDP in Canada should take note that it is only its historical electoral failures that keep it from the final resting point of Labour party trajectory: the Blair government's embrace of unsavory wars and neo-liberal economics. There social democracy was unmasked: as pseudo-socialism with a traitorous, ugly capitalist face.

Nowtopia: Part of the Solution or Part of the Problem

> *Turn on, tune in, drop out*
> Timothy Leary

The grand illusion of sixties counterculture was that one could "drop out" of the system. One can, and of course many did, reject many mainstream cultural, political and moral values. But this is not exactly the same thing. Most significantly the "system" is an economic system, a world-political-economic system. It is all-encompassing; it is beyond the scope of human choice. One can take a vow of poverty; one can leave a career in advertising; but one cannot *not* be a part of the capitalist system. You can reject its dominant values to do with consumer culture and monetary measures of success; but this does not mean you have dropped out of the game; it merely means that you are playing it differently. This is no small thing in itself. But one needs to evaluate one's choices carefully and avoid illusions about their effects.

Many of the hippies of the sixties had a self-glorifying self-deception as a baseline for their attitudes towards consumption and materialism. The hippies, at least North American hippies, were predominantly children of the suburbs. They rejected a reproduction of their parents' world, the two cars, the suburban home and. as was often said at the time, the "2.2 children." They (most anyway) thought they were rejecting consumerism. But they nonetheless appreciated a good stereo system and a VW minivan. When I travelled in the Third World during that era, I was very much surprised to learn that the common perception of my fellow hippy travelers and me was that we were rich. We may have travelled on the cheap, but the very fact that we were travelling for fun at all meant that we certainly were rich by any kind of standard of the Third World countries we backpacked and hitchhiked through. Somehow or another, too, most of the 60s hippies eventually found their way back to middle-class careers and homes in the suburbs.

But not all of them. Some forged genuinely new and different lifestyles. And that is still going on to this day; and a good deal of it is being done *without* the usual naivety of their hippy predecessors. What I am vaguely referring to here is a very culturally, politically and economically mixed bag of people. They are much more diverse with respect to beliefs, lifestyles and values than their hippy predecessors. Their beliefs and actions are also a mixed bag of varying degrees of significance to dystopia, of varying degrees of a sliding scale of hurt and harm; they are part of the solution and part of the problem.

There are people who are trying quite hard to live outside of a money economy . . . as far as possible. This is what I mean by lacking some of the naivety of the early hippies; these people know very well that, in some regards, the capitalist system is inescapable. But they are trying to live instead within a barter economy of trading resources, skills and products. This is sometimes mixed with an idea of a "gift economy," where to some degree the old communist ideal of "from each according to his means, to each according to his needs," is attempted to be put into practice.

There are people who are seeking out and utilizing alternative technologies, transport and energy sources (these groups are not at all mutually exclusive; in fact they frequently overlap; but I am listing them separately because they don't always). Others are attempting to be more food self-sufficient, even in the cities. So we have alternative cultures, if not exactly economies, of organic urban gardening, and tinkering, and bicycles and the Internet. This last is particularly significant. The self-organization and resistance to the contemporary attempted enclosure, by governments and corporations, of the electronic commons, strikes to the heart of the current stage of capitalism, as the global North moves more and more out of heavy industry towards what is frequently (and quite misleadingly) referred to as the "knowledge economy."

This all is a different kind of strategy for dealing with capitalism on the one hand and resisting it on the other. It is (to varying degrees limited) attempting to live in the capitalist world right now, in ways that somehow stand outside of its domination and control. So one grows and buys and/or trades food locally. One organizes bicycle and/or other forms of transportation and fuel collectives. These activities are limited in scope, but they are not wholly individual either. Thus, to some degree they are serious acts of resistance.

One of the most common ideologies of capitalism is that humans are by their very nature selfish. The system-innate competition of capitalism thus makes it the perfect value system so as to coincide with human nature. One can, of course, easily counter this contention with rational argument. First, one can say that we are socialized into competitiveness through the system itself, trained to be selfish as it were, rather than born that way. And secondly, it simply is not true that people are always acting selfishly, or that acts of kindness are restricted to family and friends.

The Internet provides a perfect example for the second assertion. Do you have a question about something? Anything! Ask a question on any topic from philosophy to history to technology; type it in on your search engine, and a host of people and sites and forums will likely come up to answer you. The Internet, unsurprisingly, is a particularly good source for finding advice and help to solve computer problems. It is also in the terrain of the Internet and computer programming where we see the strongest seeds of contemporary resistance to the capitalist enclosure of the commons.[5] Also we see inscribed in the Internet's very nature some of the sharpest contradictions of

---

[5] Enclosures first began taking place in 16th-century England. Hereditary rights of peasants were revoked, and they were driven from the land en masse to become the new class of laborers at the dawn of capitalism. But the enclosure of the commons also functions as the most commonly used metaphor to describe the usurpation and commoditization of publicly shared and utilized properties of any and all sorts by private capital. "The enclosure of the commons has been called the revolution of the rich against the poor," Vandana Shiva, "The Enclosure of the Commons," *TWN Third World Network*. http://www.twnside.org.sg/title/com-cn.htm

contemporary capitalism. Chris Carlsson expresses this thought very well:

> The Internet balances on radically opposite assumptions about the material basis of our lives. It is a curious hybrid of money-making business and a sprawling gift economy of avid writers, programmers, designers and inventors, mutually dependent while working (often unconsciously) towards antagonistic goals. Private ownership and its foundational fear of scarcity push the Internet to extend and intensify the exploitation of human labour. The commodity form is imposed on the "products" that traverse the Internet, while wherever possible human connections are reduced to mere transactions.
> The Internet also reveals a nearly limitless abundance that stimulates sharing and cooperation for its own sake, a digital commons reinforcing human interconnectedness and interdependence. In a late Capitalist world of numbing barbarism and alienated isolation, the powerful allure of meaningful communication inspires passionate engagement and remarkable time investments by millions.[6]

So we have an ongoing battle to shape the virtual and the real world here. The same people can be fighting on both sides, so to speak. They may work for large corporations but in their free time generously give their knowledge and advice, as well as creatively develop free software with General Public Licenses.[7] The freely available collective gift of the Linux operating system to the world has become a serious rival to the Microsoft commodity's

---

[6] *Nowtopia: How Pirate Programmers, Outlaw Bicyclists, and Vacant-Lot Gardeners are Inventing the Future Today*, AK Press, Oakland, CA, pp. 185-186.

[7] The GNU General Public License is a free copyleft license for software and other kinds of works . . . the GNU General Public License is intended to guarantee your freedom to share and change all versions of a program — to make sure it remains free software for all its users. http://www.gnu.org/licenses/gpl.html

near monopoly. Social media, such as Facebook, MySpace and Twitter, stand on the edge of a razor blade, as they both serve as social political organizational tools and become increasingly commodified.

The two main points with respect to all of the "nowtopian"[8] groups and activities are, first, that they stand in constant jeopardy of being co-opted by the capitalist system; and, secondly, that it is often easy for those involved to forget that, in addition to whatever form of alternative or resistance to the system they offer, more direct attempts at political change are *also* necessary. In both cases, it is frequently the case that their increasing success exposes them the most to these dangers. It must be remembered that the terrain of nowtopia is a terrain of constant struggle.

Utopian Dystopia: "Happy Days" in the Post-carbon World

Actually this section title is perhaps misleading. No one who has seriously engaged with the future problems of transition from our oil-dependent, energy-wasteful society to a new world order based upon energy scarcity predicts good times or an easy go of things. Of course, when I say "seriously engaged," I am not including in that definition those who believe "everything will be for the best in this best of all possible worlds,"[9] and a future where governments will interfere less and less with the market. Nor am I including those who trust absolutely that new technology will solve all problems. Such people have usually not reflected at all upon the scientific particularities of the history and present of energy production, the ways in which it is special, the ways in which it is different in kind from the constant evolution of television sets or waffle irons.

No, even the most optimistic and the most cautious with respect to considering the transition to our post-carbon energy

---

[8] The term is an invention of Chris Carlsson and provides the title for his book *Nowtopia*.

[9] An expression whose satirical origin comes from Voltaire's *Candide*.

future are rather gloomy. The Hirsh report[10] commissioned by the US government (and subsequently buried) attempted to assess the economic effects of the rising oil prices that would come about as a result of reaching the oil production peak. It concluded that if serious, that is to say *emergency*, measures were taken to prepare for a differently organized energy and transport sector, then dependent upon when such measures were begun, quite different consequences would ensue. They argued that if drastic measures were initiated 20 years prior to reaching the oil production peak, then a relatively smooth transition could be managed. This is their only "happy" possibility. If such measures were not begun until only 10 years before the peak was reached, then we could expect significant disruption to our lives and society. But if serious measures are not taken until just before the peak is actually reached, then extreme disruption and very negative consequences most certainly will result.

They have these predictions of different consequences for the different time periods for quite sensible reasons. These aspects of the problem are apparently beyond the analytical imaginations of either the technology or market worshipers. There is a physical as well as social and economic infrastructure that needs lead time to change. For example, automobiles are, for all but the rich, significant financial outlays of investment that have a time span of years attached to them. Lease agreements last for a particular length of time. Chucking away that gas hog SUV for the new hydrogen car could not simply be done at the drop of a hat. Cars have a physical lifetime through which they move through a succession of owners as they work down in price. This price chain of consumers will obviously be affected by gas prices; but again the point to be aware of is the fact that, new technology or not, the new does not *immediately* replace the old. Changing a whole transportation network, abandoning cars and highways and re-

---

[10], R.L. Hirsch, R. Besdek and R. Wendling (2005), *Peaking of World Oil Production: Impacts, Mitigation, and Risk Management*, commissioned by the United States Department of Energy. http://www.netl.doe.gov/publications/others/pdf/oil_peaking_netl.pdf

awakening the age of the train and good inner-city public transit is something whose very physical challenge (let alone all the various cultural and social changes that would have to accompany it) is one that could only be accomplished over some very significant time delay from when it was first decided to be desirable.

It seems almost certain that we will miss either the "happy" or "not so bad" alternatives put forward as forecasts by this think-tank. It is possible that the world will not reach the peak oil production peak for another 20 years. It is possible but not likely. Even so, there are absolutely *no signs* of the beginning of any *emergency* transition to a different energy and transportation system . . . anywhere in the world. And it is more likely that we already have reached the oil production peak,[11] or will within a very few years indeed.

The Long Emergency by James Howard Kunstler[12] examines the possible contours of the post-peak world. His thinking is in line with a good deal of the dystopia thesis. He sees very serious problems ahead. His analysis very particularly focuses upon the un-sustainability of American suburbia. The combinations of big-box stores, strip malls and suburban living, with the exploitation of cheap labour abroad and consequent long-distance transport of everything imaginable, he cogently argues are extraordinarily wasteful and will ultimately become impossible, as shortages and instabilities in the oil and other energy markets emerge. He rationally assesses the advantages and disadvantages of different parts of the world for surviving the "long emergency" and developing a new, more localized eco-friendly and sustainable economy.

---

[11] "We actually reached a sustainable peak in crude oil production in December 2005," Matt Simmons, an energy analyst, said at a meeting of the United States Association for the Study of Peak Oil and Gas, Reuters, October 26, 2006.

[12] James Howard Kunstler (2005), *The Long Emergency: Surviving the Converging Catastrophes of the Twenty-first Century*, Grove Atlantic.

He is quite right to emphasize differences in the way various parts of the world will be impacted. The dystopia thesis predicts a grim state of affairs for all but emphasizes that it will be the poor who feel it first and most intensely. It also argues that cultural and environmental factors will also play a significant role in the manner in which dystopia manifests itself around the globe. Kunstler would agree. He rightly argues, for example, that because of better rail networks and public transit systems, Europe will possess some advantages over the US, as the world economy is transformed by the new realities of its energy economics. He also argues that America will have a tougher time adjusting to some of the new realities because of the design of their living arrangements. As American suburbia was built, towns and cities were gutted. The big cities have crime-ridden slums surrounding their glass-and-steel skyscraper cores, while the centers of smaller cities and towns have effectively economically collapsed. People live in the suburbs and shop in the malls ("plenty of parking") miles from any town center. But this is where he begins to go a little bit wrong. The problem is to do with the timeline of prediction.

Kunstler, in addition to assessing the world's regions, looks at different parts of the United States. He sees the American Southwest as basically doomed. The dependence on cheap oil, he argues, has made what would be an eco-system scarcely able to support even a tiny population support the modern American lifestyle for millions. When the cheap oil is gone, the entire area will collapse. The area of the US he sees as best able to continue on and perhaps even healthily adapt is the rural Northeast. It is there that we find not only lakes, rivers and the survival of some small-scale farming in this agribusiness age, but also a small town infrastructure that *could* be rebuilt. This is his vision of a sustainable future.

We see a more localized economy. We see people living in towns and villages not meg-cities, and most definitely not, suburbia. The towns are surrounded by a renewed agriculture, and these regions are largely self-supporting except for trade with fairly proximate neighbours. There would be electricity, but energy usage would be far, far less than at present. Old skills would need to be revived. And, he argues, there would perhaps even be cultural human benefits to this materially less affluent new society. There would be a lessening of alienation and a revival of community spirit, mutual dependency and sharing. Yes, even in the viewpoint of the coldest rational assessment of the human condition, even in the midst of the most "alarmist" of the alarmist visions of the world, Americans seem unable to contain their Disneyland fantasies. Kunstler's vision for the survivors of the "long emergency" looks an awful lot like Main Street of 1950s America. "Happy Days" are here again.

On a different level, Kunstler's reasoning is quite sound. A different kind of economic organization *will* be forced upon us. Everything from agricultural practices to town and house design will need to change. Perhaps eventually people will live in the kind of communities Kunstler has imagined. The problem is the timescale. The problem is the transition period . . . from which perhaps we might *never emerge*. It can be found in Kunstler's own description of the different US regional scenarios. He sees the South-western desert states as likely to become totally depopulated. He sees the Southeast, America's Old South, to have a different kind of hard time. For a variety of historical and cultural factors, he deems it likely that they will resort to violence. But the Deep South is not the only home of the "redneck"; and rednecks are not the only Americans likely to resort to violence. America's largest cities will all become unsustainable, according to Kunstler. The question is: Where are all these people going to go? Some of them, many of them, perhaps, will simply and conveniently die. Many of them will take their violent social conditioning and turn it against each other. But while most of America is soft and spoiled, the people of its inner cities have grown trained in an ethos of survival. They are organized into Mafioso-style gangs, and they are well-armed. The "transition period" will not look like Main Street 1950s. It will be violent. If there is any model worth looking at to imagine the future, then something like present-day Somalia would give a much better picture.

Richard Heinberg[13] is another peak oil crisis writer. Like Kunstler and almost all others writing on the topic, he shares the dystopia perspective to quite some degree. But, also like most such authors, he presents his view of the future as a choice. He lists and elaborates the many dystopian consequences. He cogently argues that our present cheap energy-based global economic system is not sustainable. The global system will dramatically change. The question is whether or not it will change in a cooperative, fair, controlled, gradual phasing in of the changes, whereby our declining energy resources are sensibly conserved as the new, re-localized different fuel and organized system(s) emerge; or instead, whether we will engage in a brutal barbaric battle on a world scale, as today's elites attempt to maintain sole right of use upon a declining resource base.

Heinberg presents a list of valuable suggestions to overt the nightmares presented in this book and to move to a differently organized energy economy. He presents suggestions for every level. There are things individuals can do to move into a less energy-squandering lifestyle. There are energy conservation measures and some possibility of shifting to some degree to alternative power generation. Home re-modeling, the acquisition of gardening, herbology and other skills and knowledges could all be useful. Or then again, from the dystopia perspective, perhaps not. In this, Heinberg shares the double-edge of the "nowtopians." He suggests actions that communities can do. Heinberg recognizes the scale of the problem and sees limits to the potential of purely individual actions. He further realizes the limits, or at least the difficulties, of action on the local community level. Controlling their own power and water supplies, for example, are things that can be done in some places and not in other places. There are geographical differences as to the physical possibilities. There are also greater and lesser obstacles in different places,

---

[13] Richard Heinberg (2005), *The Party's Over: Oil, War and the Fate of Industrial Societies*, New Society Publishers, Gabriola Island, BC, and (2004) *Power Down: Options and Actions for a Post-Carbon World*, New Society Publishers.

which would be presented by the next organizational scale of governance and power relations. The decisions of state and national governments, as well as large corporations, all constrain the potential for progressive change to be initiated at the community level.

Heinberg moves on up the scale. He also has sensible advice for state and national government. He even has sensible advice for the world as a whole. He draws our attention to a proposal for a new global "oil protocol" prepared by the Association for the Study of Peak Oil.[14] Oil-importing nations would agree to diminish their imports by two percent a year, the approximate rate of post-peak depletion. This would moderate any wild market fluctuations in price, allowing every country to more easily plan their economic readjustments. It would also allow even the poorest countries a share in the oil, which otherwise they may be cut off from entirely. The dystopia thesis disputes none of this. Indeed, it also agrees with Heinberg when he asserts:

> In order to feel that the sacrifices they are making during the energy downturn are fair, *the people of any nation must be empowered* to participate in the process of making decisions as to how those sacrifices are allocated . . . the radical shifts can probably only happen as a result of the dramatically increased involvement of an informed citizenry at every level of a revitalized political process. Unfortunately the citizenry is currently neither informed nor involved, and the system resists fundamental change at all levels. Immense sums are invested annually to distract the public from substantive issues and to turn their attention instead toward consumption and complacency.[15]

This section has raised serious issues with respect to what can be done to understand dystopia, on the one hand, and what should be done to prevent it, on the other. The two are, of course,

---

[14] www.peakoil.net

[15] Richard Heinberg (2005), *The Party's Over*, p. 253.

crucially bound together. But we shall engage with them separately in the following two sections. First, we shall consider the problems of prediction, the knowledge *limits* of prediction. Kunstler's work in particular provokes some serious questions with respect to this issue. His analysis and predictions are plausible, but they are too detailed when you consider he is skipping to a future that passes over the transition period to get there. Too many variables could send humanity spinning off in quite a different direction than the one he plausibly envisioned. The other problem is that the vision itself seems very utopian in the sense that human existence in this world seems not too bad, perhaps even better than our present way of life in some respects. But this is to skip over the horror of the painful deaths of millions. Heinberg's suggestions for activity and change now, advice for government and so on, raises the crucially important aspect of the question of what is to be done? What is to be done by *whom*? We will look at this towards the end of the chapter.

The Limits to Prediction and the Predictions of the Dystopia Thesis

> *Prediction is very difficult, especially about the future.*
> Niels Bohr

Was the preceding chapter's year 2020 scenario a serious prediction? Yes and no. No, it was not, insofar as the future cannot be predicted so certainly and specifically. Will the Atlantic conveyer dramatically slow down in the year 2020? Will terrorists choose Beverly Hills to explode a "dirty bomb"? Will there even be any exploded anywhere? Will a hurricane hit New Orleans again? If Pakistan and India had a limited nuclear exchange, would they target Mumbai and Rawalpindi for sure? How could anyone *know* that they are even going to have a war? And there you have it. No one *can* know such things for sure. But on the other hand, the scenario did not come out of nothing. All of the events of the scenario are plausible. They are things that not only could happen, but have a certain *probability* of happening.

I recently watched a rerun of an old *National Geographic* television documentary. The experience was rather spooky and confusing at first. It took me a while to realize that the program had been made and first aired *before Hurricane Katrina* occurred. The documentary was a prediction and a warning. It was the creation of a hypothetical scenario of a hurricane hitting New Orleans. It considered problems with the levees, with the lack of evacuation plans . . . all the problems looked at in the New Orleans section in chapter 2. Everything that was considered in the scenario created by the TV producers and their scientific advisers was near identical to what actually happened two years later . . . right down to which areas of the city would be hardest hit and which sectors of the population would suffer the most. That is what made it so spooky.

The documentary was not so prescient accidentally. It was based upon sound science. New Orleans was in a hurricane zone. It had had close calls before. Sooner or later, a powerful hurricane was going to meet it head on. Detecting the problems with the levees or figuring out whether or not everyone in the city could be evacuated were not really difficult problems to work out. They merely required research and analysis. The "prediction" of the 2020 scenario above that a second hurricane will hit New Orleans and further devastation will occur is an even easier prediction to make. It rests upon equally sound reasoning to the first *National Geographic* predictions.

New Orleans has not moved. It still is in a hurricane zone. That we are beginning now to feel the effects of global warming seems clear. Even more powerful hurricanes will likely rip through the general region in the future than there have been to date. However, even should concerns over global warming or the idea about its effects upon hurricane activity prove to be exaggerated, it is at least fairly certain that hurricane activity will not significantly decrease. And were a hurricane to strike New Orleans again, would there be any less death and destruction the second time round? Well possibly so . . . but only because such a lot of the damage from Katrina still has not been repaired and has a good chance of never being fixed; only because a good-sized proportion of the city still has not returned to live there.

But everything else is in place for a new disaster. The levee system still has not been properly fixed. By that I mean not only repaired but raised to plausible predicted flood levels. A sensible, workable evacuation plan still has not been put together. So, the dystopia thesis suggests this as another accident waiting to happen in the future.

Of course, one cannot accurately predict specific accidents. Liquid natural gas terminals have certain risks attached to them. The dangers are known. Perhaps, given our collective need for energy, the risks might even be acceptable. Perhaps. But what the dystopia thesis most significantly predicts with respect to such is that an intelligent examination of those risks and a carefully considered democratic decision *will not be made.* Activists opposing such projects will be demonized in carefully plotted out public relations campaigns. Communities will simply be bullied into accepting corporate decisions.

Chapter 3 of this book looked at environmental issues. The dystopia prediction was fairly simple: the cornucopia of interrelated problems will get worse. Exactly how much worse is beyond anyone's capacity to know, except to assert vaguely "a lot worse." And of course, there were a number of specific runaway chains of consequences that would put the very existence of our species in peril. But there are too many variables, and too little knowledge concerning them, to be very certain of the odds of such catastrophes happening.

The Fight for and Against Nature

> Nature is trying very hard to make us succeed,
> but nature does not depend on us. We are not
> the only experiment.
>   R. Buckminster Fuller

The struggle against dystopia is only to a very small degree directly involved with nature. Nature imposes itself upon us indifferent to our needs or interests or desires. Nature is the context within which we enact our human dramas. Quite obviously, it profoundly affects us, and equally obviously, we

What is to be done?

affect it. So why do I say the struggle against dystopia is oi very small degree involved with nature? I say this because environmentalism is principally a struggle with human beings and social forces, a battle between eco-stewards and eco-rapists.

There is a struggle over knowledge and practices concerned with nature. What I mean here, is the struggle between science in the service of humanity and science in the service of capital.

Let us consider the latter first. Genetically modified crops are the product of science in the service of capital. Ostensibly they can increase yields and thus increase the food supply to a hungry populace. In reality, they increase the control of capital over farming, a substitution of the profit goals of cash crop agribusiness for the food needs of developing countries. The plants do not spontaneously reproduce. They are hybrids, and Monsanto, not the farmers themselves, controls the seed supplies. So here we have scientific advances, scientific knowledge, co-opted for the goals of capital with the scientists themselves becoming ideologically corrupted and mystified servants of dystopia. The struggle with nature for them is a struggle to worsen the human condition . . . though, of course, they do not understand it this way.

On the other hand, scientific knowledge may help us avoid the path of an increasingly dystopian future and do much to ameliorate present ills. Knowledge of nature may help us steward it. In fact, we crucially need such knowledge to do so responsibly. Scientific knowledge may help us feed the poor, cure disease, provide non-carbon-based energy generation, etc., etc. The Enlightenment dream of science and reason was not, and is not, merely a dream. And it is only partially a nightmare. Scientific knowledge is one of the pillars of hope for salvation from dystopia.

But there is science and science. Structural mystification is no more profoundly at work than in the scientific field. Scientists, perhaps more than any others, need to be self-aware of what they do, the forces at work upon them and the context of their research activities and findings. Structural mystification, as noted in chapter 6, works at both a sophisticated level and one that is fairly crude. The defense departments of many countries fund a disproportionate amount of research. This is particularly so in the United States. The Department of Defense provides approximately 33% of federal funding for engineering research, 70% for mechanical engineering. The Department of Defense accounts for ten percent of all federal support for academic institutions.[16] Surely, we now all know that all knowledge is not desirable. Frankenstein does not have to create the monster just because he can. We have the historical example of Einstein and Oppenheimer. One patriotically went to work to build an A-bomb. The other organized a petition of fellow scientists to send to the president of the United States, warning of its dangers and advising against its development. Scientists should heed this example. They should emulate Einstein not Oppenheimer.

Some people would say Einstein's actions were futile. If something scientifically can be done, it *will* be done. But this fatalism is only capitalist ideology. There are many wonderful applications to human betterment that could have, and should have, come from scientific discoveries that never occurred. Which discoveries? Which applications? I don`t know. The discoveries did not occur because the research *was not done*! The research was not done because the research *was not funded*! I state this only to make a point about research and knowledge and inevitability. Good things will not be discovered unless we facilitate their discovery; bad applications will not necessarily be developed . . . if we stop them.

The Logic of Historical Inevitability

> *Because things are the way they are, things will*
> *not stay the way they are.*
> Bertolt Brecht

---

[16] "Department of Defense Basic Research: Strengthening National and Economic Security Through Innovation," Task Force on the Future of American Innovation.
http://futureofinnovation.org/PDF/DoDBasicResearch.pdf

The very possibility of avoiding dystopia is questioned by many who accept many of the other tenets of the dystopia thesis. This perspective is but the flip side of that emotional rejection of the possibility that we could march like lemmings into future horror. Both perspectives are a response to the same thing: intellectual overload caused by the scope and complexity of the problems. The perspective one takes is thus, to some degree, determined by psychology and temperament. When the critical thinking and acquisition of evidence process shuts down, the emotional response is either a "Don't worry, the worst couldn't possibly happen" head-in-the-sand perspective, or its flip side, "We're doomed." This latter has as a corollary a "So what the hell difference does it make, we're doomed anyway, so we may as well make the most of it" perspective on voting Republican or Conservative, driving SUVs and not paying attention to current events.

Neither of these perspectives lends itself to the difficult assessments, decisions and actions that would work towards alleviating present suffering and preventing future barbarity. They are, in fact, responses to the situation generated by the situation that works to perpetuate the situation. They are dystopian responses to dystopia; they are part of dystopia.

There is another perspective in which dystopia is seen as inevitable but which is quite different. This is the realistic perspective that takes on-board all the painful awareness of the present conditions. Dystopia is already here for a billion or more people. The questions for the future are principally two-fold with respect to their suffering: Will their suffering be significantly ameliorated, or will their condition spread to even more of the world's population? Any realistic assessment of the present human condition asserts two clear answers to these questions. First, the dystopian conditions of that billion people will certainly persist for a number of years. Secondly, the number of people affected will increase. In short, things will continue to get worse before they could even *possibly* begin to get better. But . . . and this is crucial, though things have to get worse before they could get better . . . nonetheless we still *can* make things better. A better world *is* possible.

This is the perspective of *retrospective inevitability*. Dystopia was *inevitable* because dystopia *is*. Going back in history, we could point to this event and that one, we could say "if this and this and this had not occurred, then everything would be different." And we could even be right . . . in theory. But in fact, no other outcome was possible other than the one that actually occurred. The present human condition was inevitable . . . after the fact. The future will be too. We can extend inevitability into the future. It is inevitable that certain things will occur because we are too close to their occurrence to prevent their occurrence.

I earlier used the metaphor of a oil tanker to describe humanity's progress toward future dystopia. The metaphor illustrates the fact that to reverse directions and tendencies takes a certain amount of time. Humanity could, at some point, make a sensible and serious commitment to eradicate world hunger and commence the process that would achieve this goal. But the goal could not be achieved in a day; and those on the very brink of death by starvation will still die tomorrow. And we can predict with complete certainty quite a bit more with respect to this. We considered the "if/then" of humanity's collective serious commitment to alleviate world hunger. But there is at present no such commitment; and there are no signs on the horizon that we are even remotely close to such a commitment being made. It will take time if it is ever going to happen, and in the meantime, more and more will suffer and die. That is inevitable!

But this does not mean the future is an already-written book. We can begin *right now* to try to make a better world. And that, of course, means to struggle for socialism by all means available.

But Is Socialism Even Possible?

> *Socialism needs democracy like the human body*
> *needs oxygen.*
>   Leon Trotsky

The sad but true answer to this question is that I don't know. No one can know. Returning to the oil tanker metaphor, there comes a point when it is useless to put the engines full in reverse or spin the wheel to avoid the shipwreck . . . nothing can stop it now, it just *is* going to happen. It is perhaps difficult with an actual ship's course to calculate exactly when that point has been passed. Retrospectively, of course, it is fairly easy. Before a certain point, if this and this had been done, then all would have been well; the shipwreck occurred because the actions were not taken; but past a certain point, however, then it would not have mattered what anyone did or did not do.

There is too great a complexity with regard to dystopia to know when most of the various "tipping points" will be passed. This phrase "tipping point," is commonly used with respect to global warming. The common scientific assumption is that we have not reached it yet, with regard to most of the most significant processes affecting it (Greenland ice-shelf melt for example), though possibly we have with others. Overall, however, the problem is just too complex for us to know. And global warming is but one of the myriad processes involved with dystopia.

It is possible; I do not believe it, but it is possible, that it is *already too late* for humanity. Things may have already gone too far; complete barbaric horror is now our inevitable future. We must remember here that barbarity can come in myriad forms, some perhaps not even imagined by us. But the important thing with respect to this is that we cannot know it; we simply do not have sufficient information to make such a terrible, despairing judgment. To act as though we do is to act in accordance with what *could become* a self-fulfilling prophecy.

But what of the possibility of socialism? There are those who would assert that we *do* have enough information to judge here. Socialism has a past, a history of failure. There are those who would argue that history has shown us that socialism has built-in structural features that take us directly to barbarism . . . a different kind of barbarity than capitalism perhaps, but barbarism and horror nonetheless.

This is a hard question to answer. So let us get one quick easy one out of the way first. Is socialism *inevitable*? This has been a perspective within the history of Marxism and socialist struggle. It has been pointed out that within the Communist Manifesto, for example, Marx asserted that communism was inevitable.[17] There are two points to make with respect to this. First, one can argue that Marx was not making a literal assertion but rather articulating a political article of hope for the future. He was making a category of assertion similar to "go team go, we're gonna win." Regardless of such scholarly issues, we should not allow the question of authorial intent to distract us. Instead, we should clearly and simply conclude: Well, if Marx really believed communism was inevitable, then he was wrong.

The serious argument for socialism's inevitability is an analysis of capitalism's structure such that the contradictions within it, the increasing crises, will lead inevitably to revolution. The socialism of the future is at present a seed found within capitalism itself and beginning to germinate. Dystopia itself will engender its own solution. There are small elements of truth in this. But overall it is clearly wrong. Dystopia will *not* engender its own solution.

As things become more extreme, as problems manifest themselves more dramatically, it will be harder to hide one's head in the sand. A certain clarity may come from looking down the barrel of a gun . . . but perhaps only panic. Crises come with powerful contradictions; crises come with powerful forces pushing in opposite directions. The world financial crisis of 2008 is a perfect example of this. Capitalism had not been in such trouble for a long, long time, if ever. And yet the Left has never been weaker.

Crises always bring with them enormous suffering for ordinary people. People lose their jobs and their homes. Crises usually bring with them an intensification of repression. Crises bring with them a surfeit of mystification concerning them. For example, we have the palpable absurdity and deep ignorance of the financial

---

[17] "What the bourgeoisie therefore produces, above all, are its own grave-diggers. Its fall and the victory of the proletariat are equally inevitable." Karl Marx (1848) *The Communist Manifesto*.
http://www.marxists.org/archive/marx/works/1848/communist-manifesto/

crisis being blamed on the Jews,[18] on the one hand, and the subtler foolishness of a huge portion of the Left, at least for a time, buying the arguments of their respective governments, that billion-dollar bank bailouts were *necessary*. Both of these developments were disturbing. The first seems scarily reminiscent of Germany in the 30s and the Nazi exploitation of fear and ignorance and prejudice in the face of economic calamity. But how could present-day people of the Left think that giving tax payers' money to banks was on any level a good idea? So, the system, as Marx long ago pointed out, has structural contradictions that will produce periodic crises. But crises do not, in and of themselves, produce revolutions. They do not even automatically tear off the veil of ignorance through which most people see the world.

But they do produce opportunities. People are angered when the various bubbles (the stock market, pension schemes, real estate, etc.) are burst and cause them pain. They sometimes become ready to fight. The people of Greece went on strike and took to the streets when their pensions and other basics of life were threatened.[19] There is opportunity for serious political change to emanate from crisis. But it is not inevitable. Whether socialism is possible, whether the Earth can be saved from dystopia, is up to us.

---

[18] According to a survey of 2,768 American adults by Neil Malhotra and Yotam Margalit of Stanford University, 32 percent of Democrats and 18.4 percent of Republicans blamed Jews a moderate amount to a great deal for the current financial crisis.

[19] Between February and the end of June 2010, there were no less than five general strikes! Greece faced a rather extreme national debt crisis, and the government proposed to solve it on the backs of pensioners and workers. Unions seem prepared to seriously fight the austerity program. The final result of these actions and the winner of this struggle is not clear at the time of writing.

What Is to Be Done . . . by Whom?

> *Jeopardy means that either the leaders or*
> *the people do not realize they have all the*
> *tools required to make the revolution come*
> *true. The tools and the opportunity exist.*
> *Only the moral imagination is missing.*
>   William O. Douglas

The question of what is to be done is very tricky; all the more so, because at first glance, it would seem not to be. We have a problem: extreme inequality; people are starving, dying of easily curable diseases; they are living lives of violence, ignorance and misery; the population is increasing exponentially, further increasing the enormity of the problems. What is to be done? Solution: distribute the world's wealth more equitably; dramatically increase spending on education, particularly the education of young women, as this has been shown to be an extremely effective way of reducing the birth rate.

We have a problem: pollution. Air, water, it doesn't matter, the solution is the same. Stop or reduce the polluting practices. The same for global warming. Reorganize production, transport and the global energy usage system; significantly reduce carbon emissions. This will also reduce the negative effects of some of the myriad problems associated with the peak oil crisis. Simple. Except that these obvious global "solutions" are *useless platitudes*.

Who or what is going to make these things happen? Let's ask instead, for example, what the president of the United States should do? Well, we could give Obama a long list of things. Starting from the fairly easy, we could tell him: pull out of Iraq and Afghanistan, give the American people a proper health care system (not the one he is actually going to enact). We could then move to the more difficult suggestions: redistribute wealth both within the United States and the world at large by aggressive taxation, "fair trade" practices and suchlike measures. But questions come immediately to mind with respect to this. For example, even though Obama came to power on a wave of hope for change, a hope for *real* change, is it at all likely that he would even *want* to move along these lines? The record thus far would indicate otherwise.

Let's leave Obama for a second, so as to continue to give him the benefit of some doubt. Let's shift the question to someone for whom no such doubt exists, to someone where it is very clear what they want concerning the balance between economy and environment, for example. What is the best thing that Stephen Harper could do for Canada and/or the world? There the answer is simple: He should resign as prime minister. He could do even more good by fighting to retain the party leadership with a platform slogan of "we're not fit to govern." Perhaps he could then spend the next few years of his life rethinking his views on . . . everything . . . so as to not do any further harm to Canada or the human species.

But let's imagine that Obama really is the great man some people imagine him to be, that he really wants to substantially alter the status quo on everything from corporate profit, the media control of information, wealth distribution and so on. Well, what could he do? The watered-down pathetic excuse for a health care plan took a major battle to get through.[20] It is a cold reality of the United States' polis that it is dominated by a fearful ignorance that is truly breathtaking, on the one hand, and a very calculated ideological exploitation of that ignorance, on the other. Obama is hemmed in by the promises he made to big business during the election and their continuing power and influence over his administration at all levels and by a frequently amazingly stupid "public opinion."

---

[20] The plan provides a "health insurance market," and the White House (see http://www.whitehouse.gov/issues/health-care) alleges that 95 percent of Americans will have some kind of coverage. It is not clear what those without coverage are supposed to do. But his modest effort to cover a previously uninsured 32 million Americans has been bitterly opposed by Republicans. See, for example, Binoy Kampmark (August 8 2010) "Obama's Health Plan: The Battles Continues." http://www.globalresearch.ca/index.php?context=va&aid=18344

It has been a running argument throughout this book about the real power of corporations. But the question here is: Just how much could a CEO, a big shareholder or board member, change policy to respond to human needs when they are opposed to the bottom line of profit? The answer here is clear: *not very far . . .* before moves would begin for them to be ousted or fired or pressured into a reversal of any positive policy change. So, again we ask the question: What is to be done. . . by whom?

Solving the problems that humanity faces is not going to be done by those currently in power. They may, in a very slight way, push things one way or the other. Obama will do more good and less harm than did Bush . . . arguably anyway, hopefully anyway! And Bill Gates, through his charitable foundation, will have an effect upon Africa's malaria problem. Good for him. But he follows the same model of incorporated charity as did his 19th-century predecessors. Andrew Carnegie did indeed have a lot of libraries built, but America still is the land of the ignorant for all that.

A very simple thing that people like Bill Gates and Bono, who I believe, very genuinely want to help the poor, could do would just be to make a better selection of advisors. Bono, a leading figure and organizer in the Live 8 and the Make Poverty History projects, has, as his intellectual guru in such matters, Jeffery Sachs. Sachs was a former economic theoretical architect and policy advisor for the structural adjustment programs imposed ("economic shock therapy," it was called) on so many countries in the Third World. Yes, he has changed his mind on neo-liberal economics and now sees them as misguided[21] . . . but the thing is he was one of the guides. Though Sachs is perhaps quite sincere in his desire to eradicate poverty, I would suggest that there would be a plethora of much better-qualified instructors in the complexities of world political-economy (theorists who understand the necessary linkage between politics and economy for a start!) for Bono to listen to if he wants to use his fame to help the world.

---

[21] See, for example, Jeffery Sachs (2005) *The End of Poverty: Economic Possibilities for Our Time*, Penguin Press.

What is to be done?

Some of humanity's problems may be solved by those who are at present powerless. The enormous population who live in our "planet of slums"[22] may riot; they may take up arms and rise up in revolution. We can hope for this. And we can refuse to believe the inevitable media lies that will accompany it if it occurs. We can protest the inevitable repressive actions our governments will take to crush these peoples' struggles. We can try to help in whatever limited ways we can. But we cannot make it happen. The desperately poor will do whatever they will do. Perhaps they will be tricked, perhaps they will be ideologically manipulated by the right, and we can try and combat this; but ultimately they will do what they will do. Ultimately, they will make their own choices within their own contexts of desperation, knowledge and the lack thereof. What is very unlikely is that they will be reading this book. Literacy and access to information is not the privilege of those who are on the bottom. The struggle for literacy and better education is itself a political struggle.[23]

So the really crucial question of what is to be done is: What is to be done by *you*? It is not a question of what should the G8 or G20's new socio-political policies be. It is not a question about what BP should do (at time of writing they *still* had not properly fixed the Gulf oil leak, so it is pretty obvious what *they* should do). It is not a question of what your government should do;

---

[22] Mike Davis (2006) *Planet of Slums*, Verso.

[23] Paulo Freire did world-renowned, groundbreaking research on the connections between poverty, adult literacy and politics. He found, not very surprisingly when you come to think about it, that when sugar cane workers were able to see a useful purpose to numeracy and literacy that motivation improved results dramatically. When be briefly became Minister of Education in Brazil, he attempted to put his research results into widespread practice. It was one of the motivations for the military coup that almost immediately followed. He was then imprisoned. See Freire's classic book (2002) *Pedagogy of the Oppressed*, New York: Continuum, for a fuller explanation of his political educational theories and research.

probably the best thing they could do would be to legislate themselves out of existence. *The Yes Men* carried out a brilliant stunt in Australia while posing as senior executive representatives of the World Bank.[24] They announced that a new internal analysis of policy had concluded that it had been misguided since its inception and failed in all its worthy objectives, even having predominantly negative effects. In the light of this information, *The Yes Men* declared that it was now announcing its disbandment! If only it were true!

So the question is what should *you* do, given the full context of the world socio-political economy and your personal situation within it. You are actually in a, potentially at least, more powerful position than the millions of inhabitants of the global slums or the poverty-stricken peasantry of the Third World. Your relative affluence gives you a certain degree of relative freedom, relative power. Should you quit your job? Your job is on one level your survival but not on the same level that a Cambodian peasant's farming is for him. He literally can face starvation while you do not. The job facilitates all your other actions; we all need money to survive in this world. But if the occasion arises; if the political necessity arises, you could quit and your children would still survive as well.

But what would be the occasion to warrant the ascription of political necessity? There is no universal prescription to determine this. It is dependent upon *your* analysis, *your* conscience, *your* courage . . . *your* decision. This is not some kind

---

[24] See the movie *The Yes Men* (1999), Paramount. Also see *The Yes Men Fix the World* for further impersonations of governments, corporations and organizations, where they publicly make pronouncements that would be wonderful if they were only true. For example, it was announced in a BBC interview that a $12 billion compensation package would be given by Dow Chemical to the Bhopal victims of the Union Carbide chemical catastrophe . . . something like the compensation that would have been required had the disaster occurred in the US instead of India. This *Yes Men* hoax resulted in a $2 billion drop in Dow share prices within 15 minutes.

of all-or-nothing thing either. No, it is a matter of a moral polit. calculus that only you have the formula for. You keep your heat down and your mouth shut and live to fight the power another day; or you make your stand; or you take an intermediate moderate course. You calculate that the moderately forceful protest you make will predictably (not in an absolute sense, but in terms of risk probabilities) bring about a moderately forceful repercussion. How big are the risks? How important is the issue? Thought and analysis is required for your decision. The only thing one can say about it generally is that if it is *always* the case that your conclusion is to keep your head down, then something is wrong with your calculations. There are enough important issues to justify taking some risk to yourself in relation to them.

Should you go out in the street and shout? Should you emulate the Buddhist monks who protested the Vietnam War by pouring gasoline over themselves and setting themselves alight. Well, if you have the courage, you could inspire us all, perhaps, but I think this last one is asking too much. The other two are different and need to be answered *contextually*. Quit your job? Kind of depends upon what your job is. If you work for Wal-Mart, don't quit, try and form a union instead. Don't worry, they'll fire you for sure . . . and if you are most people, you won't have lost much except a low paying dead-end career. If on the other hand, you are trapped by desperate circumstance, if at this point in your life, you *really need* the Wal-Mart job to make ends meet . . . well, I would still say try and unionize, but be careful; this will require courage and thought and strategy and help from others. As regards the last, if you look for it you will find it.[25] The rest of us should be organizing a boycott.

Shouting in the street *is* a good idea. Not, of course, as a nutter act all by yourself. No, this too is contextual. If there isn't the context of a collective protest, think about it, talk about it and begin to organize. Yes, it does all come down to the old slogan: educate, agitate, organize! Real significant change will come not from the top but from the bottom. We can refer back to the

---

[25] See http://walmartwatch.com/ for more information.

suggestion of the previous paragraph: boycotting Wal-Mart. This would be a good idea. Wal-Mart is a company with extremely noxious policies. They were among those corporations that took out the now notorious "Dead Peasant insurance policies."[26] They have been anti-union to the point of fanaticism, preferring to shut down a store entirely rather than allow even a small portion of it to unionize.[27] They import most of their cheap goods from the Republic of China and other countries where the sweatshop conditions and exploitation of women and children are the most extreme found anywhere. Capitalism is capitalism, but Wal-Mart is not only the largest corporation in the world but possibly the best symbol of it negative features. Putting it out of business, or forcing it to dramatically change its policies, would be an incredible victory for the Left.

But simply deciding personally to no longer patronize their stores as a moral act is useless. The Left needs to completely abandon individualist moralism and its corollary practices. Moral responsibility actually demands a level of political organization.

So, we need to march and shout and boycott and agitate. We need to engage with local problems *and* global ones. They connect to one another. What is needed is less altruism and more • enlightened self-interest. If you are victim of one of capitalism's structural crises, the real estate crisis in America for example and your home is about to be repossessed, don't leave. Appeal for help from your neighbours and left-wing groups. You may be

---

[26] Dead Peasant insurance policies are life insurance policies taken out by employers on their (frequently low-paid) employees, which name themselves as beneficiaries in the event of the employee's death. Presumably the name for such policies – "Dead Peasant" – is indicative of the disdain the corporations and insurance companies feel towards their employees. See Michael Moore's film *Capitalism: A Love Story* (2009) Overture Films and Paramount Vantage.

[27] Again see http://walmartwatch.com/

surprised to find out how many people are on your side. Fight! Do not "go gently into that good-night."[28]

There are a number of problems with liberal altruism and concern for the unfortunate. The Right has always pointed to a certain hypocrisy in connection with it. Liberals often feel embarrassed about their affluence in a world of poverty and constantly strive to make those even more well-off than they are share their guilt. The underlying politics of this is that the expectation is that somehow those who are currently running the show will be more generous. But this is a complete misunderstanding of the political problem. We should not try to convince our rulers to give up their power, the rich to give up their privilege; this is a futile endeavour and contributes to the mystification process. The wealth and power they possess is not theirs to give away; we can refuse them that moral-political legitimacy. No, that wealth and power is *ours to take!* The political problem is to convince ordinary people of their real interests. The political problem is to convince them of their strength in unity. The political problem is to convince them of who their real allies are and who are their real enemies.

Let us imagine that you are a First World worker in a factory that is about to be shut down. Perhaps it will be moved to the Third World; perhaps it is about to be moved to one of the thousands of "special economic zones."[29] Again, don't go. Literally, I mean. Take over the factory! Run the company yourselves without the bosses. It can be done. Look to the history

---

[28] Dylan Thomas (1952), "Do Not Go Gentle into That Good Night." http://wikilives.info/wiki/Do_Not_Go_Gentle_into_that_Good_Night

[29] Special economic zones are found in many countries throughout the world. The Mexican Maquiladoras have special taxation, import and export regulations and other corporate friendly rules not found elsewhere in Mexico. There is increasing transfer of First World manufacture to such zones where much cheaper non-unionized labour can be found. Young women are particularly favoured for work in such areas because of their docility, among other things. When they get older, they are let go.

of the factory workers movement of Argentina with their motto: occupy, resist, produce.[30]

Most of us, of course, are not in this situation. So what should be done by us? Well, we must help the best we can. The first steps being, of course, to understand the struggles of others, to learn as much of the truth as we can, to avoid being mystified. The difficulty of this should not be underestimated. To be critical in one's appraisal of the messages of the mainstream media is only obvious; but we need to be *self-critical* as well. We need to subject our gut reactions, our first theories, our preconceptions, to rigorous critical inquiry. We need to engage in dialogue with others. The question "what should be done" should always be before us.

We need to take account of where we are ideologically in relation to others. So, for example, we should donate only to politicized charities. Of course, in the absence of significant change, there is call to ameliorate suffering now and charity in part does so. But the present state of global political consciousness among the relatively affluent (and everyone in a First World country with the exception of the bottom 10 to 15 percent or so *is* relatively affluent) is such that we can be sure there will be many more contributors to the United Way than to any of the myriad more politically focused NGOs and "charities'."

Hope: The Utopian Side of Dystopia

> *The free expression of the hopes and aspirations*
> *of a people is the greatest and only safety in a*
> *sane society.*
> Emma Goldman

If we coldly examine all the threads of causality and the trends leading into the future – and we must; it is our only hope – then the grimness of the present human condition is almost overwhelming. The situation will surely get much worse before it

---

[30] See the film *The Take* (2004) by Avi Lewis and Naomi Kline, Kline Lewis Productions.

What is to be done?

could even possibly get better. There are deep structura
work here. We are most surely on track for some kind of ultimate
calamity, some catastrophe of multi-causally linked catastrophes.
And nowhere is there to be found that growing fire of change
necessary to save the world. But we *mustn't* be overwhelmed.

We are doomed . . . or so it would appear. But we cannot know
this. No one can know this for sure. It is too big; there are too
many threads. There is no growing fire; global revolution is not
on the horizon of reality. But there are little sparks. Little sparks
of resistance is all we have. But from sparks sometimes come big
fires. To save the world is to make a better world; it is the only
way possible. The long-time socialist hopes and dreams for a
better world are conjoined with a necessary edict for survival. To
critically assess the suffering of the present and the trends leading
to the future is to imagine things being different. The problems
are structural; they are beyond individual solution. But the
problems are also humanly created. And we are not alone . . . or at
least we need not be. So those of us who see the shipwreck ahead,
those of us who see a humanly caused doomsday, must band
together. We must act collectively to fan the flames of revolution.
We must hope; we must dream; and we must act on our hopes and
dreams!

INDEX

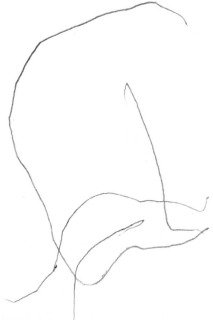

CPSIA information can be obtained at www.ICGtesting.com
Printed in the USA
LVOW10s0758150116

470735LV00001B/79/P

9 781453 822562